P9-DIG-198

The
American Medical Association

GUIDE TO
BETTER SLEEP

Revised and Updated Edition

The
American Medical Association
Home Health Library

The American Medical Association
Family Medical Guide

The American Medical Association
Handbook of First Aid and Emergency Care

The American Medical Association
Guide to BackCare—Revised and Updated Edition

The American Medical Association
Guide to HeartCare—Revised and Updated Edition

The American Medical Association
Guide to WomanCare—Revised and Updated Edition

The American Medical Association
Guide to Health and Well-Being After Fifty

The American Medical Association
Guide to Better Sleep

RA
786
.L35
1984

The
American Medical Association

GUIDE TO
BETTER SLEEP

Revised and Updated Edition

Developed by the
American Medical Association

MEDICAL ADVISORS

William C. Dement, M.D., Ph.D.

Shervert H. Frazier, M.D.

Elliot D. Weitzman, M.D.

Written by Lynne Lamberg

RANDOM HOUSE NEW YORK

KVCC WITHDRAWN KALAMAZOO VALLEY
COMMUNITY COLLEGE
LIBRARY

61440

MAR 1 4 1986

Copyright © 1984 by American Medical Association
All rights reserved under International and Pan-American Copyright Conventions. Published in the United States by Random House, Inc., New York, and simultaneously in Canada by Random House of Canada Limited, Toronto.

Grateful acknowledgment is made to the following for permission to reprint previously published material:

Harcourt Brace Jovanovich, Inc.: Excerpt by Richard Wilbur, reprinted from "Walking to Sleep," in his volume *Walking to Sleep*. Copyright © 1967 by Richard Wilbur. Used by permission of Harcourt Brace Jovanovich, Inc. First published in *The New Yorker*.
Dr. Peter Hauri and The Upjohn Co.: Two charts, "Typical Sleep Pattern of a Young Human Adult," and "Development of Sleep over a Lifetime," from *The Sleep Disorders*, Current Concept Series. Copyright © 1982 by The Upjohn Co., Kalamazoo, Michigan. Used with permission.

The recommendations and information discussed in this book are appropriate in most cases. For specific information regarding your personal medical condition, the AMA suggests that you see a physician. The names of organizations appearing in this book are given for informational purposes only. Their inclusion implies neither approval nor disapproval by the AMA.

Library of Congress Cataloging in Publication Data
Lamberg, Lynne.
The American Medical Association guide to better sleep.
(American Medical Association home health library)
Includes index.
1. Sleep. 2. Sleep disorders. I. American Medical
Association. II. Title. III. Title: Guide to better
sleep. IV. Series. [DNLM: 1. Sleep—Popular works.
2. Sleep disorders—Popular works. WM 188 A512]
RA786.L35 1984 616.8'49 83-42760
ISBN 0-394-72153-5

Manufactured in the United States of America
24689753
First Edition

MEDICAL ADVISORS

William C. Dement, M.D., Ph.D., is director of the Sleep Disorders Center at Stanford University Medical Center and professor of psychiatry at its medical school. He is president of the Association of Sleep Disorders Centers and co-editor-in-chief of the scientific journal *Sleep*.

A native of Wenatchee, Washington, Dr. Dement is a 1955 graduate of the Pritzker School of Medicine of the University of Chicago. He is a member of the National Academy of Sciences.

Shervert H. Frazier, M.D., is chief of psychiatry at McLean Hospital in Belmont, Massachusetts, and professor of psychiatry at Harvard University Medical School. He is a past president of the Association for Research of Nervous and Mental Disease and is currently chairman of its board, and is a past president of the American College of Psychiatrists.

Dr. Frazier was born in Shreveport, Louisiana, and graduated in 1943 from the medical school of the University of Illinois in Chicago. He is secretary of the American Psychiatric Association and a member of the American Psychoanalytic Association.

Elliot D. Weitzman, M.D., was until his death in late 1983 director of the Institute of Chronobiology and the Sleep-Wake Disorders Center at the New York Hospital-Cornell Medical Center, New York, and professor of neurology in psychiatry and neurology,

Cornell University Medical College. Dr. Weitzman served as vice president of the Association of Sleep Disorders Centers, coordinating secretary of the Sleep Research Society, and president of the New York Neurological Society. He formerly was chairman of the Department of Neurology at Albert Einstein College of Medicine, Montefiore Hospital, New York.

Born in Newark, New Jersey, Dr. Weitzman received his medical degree in 1955 from the Pritzker School of Medicine of the University of Chicago. He was a member of the American Academy of Neurology, the American Neurological Association, the American Electroencephalographic Society and the International Chronobiology Society.

Dr. Weitzman died while this book was on press. The author and the American Medical Association staff are grateful to have had the opportunity to work with him; his enthusiasm, knowledge and guidance were invaluable in the book's development.

American Medical Association Consumer Book Program
Thomas F. Hannon, Deputy Executive Vice President, AMA
John T. Baker, Vice President, Publishing, AMA
Charles C. Renshaw, Jr., Editorial Director, Consumer Book Program, AMA

PREFACE

Many of us are inclined to think of our waking and sleeping lives as separate and distinct, but they are, in fact, interdependent and inseparable. Your sleeping patterns have a direct influence on your waking behavior, and, in turn, your daytime habits may influence your sleep.

Aside from the common cold, perhaps the most widespread health complaint that Americans have is difficulty in sleeping. Today there is extensive activity in the field of sleep research. Sleep problems are being examined as they never have been before, and this new interest in sleep is bringing us a new understanding of it.

The purpose of this book is to tell you about the latest scientific sleep research and also—at the level of your own daily life—to explain how you can take a few simple steps to improve your sleep and your waking life. The book is one of a series of volumes collectively entitled the *American Medical Association Home Health Library*.

James H. Sammons, M.D.
Executive Vice President
American Medical Association

ACKNOWLEDGMENTS

Many people have contributed their time and expertise to the preparation of this book. In addition to our medical advisors, Drs. William C. Dement, Shervert H. Frazier and Elliot D. Weitzman, whose enthusiasm and advice have been most beneficial, we wish to express our thanks to the following individuals and organizations for their aid and encouragement in the preparation of the manuscript: Stanford, Nicole and Ryan Lamberg (Baltimore, Maryland); Richard Allen, Ph.D., Philip Smith, M.D., and the staff of the Baltimore Regional Sleep Disorders Center (Baltimore, Maryland); Ricky Fine (Baltimore, Maryland); Lynn Hassler (Stanford, California); Stephen Kennedy, Ph.D., and the staff of Project Sleep (Rockville, Maryland); Myrna Seif (Baltimore, Maryland); Elaine Snyder (Baltimore, Maryland); Marc Stern (Bethesda, Maryland); Evelyn Stone (Belmont, Massachusetts); Muriel Weitzman (White Plains, New York).

We are grateful to Charles A. Wimpfheimer and Klara Glowczewski of Random House for their guidance, enthusiasm and support.

Many of our colleagues at the AMA also helped in the development of this book. We would like to especially thank our project art director, David LaHoda, for his creative input. For their counsel and guidance we wish to thank Donald R. Bennett, M.D., Ph.D., and William T. McGivney, Ph.D., of

AMA's Division of Drugs, and to Toba Cohen, of the Division of Communications.

And special thanks also to AMA's editorial team, whose skill and dedication have been so important to the quality of this book: Lynne Lamberg, Kathleen A. Kaye, Robin Fitzpatrick Husayko, Virginia Peterson and Marie Moore.

Carole Fina
Managing Editor
Consumer Book Program
American Medical Association

CONTENTS

INTRODUCTION: HOW COMMON ARE SLEEPING PROBLEMS?

Sometimes we eagerly embrace sleep. At other times we hate to go to bed. On occasion, sleep overwhelms us when the time or place is wrong. Sometimes sleep eludes us, no matter how ardently we pursue it.

We believe we are out of touch with the world around us while we sleep. Yet we are able to hear a child's whimper, smell a hint of smoke, snuggle under the blankets or toss them aside if the room temperature changes. We are always thinking, whether awake or asleep. In our waking lives, we think primarily in words; in sleep, we use a visual language. We call our most vivid sleeping thoughts dreams. These reveries often seem so outlandish and illogical that we find it hard to acknowledge that we crafted them. If we choose to do so, we can explore through our dreams another dimension of our inner selves.

The need for sleep is so compelling that we slumber away twenty to twenty-five years of our lives. Many of us lament this as a colossal waste of time. Yet we accept sleep as necessary, because our bodies will not let us get along without it. And everyone hopes for "a good night's sleep," for we all know that sound, refreshing sleep helps us to feel our best when we are awake. We see, too, that poor sleep depletes our energy and our initiative and makes us achy and irritable.

Yet many of us regard sleep in the same casual way we regard the working of our hearts or our digestive tracts. We pay attention only if something goes wrong. Even then, disorders of sleep and arousal seldom seem as urgent as chest pain or an upset stomach. We often procrastinate before seeking help.

Today, it is increasingly difficult to maintain such complacency. "Wellness" is the watchword of the eighties. We exercise to improve our cardiac fitness. We change the foods we eat, hoping to better our odds for living a long, healthy life. Similarly, we can adopt numerous practical everyday measures to improve, reliably and dramatically, both our sleep and our waking lives.

Many of us lead a frenetic existence. We work or go to school, often commuting for sizable chunks of the day. We prepare meals, do laundry, pay bills, supervise our children's homework; we jog, swim or play squash, become engrossed in a novel or a television show, talk on the phone and visit with friends. Most of us have a long list of things we never get around to doing because "the day just isn't long enough." As a result, we often shortchange ourselves on sleep. Some of us keep odd hours, going to bed at eleven one night and two o'clock in the morning the next, and then try to catch up by sleeping late or taking naps.

One out of four of us works rotating shifts, frequently changing the times we sleep and work but usually trying to stay on the same schedule as the rest of the family and society on weekends and days off. Some of us have turned our bedrooms into living rooms; we talk on the phone, read, watch television, eat snacks and do paperwork there. Yet we seldom suspect, when we lie awake impatiently in the dark, that these practices may be the reasons we cannot get to sleep.

One in five of us reports that the quality and amount of our sleep is frequently or constantly unsatisfactory. All of us suffer an occasional fretful night or lethargic day. Some of us are troubled by nightmares so loathsome that we fear going to sleep. As parents, we continually look for better ways to contend with our children's bad dreams, bed-wetting or sleepwalking. In later life, we reconcile ourselves to stiff joints, wrinkles and fragile sleep.

Only in the last quarter century, since scientists developed and applied the tools and techniques for measuring sleep, has it become possible to match an individual's complaints with specific abnormalities of sleep and to develop remedies for many common problems. In most fields of medicine it takes many years to translate research findings from the laboratory into patient care, but the nature of sleep disorders medicine accelerates this process. The laboratory for clinical research in this field *is* the patient's bedside.

Some 120 disorders of sleep and arousal have already been identified. Most do not merely disrupt sleep; they affect a person twenty-four hours a day. Problems with sleep or with staying awake often prove more than minor annoyances. For some of us, they are lifelong illnesses that make normal work and social activities impossible.

The link between sleep and health problems, such as headaches or high blood pressure, is not always obvious; these problems may be blamed on other causes. Even more alarming, some people who seem to be healthy while awake prove to be dangerously ill while asleep.

Indeed, the identification within the past decade of a potentially life-threatening disorder known as sleep apnea provided a strong impetus for the recent surge of interest in sleep disorders. People with sleep apnea may stop breathing dozens of times during the night, upsetting heart rate and blood pressure, yet they often breathe normally while awake. Doctors now believe that sleep apnea accounts for many mysterious sudden deaths from "natural" causes during sleep in people who seem well.

Until recently, physicians seldom suspected that the course of an illness might be altered by sleep or that some illnesses might manifest themselves only in sleep. However, the "sleep connection" has proved to be the thread binding together a multiplicity of disorders.

In 1975, only five medical institutions in the United States had centers devoted to the diagnosis and treatment of these problems. By 1984, more than seventy sleep disorders centers had opened and more were in the planning stages. It seems likely that by the end of the decade, most of the nation's medical schools and many hospitals will house sleep clinics.

Worldwide, about five hundred scientists now identify themselves as somnologists, specialists in the study of sleep and in the diagnosis and treatment of disorders of sleep and waking. They bring their expertise from the fields of neurology, psychiatry, clinical and experimental psychology, internal medicine, pediatrics, biochemistry, physiology, pharmacology and numerous other disciplines.

Project Sleep, a program to educate physicians and the general public about disorders of sleep and arousal, was launched in the United States in 1979 by the Surgeon General's office, in collaboration with the Association of Sleep Disorders Centers, various medical professional organizations, including the American Medical Association, and the pharmaceutical industry and consumers' groups.

The message is getting out: Problems of sleeping and waking are not trivial, and they can no longer be viewed as obscure or unfathomable.

The various disorders of sleeping and waking are now divided into categories that reflect the kinds of symptoms you might complain about when you go to see your doctor. These are the four main groups: problems with falling asleep or staying asleep, problems with staying awake, problems with the timing of sleep and waking and problems that occur during sleep.

Problems with Falling Asleep or Staying Asleep

Insomnia, the most frequent sleep complaint, is a complex disorder. Few of us suffer total insomnia—that is, no sleep. Instead, we may take too long to fall asleep, wake too often during the night or too early in the morning, or feel our sleep is too light, uneasy or restless. We may believe that our ability to fall asleep and stay asleep varies too much from night to night. Most people with these complaints say that bad nights make them feel groggy and out of sorts the next day.

It is common to have trouble sleeping when we are excited or anxious; few of us, for example, sleep well the night before we are to depart for a long-awaited vacation or go to an important job interview, or the night after we learn that someone close to us is seriously ill. At times we may be bothered by unpleasant, repetitive dreams that center on problems we have not been able to resolve in our waking lives. Hence, when insomnia continues for weeks or months, it is tempting to blame everyday stress. But anxiety and depression are not the only causes of insomnia.

In the hope that the problems of our waking lives can be "cured" by more sleep, we may try sleeping pills or alcohol to ease our entry into the night. But these substances do not solve any of our problems and they may worsen our sleep. By the time our suspicions are aroused, our bodies have come to "need" the drugs, and attempts at withdrawal disturb sleep further. It's a vicious circle; understanding and great persistence are needed to escape from it.

Some of us have leg jerks for a second or two every thirty seconds, for hours at a time, while we sleep. The leg movements don't awaken us fully; yet in the morning we sense that we've had a restless night. These leg movements become increasingly common as we grow older. Often it is a spouse who provides the first clue by complaining of being kicked repeatedly during the night.

Some of us stop breathing over and over again while we sleep, too briefly to awaken us fully but long enough so that we know our sleep was fitful. Arthritis, back trouble, pregnancy and a host of other conditions that alter our waking lives may also disturb our sleep. Noise from frequent airplane flyovers, heavy road traffic or other sources will probably cause us to sleep less well than we would if we lived in a quieter spot. We may resign ourselves to the noise but our bodies seldom get used to it. Finally, we may unwittingly bring insomnia upon ourselves if we habitually drink several cups of coffee in the evening or keep irregular hours.

You'll find more about the many causes of insomnia, along with practical guidelines for better sleep, in the following chapters:

Problems with Staying Awake

Sleepiness is one of the most insidious of states. Most of us think of it as the feeling we get when it's time for bed. Our eyelids feel heavy and may itch or burn; we have to strain to keep our eyes open. Our heads nod. We're overcome by inertia; if we are relaxing on the living room couch, we find it almost too much trouble to get up, turn off the lights and head for bed. As sleepiness grows, we lose interest in whatever we have been doing. We can fight sleepiness by yawning, stretching, standing or moving around, but the idea of finding a quiet spot, lying down and closing our eyes becomes more and more attractive. Eventually, sleep proves irresistible.

All of us feel more alert at certain times of the day and more sleepy at other times; such fluctuations are perfectly normal and follow a predictable pattern. Most of us try to hold sleep at bay when at work or behind the wheel of a car, but, as accident statistics testify, we don't always succeed. As one example, a head-on collision between two freight trains in West Virginia in 1980 occurred when both the engineer and the head brakeman of one train apparently fell asleep at the controls. Some of us go through periods of feeling "fatigued," "tired all the time" or "exhausted." These feelings often are confused with sleepiness and, if we discribe ourselves this way, we pose a challenge to our physicians to determine whether we have a disorder of sleep or some other physical illness, or whether psychological stress is to blame.

Excessive sleepiness is currently thought to affect about 4 percent of the population, while insomnia bothers perhaps 15 to 20 percent of us. However, according to a national survey of 8,000 patients sponsored by the Association of Sleep Disorders Centers, excessive sleepiness accounts for more than half of the people with sleep disorders who seek treatment at sleep disorders centers. It is probable that excessive sleepiness brings more people to sleep specialists than does insomnia, because physicians are now aware that this symptom may reflect the potentially lethal disorder of sleep apnea.

People with sleep apnea stop breathing dozens, often hundreds, of times while they sleep. The pauses cause them to awaken, and only then does breathing restart. If the awakenings are long enough, the person may complain of a restless night; but, in the more typical case, the awakenings are so brief that the sleeper has no memory of broken sleep in the morning. He—for this problem is far more common in men than women—is more likely to describe his sleep as "unrefreshing" and say he feels "worn out." A prominent sign of the most common form of sleep apnea is a particular pattern of extremely noisy snoring, followed by silence as breathing stops, and then a gasp as breathing restarts. Snoring, long treated as a joking matter, is now recognized as an important early warning signal.

After sleep apnea, the next most common reason for excessive sleepiness is a neurological disorder, narcolepsy. This illness leaves people relentlessly sleepy, not just now and then but most of the time. They might fall asleep while eating dinner, talking on the phone or riding a bicycle, an experience frequently described as a sleep attack. People with narcolepsy are often stigmatized as slackers or incompetents, and, although treatment is available to curb the most severe symptoms, they typically struggle with their symptoms for many years before the problem is correctly diagnosed.

While narcolepsy and sleep apnea account for two thirds of all cases of excessive sleepiness, the symptom may also stem from metabolic and endocrine disorders, such as diabetes and thyroid disease. Some women are excessively sleepy just before their menstrual periods, and sleepiness is often an early sign of pregnancy. As we get older, we usually sleep less well and, as a result, feel sleepier during the day. Erratic sleeping habits, frequent but irregular naps and even boredom can all contribute to the feeling of weariness. And sleepiness may be a hangover effect from the use of sleeping pills, alcohol or other drugs the night before.

You'll find more about the most common causes of excessive sleepiness and suggestions for coping with this problem in the following chapters:

Problems with the Timing of Sleep and Waking

The times at which we choose to get up and go to bed each day serve as powerful anchors for a whole host of bodily activities, including predictable variations in body temperature, release of hormones, and other metabolic processes. If we change our normal pattern, we upset the synchrony of these inner rhythms. Then we are likely to find that we can't sleep when we want to, need to or expect to, and that while we are awake, our attention flags and we feel edgy. If you've ever traveled rapidly across many time zones, you've probably experienced jet lag, a complex constellation of symptoms that includes not only sleep problems but also digestive upsets and malaise. If you work rotating shifts, you probably find that it takes several days before you're comfortable with your new schedule. If you follow still another schedule on weekends and days off, you may be afflicted with a kind of permanent "jet lag."

People who stay up late on weekends and try to "sleep in" Sunday mornings may end up paying for their folly with the Monday morning blahs. Some of us find ourselves chronically out of sync; we can't fall asleep until two or three in the morning, even though we've tried to do so since eleven. If we must get up at seven o'clock for work, we end up dragging ourselves stuporously through the day. Until recently, these problems were lumped under the term "insomnia." Now it's realized that the trouble lies in the timing of sleep. A method of treatment known as chronotherapy—literally, "time therapy"—has been developed to help people with these problems acquire a normal schedule.

Disturbances of the sleep/wake cycle may also occur in people with certain mental illnesses, including manic-depressive disease and schizophrenia. The switch from the high of mania to the low of depression, for example, is often preceded by a night with significantly less sleep than usual. People with schizophrenia sometimes reverse night and day, an activity consonant with their withdrawal from reality. Manipulations of the amount and timing of sleep are being used experimentally to treat these disorders, often with dramatic results.

If you're interested in these problems you'll want to look at the following chapters:

Chapter 1: Why Sleep?

Chapter 11: The Time of Our Lives

Chapter 14: Troubled Minds/Troubled Sleep

Problems That Occur During Sleep

Sleep is not always a peaceful and quiet state. Sleepers sometimes start to awaken but, for unknown reasons, go only part of the way. They straddle sleep and wakefulness simultaneously. That's the reason someone can get up out of bed and walk around the house, put on clothes and open doors, yet have no memory of the events in the morning. Contrary to popular myth, sleepwalkers aren't magically protected from harm; they may bump their heads, bruise their shins, stumble and fall.

Sleepwalking, bed-wetting and sleep terrors (feelings of nameless dread that often prompt horrific screaming) are disorders of partial arousal. Once they were thought to represent the acting-out of dreams; now it is recognized that they start during non-dreaming sleep. These problems are far more common among children than among adults, a fact that suggests that immaturity fosters their appearance, particularly in those who are genetically predisposed to them.

All of us occasionally experience nightmares. These are violent and often threatening events from which, just as doom is about to strike, we burst into wakefulness, drenched in perspiration, with heart pounding and breath short. Nightmares frequently follow a frightening experience, such as being in or witnessing an automobile accident or seeing a horror film. Unpleasant, repetitive nightmares are a key component of the post-traumatic stress syndrome, a condition that affects some people for months or years after they have been involved in a plane crash, a house fire or other catastrophes. Ten years or more after leaving the service, some Vietnam veterans report that they still have horrible dreams in which they re-experience actual war events, such as an ambush in which comrades were killed or mutilated.

Some illnesses are worsened by sleep or emerge only then. The chest pain of angina, for example, often occurs during periods of vivid dreaming, a time when our breathing and heart rate are more irregular.

Among healthy males of all ages, from newborn babies to octogenarians, the penis normally becomes erect during a specific state of sleep. Recognition of this fact has led to a quick and reliable way to determine the probable cause of impotence. When a man complains of impotence, his ability to have erections during sleep can be monitored in a sleep laboratory. The absence of erections or abnormal erections during sleep suggest that his impotence has a physical basis; normal erections suggest that it is of psychological origin.

For more information on these disorders, turn to the following chapters:

Chapter 4: The Stuff of Dreams
Chapter 5: The Growing Years
Chapter 12: Things That Go Bump in the Night
Chapter 13: In Sickness and Health

An Achievable Goal: Better Sleep

Why do we sleep? What do our dreams mean? Does everybody need eight hours of sleep? What happens if we stay up late or get up early and get less sleep than usual? What can I do when my child won't go to sleep? Is there a cure for bed-wetting? Why, now that I'm getting older, can't I sleep as well as I used to? What can I do about my insomnia? What's the best sleeping pill? How can I get over being sleepy all the time? Is there any way to make my husband stop snoring? These are among the questions most frequently asked of sleep specialists. Their answers, based on studies of thousands of sleepers, are found in the following pages.

This is a self-help book in the best sense of the term. It aims to make you more knowledgeable about your own sleep and about the factors that interfere with sound sleep and those that enhance it. It offers ways to improve your sleep and your waking life. It provides a guide to the most common disorders of sleep, not to encourage you to act on the basis of a self-diagnosis, but rather to help you assess any difficulties you may be having. It describes current treatment and explains what you can expect in your doctor's office and at a sleep disorders center. This book's aim is to help you fulfill the familiar exhortation with which many of us end the day: *Sleep WELL!*

PART I

NORMAL SLEEP

1

WHY SLEEP?

Sleeping, intertwined with waking, creates the framework within which we conduct our daily lives. We spend one third of our lives asleep—220,000 hours in an average life span. Our need for sleep determines how we organize the rest of our time. It influences the way we schedule our work and leisure activities and even how we design our homes.

The need for sleep is built in to living things. Sleep is not a skill, like talking or riding a bicycle; we don't have to learn to do it. An animal taken from its mother at the moment of birth and kept in total light or total darkness would sleep part of the day and be active at other times; its offspring would, too.

We can't go without sleep. We can keep it at bay, for hours or even days, but inevitably we must surrender to it.

Our obdurate need for sleep suggests that sleep is indispensable to life itself. In recent years scientists have begun to chart what happens in body and brain as we sleep. In this chapter we will look at some of the leading theories of why we sleep and explore the impact of sleep on the way we live.

Home Is Where Your Bed Is

A special place for sleeping—a bed, a straw mat, animal skins, a hammock—is central to our concept of home. We live where we sleep. The size of a house or an apartment is identified by the number of bedrooms it has. Whole towns may be referred to as bedroom communities.

Billions of dollars and millions of jobs depend on our daily need to sleep. Mattresses, bedding, nightclothes, alarm clocks, sleeping pills, hotel rooms and even books on better sleep are all necessitated by this curious daily habit.

Although we set aside our outer clothes at night, we seldom drop our daytime roles. In primitive societies, in a hut with only a small fire for warmth, the person with the highest status in the family sleeps closest to the fire. In the United States, parents typically assign to themselves the master bedroom. A child's crib is more likely to be on the mother's side of the bed than on the father's. A child old enough to go on "sleepovers" is starting to leave the parental nest. A teenager's declaration of independence is often marked by the creation of a new bedroom in the attic or the basement, and a young adult moves out to a place of his or her own.

The bedroom is a private place; company comes, and we shut the door. Grunts and snorts, various states of undress—behaviors that would be frowned on in the living room—are permissible in the bedroom.

Think about beds. The bed is a microcosm of life—the setting for birth, sexual union, sickness and death. We use the word "sleep" as a euphemism for sex. To "sleep with" someone is to share one of the most intimate of human experiences. Handing down grandmother's bed quilt from one generation to the next is, quite literally, passing on one's heritage.

Alexander the Great and Louis XIV, among others, conducted business of state from their beds. John Milton, Jonathan Swift, Marcel Proust and Elizabeth Barrett Browning are among the many authors who wrote major works in bed; Rossini frequently composed music there.

Charles Dickens insisted, both at home and while traveling, that the head of his bed point directly north. A theory prominent in his day held that magnetic currents surging between the North Pole and the South Pole would revitalize a person if they passed directly through his body.

In earlier cultures, people often positioned themselves at night to face protective spirits or to confront predators. It's easy to see that in a cave or hut it would be advantageous in case of attack to sleep with feet toward the door. Even today, most of us favor a specific position in which to fall asleep; you'd probably feel ill at ease tonight if, for example, you tried to sleep with your head at the foot end of the bed.

The act of going to sleep has long stirred fears of dying. Sleep has been described as "the brother of death" and even as "a small death." At one time in Tibet, the worry that a sick person would die if allowed to sleep prompted measures such as sprinkling water in the person's face and keeping the person in a sitting position.

The belief that the soul wanders from the body during sleep is an ancient one. Even today, a widely used bedtime prayer begins, "Now I lay me down to sleep, I pray the Lord my soul to keep." Morning prayers of many religions offer thanks to God for the return of the soul.

Some people are afraid that evil inner impulses will be unleashed during sleep. We calm our fears with lullabies and learn to bypass them with bedtime rituals. Donning nightclothes, washing the face, checking the doors, setting the alarm and similar routines are not simply a response to feelings of sleepiness; they actually encourage it. Should you neglect a customary bedtime habit, you may find yourself restless. Could you, for example, fall asleep easily at night without brushing your teeth?

Sleep brings dreams, long regarded as a source of information, or even as communication from the supernatural world. The Bible contains dozens of dreams and visions. In Genesis, the Pharaoh of Egypt reports two dreams: seven plump cows are devoured by seven lean ones, and seven fat ears of corn are swallowed up by seven withered ones. Joseph correctly forecasts seven years of plenty followed by seven years of famine, and because of the dreams, provisions are stockpiled during the good years to save the country from starvation in the succeeding ones.

In many cultures, sacred temples have been built to a god of dreams; people have followed elaborate rituals to induce dreams with specific content, including solutions to problems. Among the Senoi of Malaysia, the day begins with a discussion of the dreams of family members, who then proceed to share, interpret and act on these dreams with others; dreams set the direction of village life. A Chinese parable addresses the illusive nature of reality by describing a man who dreamed he was a butterfly. On awakening, he could not decide if he was a man who had been dreaming he was a butterfly or a butterfly dreaming he was a man. We don't sleep merely to dream. Or do we?

What Is Sleep For?

Most of us believe that, as a rule, sleep is good for us. We often say, "I know I'll feel better after a good night's sleep." We postpone an important decision until we can "sleep on it." We urge someone who is ill to "get some sleep." Millions of us swallow sleeping pills night after night in the hope of getting more or better sleep. We intuitively feel that sleep restores both the body and the mind. Shakespeare addressed this concept, calling sleep "sore labour's bath, balm of hurt minds . . . chief nourisher in life's feast."

Attempts to track down exactly what is "lost" during wakefulness and "recovered" during sleep have, so far, proved fruitless. However, proponents of the restorative theory note that growth hormone is secreted mainly during sleep; this hormone is necessary for normal development in children and is believed to be important for tissue repair in adults. It may be that, like your car, your body cannot simultaneously be driven and tuned up. Certain waking functions may have to be turned off so that nightly readjustments can be made to keep things running smoothly.

Certainly, rest is no substitute for sleep. Sedentary secretaries or editors do not differ from physically active people, such as athletes and construction workers, in their need for sleep. Even persons confined to bed or a wheelchair need to sleep every day. We can rest by sitting quietly, lying down, or sinking into a warm bath. But sleep gives us something more than, or other than, physical rest. Indeed, physical rest may occur only coincidentally with sleep.

Some people report that they need more sleep in times of stress and less when things are going well, a fact that suggests sleep may be important for our emotional well-being. There are, however, paradoxes in the notion that sleep abates mental fatigue. After a stimulating day, it often is hard to sleep because interesting ideas continue to spark; conversely, while we are doing nothing, trapped, for example, in a vacation cabin on a rainy day, we are likely to find that sleep comes easily.

During sleep the mind does not truly rest. We continue to think, expressing our thoughts as dreams. We are able to differentiate between important and trivial events in our immediate surroundings: we are more disturbed by our baby's whimpering than by the wail of a siren from a passing fire engine; we can be aroused by a whiff of smoke. If awakened, we can even estimate accurately how much time has elapsed since we fell asleep.

Sleep is not, then, a state of total unconsciousness, nor is it as extreme a state as the winter hibernation of certain mammals. During this long period of inactivity, however, most aspects of responsiveness are dramatically lowered. At such times a crocodile, lying on its belly with all legs pointing backward, can safely be approached and even picked up briefly.

Even fish sleep. They are oriented to light and dark, like other species, and the majority are active during the day. At dusk, the parrot fish secretes a mucous cocoon around itself for protection from predators through the night. In the morning it swims out of this cocoon. At the National Aquarium, Baltimore, Maryland, the lights in the tanks are used to replicate the patterns of light and darkness in the natural habitats of the various species; those of night-active species, such as the octopus, are reversed, to benefit visitors. When fish are sleeping, their breathing slows and their coloration changes, often becoming less intense. During these times, not even the touch of a human hand or a light flashed in their eyes makes them scurry. Fish that must remain in motion may hover in one spot or rest and glide instead of swimming actively. Such behavior underscores the inborn nature of sleep.

Cats fall asleep and awaken perhaps a thousand times in a single day. Human beings are exceptional animals in that most of us take the bulk of our sleep in a single daily chunk. Further, most of us prefer to sleep at night, apparently by nature's design. We function best when we can easily see the world around us; only in the last century, since the invention of the electric light, have we had the option of turning night into day. Animals tend to be most active at the times when their food sources are most readily accessible. Honeybees, butterflies, songbirds, hawks, and lizards work the day shift; bats, owls, moths, raccoons, and cockroaches are among the creatures of the night.

Sleep as humans and other mammals and birds experience it is a more discrete state than the periods of sleeplike immobility experienced by lower life forms, such as reptiles and amphibia. True sleep may have developed in tandem with body temperature regulation. Higher forms of life—mammals and birds—stay at a nearly constant body temperature regardless of the temperature of their environment. This permits far more activity than is possible for lower species, who are active only within a fixed range, but one drawback is that mammals and birds require more food.

Hence, once, when food supplies were scarce, sleep may have prevented higher life forms from running around and burning up all the calories they had worked hard to obtain. At the same time, the lack of vigilance that sleep entails may have forced them to find places where they would be safe from predators.

"Sleep serves the purpose of keeping animals out of harm's way," asserts Ray Meddis, of the University of Technology in Loughborough, England. Baboons sleep in trees; the most dominant males sleep in the lower branches, where they can best deal with attackers. Birds often pick high ledges, and rabbits choose holes. We lock the doors to our homes.

Yet the concept that sleep is a developmental leftover, like the appendix, leaves some scientists skeptical. Allan Rechtschaffen, Ph.D., director of the Sleep Research Laboratory at the University of Chicago, contends, "If sleep does not serve an absolutely vital function, then it is the biggest mistake the evolutionary process has ever made."

In support of this assertion he asks, "How could natural selection, with its irrevocable logic, have 'permitted' the animal kingdom to pay the price of sleep for no good reason? How could sleep have remained virtually unchanged throughout the whole of mammalian evolution while, during the same period of time, selection has been able to achieve all kinds of delicate, finely tuned adjustments in the shape of fingers and toes?"

The one third of our lives that we spend sleeping may make the other two thirds possible. Nathaniel Kleitman, M.D., the father of modern sleep research, suggests that sleep is related to waking as the trough of a wave is related to the crest. It is a part of a perpetual cycle and the most powerful organizer of our lives.

The Beat Goes On

The cyclic alteration of sleeping with waking is only one of dozens of persistent rhythms within our bodies and in the world around us.

Night follows day, tides ebb and flow, the seasons change. Within the body, every day, temperature normally fluctuates from a low of 97°F to a high of 99°F. Most of us feel a postlunch dip around one-thirty, regardless of when, or even whether, we ate lunch. The heart beats faster and slower at different times of day; blood pressure, the rate of breathing, the secretion of hormones and over a hundred other bodily activities change. Indeed, daily variations occur in every cell of the body. Moreover, there are daily fluctuations in our ability to perform a wide range of tasks. Our short-term memory, for example, works best in the morning, while long-term memory works best in the afternoon, a fact that suggests we can learn math best early in the day but will do better at history or languages later on. We are more or less cheerful, friendly, alert and sleepy at different times of the day, too.

Twenty-four-hour rhythms are prominent in our lives; they are a direct consequence of living on a twenty-four-hour planet. But shorter and longer rhythms also figure in our lives. Within sleep, for example, dreams occur roughly every ninety minutes; during waking, daydreaming occurs at about the same frequency. Heart-beats, breathing, digestive contractions, hair growth, menstruation and numerous other bodily functions also follow predictable cycles. In the world at large, even the rise and fall of the stock market, fashions in hemlines and the outbreaks of wars seem to occur in a periodic fashion.

Studies of the way our inner clocks work require special surroundings that are free of all indicators of time. Such studies are under way at the Institute of Chronobiology of the New York Hospital-Cornell Medical Center in White Plains, New York, for example.

Here, there are four windowless apartments, each with a sleeping area, activity area and bathroom. People taking part in studies live here for as long as six months. For the bulk of the time, they go to sleep, get up and eat when they wish.

They never see clocks. They do not watch television or listen to the radio. They see newspapers and magazines long after publication and are given mail many days after it arrives. One man voted by absentee ballot early in October in a federal election to be held in November. When he learned the results, it was late in December. To further keep the individuals living in the laboratory cut loose from time, the staff members who bring meals and conduct tests work irregularly rotating shifts. There is no contact between any of the study participants.

During the entire study, numerous bodily functions are measured. Body temperature is recorded automatically every minute, with a thermometer worn in the rectum. A catheter remains in a vein in the arm so that samples of blood can be taken for hormone studies at any time, even when the person is sleeping. Sleep is recorded but it is not disturbed; a tube connected to the catheter runs through an opening in the wall to the control room outside the apartment. Video monitors and intercoms permit staff members to observe and talk with the study participants at all times. Computer terminals are on hand for tests of thinking ability, alertness and mood. Computers help process the vast volume of information that is generated.

Studies such as these reveal that, even though we plan our daily activities on a twenty-four-hour schedule, our inner clocks for waking and sleeping have a different tempo. Deprived from time cues, most of us would naturally follow a schedule of about twenty-five hours; that is, we would tend to go to sleep and to get up approximately an hour later each day. Studies of dozens of people living in time-free environments for weeks and even months have revealed that this pattern is common. However, it is not true for every living thing; a few people and many other animals have a natural rhythm that cycles in fewer than twenty-four hours. All such inner clocks are called circadian (from the Latin *circa*, meaning "approximately," and *dies*, a "day"), a term coined by Franz Halberg, M.D., of the University of Minnesota.

The powerful nature of the inborn circadian clock in humans is confirmed by jet travel; a person transported to a different time zone is ready to sleep or to be awake on "home" time, usually for several days, until he or she adjusts to the new schedule.

All of us, every day, must reset our internal clocks to live on a twenty-four-hour schedule. Light and dark help us make this adjustment. Perhaps you can recall the eerie sensation of time being "out of joint" if you have visited the night-into-day world of Las Vegas, Nevada, or even if you have awakened in total darkness after stretching out in midafternoon to take a brief nap. We can understand the power of light and dark in our lives by looking at people who are unable to respond to these signals. The blind must depend on clocks, mealtimes and interactions with other people to order daily rhythms in their lives; some complain that they lack a time sense.

"Body time" may affect the course of treatment for illness. The time of day when your physical processes are monitored, or when you take medicine, undergo surgery or receive X-ray therapy may alter your response. For example, in people with high blood pressure, readings are sometimes 30 percent lower in the evening than in the morning; a dose of medication that's appropriate in the morning may be too strong twelve hours later. Some people with bronchial asthma have increased bronchial constriction around six in the morning; they may need therapy concentrated in the early morning and also may need to be watched particularly carefully then. Aspirin taken at seven in the morning stays in the body for twenty-two hours; taken at seven in the evening, it is used up five hours sooner. A poison, *Escherichia coli* endotoxin, given to mice at three in the afternoon, kills 85 percent of them; given at midnight, it kills only 4 percent. Mice that are exposed to a certain level of noise at one time of day will suffer fatal convulsions; at another time, they will show no ill effects.

Some people seem to be running on a clock that is set a few hours later than those of the rest of the world. They often describe themselves as insomniacs because they can't fall asleep until three in the morning. But if workday demands do not intrude, they are able to sleep through until ten or eleven. The recognition that this is not a disorder of sleep but rather of the timing of sleep has led to the development of an effective remedy. The person stays up two or three hours later each day for several successive days, moving bedtime around the clock until the desired time is reached; then he adheres strictly to the new schedule.

The smooth functioning of our inner clocks is now recognized as critical to our health and happiness.

Must We Sleep?

More than two thousand years ago, a scribe of Alexander the Great observed that the tamarind tree opened its leaves during the day and closed them at night. He thought the plant was worshiping the sun. In fact, the plant was sleeping and waking.

Sleeping and waking, in humans and other animals as well as plants, were once regarded as passive responses to light and dark. But in 1729, a French astronomer, Jean Jacques de Mairan, showed that even if a plant is kept in total darkness it will continue to raise and lower its leaves regularly.

In surroundings without clues to reveal time, people respond on a predictable schedule to inner voices that say "Go to bed" and "Time to get up."

Indeed, people sleep under the most adverse conditions. Prisoners in concentration camps, soldiers in foxholes and patients in hospitals sleep. An Antarctic explorer's diary described sleeping at minus 76°F, after struggling fiercely, fighting cramps, for more than an hour to thaw his frozen sleeping bag. Although astronauts must strap themselves down to keep from floating, they manage to sleep while spinning through space.

Sleepiness is a "drive state," comparable to thirst or hunger, suggests William Dement, M.D., director of the Sleep Disorders Center at Stanford University. Just as these feelings prod us to drink or eat, sleepiness makes us seek sleep. Whether sleepiness is pleasant or unpleasant, he notes, depends largely on whether we're able to satisfy the need for sleep. Just as intense thirst makes drinking pleasurable, whereas the absence of liquid makes thirst a torture, so a very sleepy person finds getting into bed, snuggling down, relaxing and letting the mind drift very pleasant. A sleepy person required to maintain vigilant behavior finds the task exceedingly painful.

The time-honored way to understand the importance of a bodily process for survival is to take it away and see how—or if—the body manages without it. A person who does not eat or drink will suffer weight loss, extreme thirst, coma and finally death. What happens when people do not sleep?

In a study done in 1922, a whole class of students at the University of Chicago stayed awake for twenty-four hours. The group's performance on a number of tasks was compared with that of students who had their usual amount of sleep. The groups did equally well.

However, a thirty-two-year-old disk jockey who went without sleep for two hundred hours to raise money for the March of Dimes in 1959 developed some worrisome symptoms. After about five days without sleep, Peter Tripp began to experience hallucinations. He saw flames pouring from a drawer. He imagined that a doctor's tweed suit was composed of worms. Although he managed to complete his daytime broadcasts, his nights were haunted by the feeling that he was in mortal danger. The doctors caring for him during his ordeal later described his reaction as a "psychosis of sleeplessness." Essentially back to himself after thirteen hours of sleep, Tripp reported slight feelings of depression for several months.

Randy Gardner, a seventeen-year-old high school senior, decided in 1964 to beat a record of 260 hours of sleeplessness as a research project for his local science fair. The study was conducted during the winter vacation. Two close friends acted as co-investigators to help him stay awake. For the final 90 hours of the vigil, sleep researchers also stayed with Randy.

He took no drugs or stimulants, not even coffee. Though his irritability increased after about the fourth day of the study, he never had delusions, hallucinations or delirium. Particularly toward the end, lack of movement and stimulation brought on extreme drowsiness, while activity restored him. On the night before the final day, after 230 hours of sleep loss, Randy held his own against one of his friends and sleep researcher Dr. Dement in a hundred-game competition on a complicated pinball machine. At the same time, he couldn't say the alphabet without mistakes. His most prominent complaints were a feeling of fatigue and heaviness and burning of the eyelids.

After 264 hours and 12 minutes without sleep, an amazing eleven days, having surpassed his goal, Randy concluded the study. He responded intelligently to questions at a press conference. He appeared able to push onward had he decided to do so. Once in bed, he fell asleep within two minutes. He woke spontaneously 14 hours and 40 minutes later, feeling fine. He suffered no ill aftereffects from his adventure.

Randy's record achievement showed that extreme sleep loss does not invariably produce mental or physical breakdown, and the experiment helped clarify how the amount of sleep loss and the circumstances under which it is experienced are related to its effects.

His experience, like that of Peter Tripp and the students at the University of Chicago, demonstrated that motivation can override sleepiness, particularly if the task being scrutinized is brief and involves physical activity. A drop in performance and an increase in psychological disturbances, such as hallucinations, after sleep loss become most noticeable when tasks continue for a long time and are repetitive. Circadian rhythms of sleepiness and alertness continue to affect the way people function, despite the length of time they are without sleep. You are more alert at ten in the morning than you were the previous night at two, even though you have gone longer without sleep.

Without your usual sleep, you're likely to feel irritable and have difficulty concentrating. If you undergo a prolonged loss of sleep, you're more likely to be troubled by it if you see the sleep loss as stressful rather than as a challenge or an adventure. Age is a factor, too; young adults generally handle sleep loss more easily than older ones. The environment and social setting in which sleep loss occurs has a lot to do with an individual's willingness and ability to tolerate it. Most of us don't mind staying up late with pleasant company at a party but find it unpleasant to keep late hours while cramming alone for an exam; in the same way, comfortable surroundings and supportive companions make prolonged sleep loss more bearable.

Today it's recognized that Randy probably did not entirely forgo sleep. The longer a person tries to stay awake, the more likely it is that he will experience brief sleep episodes, known as microsleeps. Physically fit people seem to have such episodes less often than out-of-shape people; moreover, vigorous physical activity can reduce the frequency of microsleeps. That's why the tendency to doze off over paperwork, particularly common in midafternoon and late evening, can be countered by standing up and walking around.

However, we cannot stay awake indefinitely, no matter how hard we try. The fact that nobody dies from lack of sleep may demonstrate the effectiveness of the sleep process as nature's powerful built-in system for our self-protection. Sleep may overwhelm us to keep us from mortal danger.

It would be unethical to try to make people stay awake in order to prove this theory; however, animal studies conducted by Dr. Rechtschaffen and his colleagues at the University of Chicago offer impressive evidence that sleep serves a vital function. Rats that stay awake virtually all the time, walking at a moderate pace to avoid falling into a pool of water, become scrawny and weak and die within a few days. Identical rats, following the same routine but allowed brief periods of sleep, survive with few ill effects.

The flippant statement has been made that, in humans, the only certain consequence of lack of sleep is sleepiness. It's a mistake, however, to view sleepiness as an innocuous state. Some people put their lives on the line when they lapse into "automatic behavior" states, driving, for example, without paying full attention to what they are doing. "One could safely doze off while driving a horse cart because 'Old Dobbin' would never leave the road," Dr. Dement observes, but today a momentary lapse behind the wheel can be fatal. Sleepiness may even be so painful that a person will do nearly anything to end it; this is one reason why prisoners who are tortured by being kept awake often produce "confessions." Many of us may suffer significant disability from sleepiness. We may be functioning at less than our best every day, yet be so fatigued that we aren't aware of it.

"Even if the only function of sleep is to enable us to stay alert while awake, this function must be recognized, understood and respected in our day-to-day lives," says Dr. Dement.

We have no choice but to accept sleep as one of life's givens. We sleep because we have to. Happily, sleep provides for our waking lives the ultimate natural high. Dr. Dement ticks off the rewards: "High initiative, high motivation, high energy and a sense of clearheaded well-being."

2

WHAT IS NORMAL SLEEP?

Imagine a large apartment complex. Midnight approaches and most lights blink out. But some flip on, as the night workers embark on a myriad of tasks. At no time is there silence everywhere. Some ventures always are under way. Our bodies may work in much the same manner.

In the course of our everyday lives, it is easy to view sleep as a time-out from the business of living. But sleep is not merely the absence of wakefulness, nor a state in which we completely "turn off" shortly after the head hits the pillow. Rather, sleep is an active process. We turn on to it, just as we turn on to wakefulness.

The phenomenon of sleep was once as mysterious and inaccessible to study as the dark side of the moon. Today scientists routinely go along with us as we journey to inner space. The technology that makes this trip possible relies on a device known as an electroencephalograph (EEG), developed only a half century ago by Hans Berger, an Austrian psychiatrist. As its name indicates, it provides a record of the natural electrical activity of the brain. In examining continuous recordings made during sleep, scientists saw certain discrete brain-wave patterns occurring in regular cycles.

Sleep was still thought to be a time of rest for body and brain. Then, in 1952, in the physiology department at the University of Chicago, Nathaniel Kleitman, M.D., noticed the slow, rolling eye movements that take place when a person is falling asleep. He decided to see if these eye movements occurred at other times during the night. A young graduate student, Eugene Aserinsky, was assigned the task. Electrodes were taped near a number of sleepers' eyes to aid in monitoring their movement. Aserinsky was startled to find that, at certain times during the night, the subjects' eyes darted beneath closed lids, in a manner similar to, but often faster than, the movements that occurred during wakefulness. If sleepers were awakened during these times and asked what they were thinking, they nearly always reported visual dreams. Awakening sleepers at other times seldom produced such reports.

The realization that there were two distinct types of sleep—quiet and active—fired further study. William Dement, M.D., now director of the Sleep Disorders Center at Stanford University, then a second-year medical student at the University of Chicago and soon to be an enthusiastic participant in this research, recalls, "This was *the* breakthrough—the discovery that changed sleep research from a relatively pedestrian inquiry into an intensely exciting endeavor pursued with great determination in laboratories and clinics all over the world." Researchers began to investigate the events of the night, monitoring the sleep of thousands of people of all ages.

A Night of Normal Sleep

Quiet sleep alternates with active sleep in cycles lasting approximately ninety minutes. Active sleep is called REM, because of its characteristic rapid eye movements. Quiet sleep is known as non-REM, or NREM.

NREM sleep is what sleep is conventionally thought to be, a restful state. Brain waves are slow and regular. Most of the time we lie quietly. REM sleep offers a startling counterpoint. During REM sleep, brain waves resemble those of wakefulness, yet our bodies are paralyzed. Messages from the brain telling arms and legs to move cause mere twitching, perhaps to keep us from acting out our dreams. Some sleep specialists call REM sleep a third state of existence, a true time of altered consciousness, as different from NREM sleep as it is from wakefulness.

NREM sleep is divided into stages 1, 2 and 3-4 combined, with stage 1 representing the lightest and stage 3-4 the deepest sleep, measured by the ease with which the sleeper can be awakened by sound. REM sleep is not conventionally subdivided; moreover, it cannot be labeled either light or deep.

In order to distinguish the different stages of NREM and to tell NREM from REM, at least two bodily functions must be recorded during sleep: brain activity and eye movements.

Brain activity is monitored by electrodes placed on the top of the head and behind the ears, and eye movements are monitored by electrodes placed near the outer corners of the eyes. To better discriminate REM from NREM, many laboratories also monitor muscle activity, with electrodes on the sides of the chin. The beating of the heart, breathing, movements of the leg muscles, body temperature and other processes are often also recorded during sleep with the aid of electrodes at various spots on the body; such recordings are necessary for the diagnosis of specific disorders of sleep.

The electrodes are attached to color-coded wires, about the thickness of household string, gathered together like a ponytail, and plugged into a panel at the head of the bed. The electrical activity that's generated by the natural activity within the cells of brain and body runs through the wires to a device known as a *polygraph* to produce, as the name states, "many tracings." The electrical signals, amplified as much as a million times, drive a row of pens over a moving strip of graph paper. Each pen records the activity of a single electrode, or one "channel" of biological activity. A technician monitors the activities throughout the sleep period. An intercom and often a video camera enable the technician to hear, respond to and observe the sleeper.

At the rate of fifteen or thirty seconds per foot-wide page, a typical night's sleep creates a trail one thousand to two thousand feet long. The electrical signals, incidentally, are all one-way, from the sleeper to the amplifiers. People spending their first night in a sleep laboratory, often holding stereotypes spawned by Grade B mad-scientist films, frequently want reassurance that there's no chance they could be electrocuted.

A typical young adult takes from about thirty seconds to seven minutes to move from wakefulness to sleep. Nathaniel Kleitman, M.D., compares the drowsiness level, or intermediate state between wakefulness and sleep, to the melting point of ice or the freezing point of water. Tonight try to take note of the instant you fall asleep. You'll find in the morning that it is astoundingly difficult to recall. Yet, if you think of all the other contrasts in the world around you, none is so distinct as that between the "here" of wakefulness and the "there" of sleep. Falling asleep and waking up again are the happiest of everyday miracles.

Sleep normally begins with NREM sleep. In the period of drowsiness, or stage 1, thoughts drift. A sensation of falling or floating is common. Dreamlike hallucinations may dart through the mind. Eyes roll slowly, a phenomenon most of us have witnessed in others or been aware of in ourselves. During this time, brain waves characteristic of relaxed wakefulness, known as alpha waves, gradually disappear and are replaced by the slower and more regular theta waves. The printout on an EEG resembles the cutting edge of a household saw, with small, closely spaced peaks and valleys.

At some point, detectable on a sleep record within a second or two, even if eyes are taped open, flashes of light go unnoticed. Noises and touches, which the person previously acknowledged, fail to generate a response. The shutdown of perception is sudden and massive.

The process of sinking into sleep sometimes is interrupted by a sudden jerk, a muscle contraction of the leg, arm or entire body. Known as a hypnagogic (or sleep) startle, this experience does not indicate that anything is wrong; rather, it is simply one of those funny tricks that our bodies sometimes play. We awaken but usually only momentarily.

Sleep scientists generally consider that stage 2 sleep has begun when the EEG records the first "spindles," or bursts of twelve to fourteen distinct peaks and valleys per second, each burst lasting one-half second to two seconds. Another distinct marker is the "K complex," a sharp spike of high-voltage brain activity.

Some experts call stage 2 the first bona fide sleep stage. People aroused during this time usually report short, mundane and fragmented thoughts, but sometimes they describe vivid and complex dreams similar to those of REM sleep. Although it takes a stronger stimulus to arouse people from stage 2 than from stage 1, some people awakened in stage 2 insist, "I was not asleep." The EEG is a superb tool for detecting brain activity, but it does not capture all aspects of consciousness.

About fifteen to thirty minutes after sleep starts, stage 3-4 begins. The brain waves become slower and larger. The polygraph tracings undulate like the humps of a camel plodding through sand. The characteristic wave forms, occurring at about one-half cycle to two cycles per second, are called delta waves. In the past, the frequency of these large slow waves prompted distinctions between stages 3 and 4, but today, the debate over "lumping" or "splitting" the categories has largely subsided. This is the deepest stage of sleep; most people, if awakened at this time, confidently state that they were asleep. In a young adult, stage 3-4 lasts about an hour; then the sleeper climbs back to stage 2 and almost immediately into REM.

The first REM period of the night, starting about ninety minutes after the onset of sleep, lasts perhaps ten to fifteen minutes. The rapid eye movements that give this state its name do not occur continuously but, more typically, appear in short bursts, sometimes as many as ten per second.

Researchers have found that the percentage of people who recall dreams when awakened from REM sleep ranges from 60 to 88 percent. The percentage of people who recall dreams after NREM awakenings ranges from 7 to 64 percent. These wide ranges are attributed to variations in the definition of the word "dream" and the specific question posed to sleepers. For example, the question "What was going through your mind before you woke up?" is more likely to produce a response involving some mental content than "What were you dreaming about?"

The mental fireworks, the reports of visual, storylike and often hallucinatory events, are associated with waking from REM. "My father came to visit me in my new house; I was not surprised even though I knew he had been dead for eight years" is one such account. By contrast, NREM awakenings are more likely to produce thoughtlike and realistic reports, such as "I was thinking about straightening the house," or possibly, "I wasn't sleeping, just thinking." Both REM and NREM awakenings may elicit the report "I know I was thinking about something, but I can't exactly say what it was," which, although vague, is still an indicator that our minds continue to work while we sleep as well as when we are awake.

Each NREM/REM cycle lasts about ninety minutes; hence, in seven or eight hours of sleep, a person will go through four or five cycles. As sleep progresses, deep sleep periods become increasingly shorter and REM periods grow progressively longer, lasting up to an hour toward the end of sleep. Indeed, nearly all the deep sleep occurs in the first half of a sleep period, confirming the long-held folk wisdom that the first hour of sleep is the soundest.

Think of your sleep as a ride on a carousel. You glide down, then up, remaining a while at each level, sometimes down, sometimes up, sometimes in between, while at the same time you promenade forward and around. You mount the carousel at one spot but step off at another, coming back to a wakeful world that usually is much as you left it, although subtly altered by the passage of time. For the legendary Rip Van Winkle, this experience was greatly magnified; he returned with a long beard and creaky joints after sleeping for twenty years.

Young adults spend about 10 percent of a typical night in stage 1, the transition between wakefulness and drowsy detachment. They spend half of their time asleep in the light sleep of stage 2 and 20 percent in the deep sleep of stage 3-4. They log about an hour and a half, or 20 percent of their time asleep, in REM.

Night Life

The part of the brain that is critical for sleep is the brain stem, the lowest sector of the brain, lying at the base of the skull. Through this structure, which is about the size and shape of your thumb, nerve messages flow between the brain and the rest of the body, as sensations are transmitted and commands for action are executed. In addition to regulating sleep, the brain stem controls other automatic functions, including heartbeat, blood pressure, body temperature and breathing. In the search to identify the functions of various parts of the brain stem, experiments with animals have involved the removal of specific areas. An injury at one location, for example, disrupts the normal muscle inhibition of REM sleep, permitting sleeping cats to sit up, run and arch their backs, as if they were acting out their dreams. But because brain-stem injuries have other effects, including disruption of other nerve pathways, scientists are not yet able to pinpoint precisely the location of a "sleep center."

Brain and body function differently in many ways in sleep and wakefulness. During NREM sleep, the rate of metabolic activity throughout the brain slows by 30 percent, scientists at the National Institute of Mental Health have recently found. This finding supports the hypothesis that the brain "rests" in NREM sleep. As of this writing, REM sleep has yet to be assessed, since the studies involve the measurement of the rate at which the brain uses glucose to which a radioactive carbon has been added, and at present such measurements require study periods longer than REM sleep usually lasts.

Although going to sleep sometimes provokes anxiety about dying, we are actually more likely to die while pursuing our waking activities than while we sleep. Death comes most often in the hours between six in the evening and midnight.

Throughout sleep, blood pressure, heart rate and breathing show a steady overall decline to their twenty-four-hour low points. During REM sleep, even in people in perfect health, blood pressure, heart rate and breathing all fluctuate considerably. In people with chronically elevated blood pressure, the REM surges may further strain the heart and damage arteries. Some physicians suspect that, in people with heart and blood-vessel disorders, this added stress may trigger a heart attack or stroke.

However, statistics on the exact time that deaths occur in sleep are scanty; the time recorded often is the time the person was found dead in bed in the morning. The most common time of death from heart attacks and strokes theoretically would be the REM-rich period toward the end of sleep, or four to six in the morning in people who sleep at night. This theory—and it is only that—seems to have been elevated to a "fact" by frequent repetition in medical journals, newspapers and magazines. Studies of heart attack patients in intensive care units have not, however, implicated REM sleep as a time of added danger.

Body temperature falls while we sleep; it goes up slightly during

REM sleep in a warm room and down in a cool one, evidence that internal temperature control clicks off during this state. Usually, body temperature starts to rise shortly before the time we habitually awaken.

The secretion of many hormones is tied to sleep. One of the most important, growth hormone, is primarily released early in sleep in stage 3-4. Children need this hormone for normal development. Some victims of child abuse, afraid to sleep or repeatedly forced to awaken, simply do not grow. Their dwarfism results from lack of growth hormone; once they are removed from their homes and permitted to sleep, their growth resumes, often at a rapid pace. In adults, the hormone is thought to be useful in the healing of wounds and other bodily repair. Growth hormone secretion declines with age, along with the decline in the time we spend in slow-wave sleep.

During REM sleep, males of all ages, even newborn babies, have partial or full erections of the penis. In females, the clitoris becomes engorged with blood and vaginal pulse and lubrication both increase. These physiological responses occur in all REM periods, regardless of dream content. Their presence or absence already has been utilized to aid the diagnosis of impotence in men and is being applied experimentally to provide information about sexual disorders in women. (The relationship of sleep to various medical disorders is described further in Chapter 13, "In Sickness and Health.")

While asleep, we do not remain in one place, like a car with the motor idling. Yet the activity of body and brain are paradoxical. During "quiet" sleep (NREM) we move around, although we do so less often than while awake. During "active" sleep (REM) our ability to move is turned off; we lie paralyzed. A REM dream message from the brain to kick a football would be reflected as a slight twitch in the big toe.

People who insist, "I slept like a log," or note that they are in the same position in the morning that they assumed when going to sleep, often are astonished to see a series of time-lapse photos taken at regular intervals throughout the night. We curl up, stretch out, fling an arm or leg to the side, bury the head under a pillow, shed the blankets or wrap them tightly, changing positions an average of thirty times a night. Major posture shifts, including turning over, occur regularly before and after REM periods; a Harvard study showed that 60 percent of all large body movements occurred in the two minutes before or after REM.

Movements during sleep are thought to serve the important function of keeping the body in a state of readiness for waking. In fact, movements often prompt partial or full awakenings, although we generally remain awake for less than fifteen seconds, too briefly to remember the event in the morning. Of course, no one wants to be aware of tossing and turning all night. It's not moving around per se that makes us describe the night as "good" or "bad" but rather awakening without being able to fall back to sleep quickly. Poor sleepers move around more and wake more often than good sleepers. Awakenings also occur more often and last longer as we grow older, supporting the impression that sleep worsens with age.

Two people who sleep together learn to synchronize their movements. The smaller the bed, the greater the synchrony, an interesting demonstration that we maintain conscious awareness during sleep. Yet couples who sleep together do not get quite as much deep sleep as either partner does when sleeping alone.

Individual sleep patterns are so distinctive that they have been likened to fingerprints. However, the sleep patterns of normal healthy people of the same age show many similarities. Hence, sleep specialists can compare an individual's records to norms for his age in order to diagnose the nature of a sleep disturbance.

Sleep Changes Over Life

Babies still in the womb exhibit behavior that resembles waking and sleeping. The unborn child has quiet periods with chest wall movements similar to those of a breathing newborn; fluid, not air, moves in and out of mouth and lungs. Ultrasound studies show that, at the same time, eyes are inactive, implying a period of quiet sleep. Rapid eye movements appear to begin at twenty-three weeks and then to become increasingly frequent. In fact, eye movements may be a good predictor of normal fetal development.

Newborns usually sleep from sixteen to eighteen hours a day. Infants born too early, and full-term infants who are small, as you might expect, sleep more erratically than other newborn babies.

More than fifty years ago, psychologist Arnold Gesell categorized infant sleep behavior into four phases: going to sleep, staying asleep, waking up and staying awake. In its first four months, the infant isn't good at any of these, he felt. Today's sleep specialists, drawing on new understanding of circadian rhythms, emphasize instead the remarkably speedy way a baby adapts to the ways of its parent's world. In the early months a baby falls asleep while nursing and often awakens crying. By four months, however, he finishes eating before falling asleep, falls soundly asleep, stays asleep for longer periods and does not awaken crying.

The newborn's sixteen to eighteen hours of sleep are spread out over six to eight sleep periods, approximately equal in length. By three months of age, the infant usually sleeps mainly at night, and the longest period of wakefulness predictably occurs in late afternoon and early evening. By six months of age, the infant's sleep pattern already resembles that of the adult, with the longest sleep period occurring between ten at night and eight in the morning. In addition, the baby usually takes a morning and afternoon nap.

By their second birthdays, two thirds of all children take just a single nap in the afternoon. The average two-year-old gets about twelve hours of sleep a day. By age four, most children rebel against taking a nap. As a rule, they require only a single nighttime sleep period. From about age six until they are well into puberty, at about fourteen, most children spend eight and one-half to nine hours asleep. From puberty through late adolescence, the average time in bed decreases by about an hour. (Children's sleep behavior is a major source of concern to parents. For more information, turn to Chapter 5, "The Growing Years.")

Adolescence, after infancy the time of life with the most rapid body growth and development, is marked by striking changes in sleep. Work at Stanford University indicates that even when adolescents sleep as long as they wish at night, they are still sleepy during the day. While the reasons for this excessive sleepiness during the teenage years are not yet well defined, recognition that it is normal may alleviate family squabbles over sleeping late on weekends.

Adults average seven to eight hours of sleep a night, although most of us tend to sleep about an hour more on weekends than weekdays, trying to compensate for lost sleep during the week. The changes in sleep that occur from young adulthood to old age are described by Wilse Webb, Ph.D., of the University of Florida, as a "fraying" of the sleep process. The changes are gradual, much like the graying of the hair or the development of wrinkles.

As we grow older, we have more trouble sustaining sleep at night and we begin to nap more during the day. The often-voiced wish "to sleep like a baby" is granted in old age, but it does not bring us joy. Ideally, we'd all sleep like preteen children; they slumber soundly through the night and are on the go all day. (For more on sleep and aging, see Chapter 6, "The Later Years.")

The changes in amount of sleep from infancy to adulthood are paralleled by changes in the percentage of total sleep time spent in the various sleep stages. Full-term newborn babies spend half of their sleep time in REM, or "active," sleep and half in NREM, or "quiet," sleep. Sleep that can be distinguished as NREM stages 2 and 3-4 develops by three months of age. By six months, only a quarter of sleep time is spent in REM sleep.

These early, major changes in sleep have led some researchers to conclude that REM sleep must be a primitive state and that sleep, especially REM sleep, must perform some essential function, most likely involving learning or maturation of the brain. The corollary of this concept is that NREM sleep must be a more complex state, since its development parallels maturation of the central nervous system. Of course, the fact that we get both states of sleep in cyclic fashion also suggests that both are necessary.

From the age of six until they enter puberty, children spend about one quarter of their time in the deep sleep of stage 3-4, about one quarter in REM sleep, half in the lighter sleep of stage 2 and only a tiny proportion in the transition between sleeping and waking of stage 1. After adolescence and throughout adulthood, the proportion of deep sleep decreases, while that of lighter sleep and time awake during the night increases. At puberty, REM falls to about 20 percent of sleep and then holds constant in healthy people until extreme old age when it declines slightly.

Our Waking Lives: Larks and Owls

Some of us feel and function best at a favorite time of day. Indeed, one in four of us is distinctly a "morning person," a "lark," and one in four is an "evening person," an "owl"; the rest of us show no strong bent in either direction.

The larks are out jogging at seven; the owls take to the streets late in the day. Larks open up the office; owls get docked for coming in late. The larks' hero is featured in an early morning television commercial; he's the stockbroker with the "winning attitude" for whom "the day can't start too early." The owls, struggling to get out of bed when they hear those words, heave a pillow at the tube. Larks won't stop at a restaurant for ice cream after the theater; owls make dinner reservations for ten. Larks photograph sunrises; owls go swimming in the moonlight. If there's an important job that must get done, larks get up early, while owls stay up late. Early birds make great surgeons or school bus drivers, but it's harder for them than for owls to adapt to the changing demands of shift work.

Are we owls or larks by nature or by habit? Or both? To find out, researchers have studied personality and circadian temperature rhythms. Larks are more likely to be introverts and owls to be extraverts, particularly from age forty on.

In morning types, body temperature rises rapidly after awakening, stays at a plateau and begins to fall at about seven-thirty in the evening. In evening types, temperature rises gradually through the day; it peaks and starts to drop about an hour later than in morning types. Since a rise in body temperature is associated with a rise in alertness and a dip in temperature with diminished alertness, the dynamics of the temperature curves reflect a difference that cannot be accounted for simply by differences in the times the two groups go to bed and wake up, say James Horne, of the University of Technology, Loughborough, England, and Olov Östberg, of the Swedish National Board of Occupational Safety and Health.

Another study of 100 college students found, in addition to sleep-pattern differences between larks and owls, that the larks reported better sleep quality, fewer worries and thoughts, fewer night problems and a better feeling in the morning. When Wilse Webb, Ph.D., and his colleague Michael Bonnet, Ph.D., of the University of Florida asked the owls to attempt to get up at lark arousal times, they found that these differences persisted even when the time of sleep was shifted.

Social surroundings may modify natural tendencies. In the college environment, for example, social life promotes evening activity, thus eventually redefining both the point of peak body temperature and the distribution of temperature across the day. If the students had to face a nine-to-five job, their body temperature peak would be earlier in the day. Hence, tendencies toward being a morning or an evening person may change over life.

There may be some truth to Ben Franklin's aphorism "Early to bed, early to rise, makes a man healthy, wealthy and wise." A study of 104 medical students found that those who earned better grades got up early and reported better sleep quality.

A marriage between a lark and an owl has more conflicts than one between two larks or two owls. When compared with a matched couple, the partners in a "mixed" marriage have sexual relations less frequently, go out together less often and spend less time talking to each other, according to Bert Adams, Ph.D., professor of sociology at the University of Wisconsin, and Ronald Cromwell, Ph.D., director of the University of Missouri's Family Study Center.

The matched couples may have difficulty creating distance, the mismatched couples, togetherness. The best-adjusted couples create a balance, the researchers say. Sometimes one spouse becomes a lark or an owl to avoid the other; one who putters around the house long after the other is in bed may be trying to escape sexual relations, for example.

Family harmony and interaction are also influenced by these factors. When family members go to sleep and arise at approximately the same times, they rate family life as more satisfactory than do families with different patterns. Of nearly 500 college students surveyed, one explained, "Because we are all similar, we do a lot of things together." Another told how conflicts arise, saying, "My parents don't want me to sleep when they're up and working."

Ups and Downs

Not all of us are morning or evening people. However, everyone is subject to many daily fluctuations in mood and performance.

This clear twenty-four-hour rhythm in our sleepiness and alertness was demonstrated by experiments at Stanford University involving a "ninety-minute day." Volunteers agreed to go to bed every ninety minutes around the clock, staying in bed for thirty minutes each time. If they fell asleep, they were permitted to stay asleep for the remainder of their time in bed.

If they were able to fall asleep instantly and stay asleep for the full thirty minutes each "day," they would get a total of eight hours sleep in every twenty-four hours. But no one did. Sometimes they fell asleep nearly as soon as they got to bed. Other times they stayed awake for the entire thirty minutes.

People were sleepier at four in the afternoon than at ten o'clock in the evening. Maximum sleepiness—reflected by falling asleep the fastest—did not coincide with conventional sleeping hours in the real world, showing researchers that the ease of falling asleep does not occur at precisely the same time we usually sleep, even though, under normal circumstances, the two times clearly are linked. Certainly it's possible for us to stay up when we are at our most sleepy and to go to sleep when we are at our most alert, although it isn't easy, as anyone who has ever traveled across time zones knows.

Following the discovery of a ninety-minute NREM/REM cycle during sleep, Dr. Nathaniel Kleitman theorized that the sleep cycle is only part of a continuous daily rhythm, which he labeled the "Basic Rest-Activity Cycle" or BRAC. In recent years, researchers have uncovered a number of regular cycles, many recurring approximately every ninety minutes. However, they do not appear to be synchronized; the highs of one may be the lows or midcycles of others.

When individuals are left in a room with food and told that they can eat whenever they wish, they start munching every eighty to one hundred minutes. Even without eating, stomach contractions occur about every hundred minutes. There are ninety-minute cycles in urine flow. People pursuing their normal daily activities —working as a computer programmer, clerking in a hotel, going to the beach, taking a shower or watching television—when asked to describe their ongoing thoughts into a dictaphone every ten minutes, turn out to be daydreaming roughly every ninety minutes. When the diameter of the pupil of the eye is checked every fifteen minutes over a ten-hour period, it is noted to change every seventy to ninety minutes.

Such studies have many implications for daily life. If we could learn to eat only when we are hungry, fewer of us might become fat. Artists and writers might be able to tap their most creative, imaginative times. Air-traffic controllers and long-distance drivers could schedule work breaks when they are most prone to be inattentive and to make mistakes. And finally, if more of us learned to go to sleep at a time most propitious for sleep, there might be fewer complaints of insomnia. Indeed, we might all feel and function much better all day.

Such goals are within the realm of the possible. To achieve them most of us need only to pay sustained attention to the expression of "body time" and then to adjust, as best we can, the schedule of the outer world to the demands of our inner clocks.

If we stay up late, get up early, get less or more sleep than usual, take naps, cross time zones or simply set a clock forward or backward twice a year to conform to daylight-saving time, we alter our sleep. The one question that is central to our understanding of how much manipulation of sleep we as individuals can handle well is also the question most frequently asked of sleep researchers: "How much sleep do I need?" That's the subject of the next chapter.

3

HOW MUCH SLEEP DO WE NEED?

None of us would walk into a store expecting to get a comfortable fit from shoes of an "average" size. But many of us firmly believe that all adults should spend eight hours asleep each night. We worry that not getting that magic number of hours will have dire effects, not only on the next day, but over a lifetime, making our minds crumble or our lives shorter. On the other hand, many of us also think that eight hours are enough and that long-sleepers are lazy.

Seven to eight hours of sleep per day is, indeed, the norm, or average, for adults, numerous studies show. About two thirds of a population sample of 23,000 Americans over the age of twenty, including equal numbers of men and women, reported getting this amount of sleep when surveyed by the National Center for Health Statistics in 1977. Nearly half of 4,000 freshmen at the University of Florida, Gainesville, said they averaged 7.5 to 8.5 hours a night in the previous year. The average of seven to eight hours holds true even in far northern latitudes, where there are extreme shifts in the ratio of light to darkness over the course of a year. People who live for weeks or months in caves, research laboratories or other isolated environments without clocks, windows or other indicators of time, sleeping and arising whenever they choose, spend one third of their time asleep.

Some people interpret these averages to mean that sleeping seven to eight hours is good for us, a goal toward which we all should work. But that's as unrealistic as aiming to be exactly 5 feet 4 inches tall or to have an intelligence quotient of 125. "One size fits all" does not apply to sleep.

The amount of sleep that's right for you is part of your genetic makeup. Your age, physical and emotional health and life-style may affect the amount that your body demands at different times. Yet individual needs, like shoe sizes, have a limited range. No one sleeps constantly. No one goes without sleep at all.

About two people in ten, slightly more men than women, sleep less than six hours a night, the National Center for Health Statistics reports. About one in ten, slightly more women than men, sleeps nine hours or more a night. Six and nine are the numbers sleep specialists generally use when they talk about short- or long-sleepers.

People who sleep less than six or more than nine hours a night do seem to have a higher risk of dying from heart disease, cancer or stroke than people who average seven to eight hours of sleep a night, according to a recent study of seven thousand adults by researchers at the University of California, San Diego. But sleep experts caution that although very short or very long sleep, particularly if it represents a change in customary habits, may reflect an underlying illness, many healthy people differ considerably from the average in the amount they sleep at night.

Perhaps one person in twenty-five sleeps less than five or more than ten hours each night. Very short sleepers are so unusual that they generate reports in scientific journals. Several healthy people who claimed to sleep only a few hours a night responded to a newspaper ad placed by sleep researchers Henry Jones and Ian Oswald of the University of Western Australia. Among them were a fifty-four-year-old businessman and a thirty-year-old draftsman who agreed to be monitored for a week in a sleep lab. Both averaged only three hours, their usual amount, as their wives confirmed. Neither felt the need for more sleep.

A seventy-year-old nurse had an even more extreme case of "healthy insomnia." She slept an average of only sixty-seven minutes per night on five successive nights in the sleep laboratory, with no naps at other times during the day and no signs of tiredness. It was a mystery to her why other people waste so much time sleeping, she told Dr. Meddis, of the University of Technology, Loughborough, England. She said she had averaged only an hour of sleep a day since childhood.

The hours we sleep may vary considerably from one day to the next. We lead busy lives; sometimes the amount of sleep we get is less than the amount we truly need. Women employed full-time sleep less than women employed part-time, for example, and shift workers on rotating schedules get less sleep than permanent day-shift workers. Full-time working women and shift workers often complain that they get less sleep than they would like.

By inventing electricity, Thomas Edison robbed us of sleep, asserts Wilse Webb, Ph.D., director of the sleep laboratory at the University of Florida. Edison himself was a notorious owl; he often fumed that "sleep is a waste of time." School children surveyed by Dr. Webb in the sixties got an hour less sleep than children of the same age questioned in 1900. Researchers at the Annenberg School of Communications, Philadelphia, say television-viewing is a factor in the decline in time spent sleeping; late-night news or entertainment proves more attractive than sleep.

In the animal world, creatures that need to spend more time foraging for food or avoiding predators often sleep less. The lion sleeps longer than its prey, the antelope. Elephants in the wild, who need to find an enormous quantity of food, sleep less than elephants in zoos and circuses.

While sleep schedules may have developed throughout evolution to suit the life-style of each species, it's hard to account for all variations. The giant sloth, true to its name, sleeps twenty hours a day. Cats and mice sleep about thirteen hours. Like humans, pigs and rabbits average eight hours, while cows, goats and horses get only two or three. Each species seems to have its own range. However, when, for example, mice at the same end of the sleep-length spectrum are mated, their offspring tend to resemble the parents and to be either long-sleepers or short-sleepers.

You may find compatibility in sleep needs desirable in a mate; two people who require widely different amounts of sleep may find this matter hard to reconcile.

The Long and Short of It

Apart from the variation in hours spent snoozing, do long-sleepers and short-sleepers differ? This question has long intrigued researchers.

Worldly success does not seem to depend on getting by with less sleep than the average person requires. When 509 "men of distinction" were surveyed, they reported sleeping an average of 7.4 hours per day. While the achievements of Thomas Edison and Napoleon Bonaparte are frequently attributed to their sleeping only four to six hours a day, it's less well publicized that both took regular naps. Albert Einstein reportedly was a long-sleeper.

People whose work involves physical labor don't, on the average, sleep more or less than people whose work is primarily mental. Construction workers and professional football players don't get more or less sleep than file clerks or college professors. Soccer players get the same amount of sleep as their fans. The mentally retarded get about as much sleep as geniuses.

No differences in personality, intellectual ability or physical health were turned up by Dr. Webb and his colleagues at the University of Florida when twenty-two college students who regularly slept 6.5 hours or less were compared with thirty-two students who slept 9.5 hours or more.

However, the opposite conclusion emerged from a study of men over the age of twenty conducted by Ernest Hartmann, M.D., director of the sleep laboratory at the Lemuel Shattuck Hospital, Boston. He compared people averaging 5.6 hours with those averaging 9.7 hours per night. The short-sleepers tended to be efficient, energetic and ambitious. Socially adept, secure, satisfied with themselves and their lives, several short-sleepers claimed, "I never let my worries go to my head." They tended to be conformist in their social and political views. Though relatively free of emotional disturbances, short-sleepers tended to avoid problems by keeping busy and by denying that problems existed. The long-sleepers, as a group, showed more doubts about their career choices and their life situations; several were artistic and creative. Many complained of a variety of minor aches and pains and tended to hold nonconformist and critical views of social and political affairs. A few admitted that they sometimes used sleep as an escape when reality became unpleasant. They tended to be worriers. None had serious psychiatric illnesses but most had such neurotic problems as anxiety, inhibition in aggressive and sexual functioning or mild depression. Both long- and short-sleepers got about the same amounts of deep stage 3-4 sleep. Because they slept longer, long-sleepers got more REM (rapid eye movement) sleep, the state in which mental activity in the form of dreaming most often occurs. Hence, Dr. Hartmann postulates that worriers may need extra dreaming sleep and that dreaming sleep may play a role in restoring the brain and psyche.

Some of us need less sleep when things are going well and more sleep when life is tough. When Dr. Hartmann surveyed some five hundred "variable" sleepers, he found that, as a rule, they needed less sleep when their lives were without change or stress, when they were happy and healthy and involved in interesting or enjoyable tasks. By contrast, they needed more sleep when they were ill or burdened by unwanted extra physical work, as well as when they had mental stresses, such as those caused by a job change, heavy work responsibilities or a depressed mood. The ability of some people to escape from their problems in sleep, at least temporarily, was addressed by Shakespeare, who called sleep "surcease from sorrow."

Self-imposed stress may also influence the number of hours we set aside for sleep. People with the hard-driving coronary-prone "Type A" personality often have habitually shortened sleep, reports Robert Hicks, Ph.D., of San Jose (California) State University. Those who willingly sacrifice sleep in favor of a frenetic life-style may have certain personality characteristics in common. However, if personality traits really accounted for differences in the number of hours people sleep, this fact surely would be more obvious to all of us.

Length of Sleep

Most of us go to sleep when we want to but get up when we have to. How long we could sleep if not awakened by an alarm clock is not as unpredictable as it may seem.

One factor is how long we were previously awake. The longer we have gone without our usual sleep, the more likely we are to make up for some of our "lost" sleep. But a more important determinant of the amount of time we could sleep is the cyclic rise and fall in our body temperature (from about 97°F to 99°F every day).

If we usually sleep from about eleven at night to seven in the morning, body temperature starts to fall in the early evening, decreasing our alertness and making us ready for bed. It is lowest between two and four in the morning and starts to rise an hour or two before we customarily awaken.

If we were living in an environment free of time cues—such as a windowless apartment or a cave—the relationship between body temperature and the length of time we sleep would become more obvious. In a study conducted by Charles Czeisler, M.D., Ph.D., and his colleagues at Montefiore Hospital, New York, twelve men lived separately for 16 to 189 days on a self-scheduled routine without any knowledge of time or of their body temperature.

When the men went to sleep just after the low point of their body temperature, they slept an average of 7.8 hours. By contrast, when they went to sleep at or after the temperature peaked, they slept an average of 14.4 hours. (Once, one man slept twenty hours straight.) If they had been awake for at least fourteen hours, further hours of wakefulness did not affect how long they slept.

Nearly all of their waking times occurred as their temperatures were rising. The most frequently chosen time to go to sleep was just after the temperature low point. Hence, there were more short sleep periods than long ones. This same pattern of shorter sleep periods alternating with longer sleep periods has been documented in people living for long periods in caves or isolation environments, although no one previously had identified the critical role of body temperature.

This finding has practical implications for everyday life. It explains why it is hard to get restful sleep or enough sleep when we sleep at the wrong time with respect to the temperature cycle, regardless of how long we previously have been awake, and why changing our times for sleeping and waking often makes us feel out of sorts while awake. You don't have to take your temperature periodically during the day to benefit from this knowledge. If you go to sleep and get up at regular times, your temperature will fall before your accustomed bedtime and rise before your usual time of awakening. Stabilizing your temperature rhythms will enable you to sleep your best at night and feel most alert during the day. If you are traveling across many time zones or working on rotating shifts, you can minimize your discomfort by sticking as close as possible to a consistent time for sleeping. Ideally, you would allow yourself to sleep until you awaken naturally, letting your body tell you how much sleep is enough for you.

After his eleven-day marathon, Randy Gardner slept for just under fifteen hours. Even if you undergo a prolonged period without sleep, fifteen to eighteen hours of "recovery" sleep is as much as the body demands. You don't have to "pay back" one hour of sleep for every extra hour you stay awake. You will spontaneously wake up as your body temperature follows its cyclic upswing.

Time to Wake Up

Have you ever awakened just seconds before the alarm went off? Many of us have done so before an early job interview, trip or other exciting event. Could you prime yourself to do it every day?

Before modern sleep-laboratory research started, scientists tested the notion that some people could consistently wake up at a predetermined time. Early in this century, a German researcher observed five people for 250 nights. His subjects usually woke up five minutes ahead of an agreed-upon time. They woke up suddenly, and some said that, in the midst of a dream, they felt as though they were interrupted by the words: "It's time, you must wake up now."

If sufficiently motivated, you probably can awaken yourself at an unusual hour. But you pay a price: You awaken more frequently to check the time. Hence, most of us will sleep better if we place our trust in an alarm clock or a wake-up service.

In people who sleep regular amounts and normally awaken by themselves, partial or even complete brief awakenings do not mark the end of sleep. Rather, sleep continues in its orderly, cyclic fashion until we awaken fully and finally. At the end of sleep, we spend most of our time in light stage 2 sleep and in REM sleep. We are equally likely to awaken from either; but if we awaken from REM sleep, we are more likely to recall a dream. We also may feel more alert.

Not all of us awaken cheerfully. "It is about time that someone exploded the myth that a good sleep causes you to wake refreshed," asserts Dr. Meddis. The person who discovers a marketable potion to make us awaken in good spirits will earn a fortune, he conjectures.

How you wake up may affect how you feel. A sudden awakening sometimes produces the sensation of "sleep inertia," or "sleep drunkenness." If your phone rings in the middle of the night, and you are awakened from deep stage 3-4 sleep, you may find yourself confused and disoriented. Some of us feel this way even when we wake in the morning. You fall out of bed to stifle the alarm clock and lurch into the bathroom, stubbing your toe on the way. You splash cold water on your face, grope for the towel—and miss it. Your family knows that you don't start perking until well after the coffee is done.

Although the process of awakening normally takes only a few seconds, some of us do not feel mentally awake until some time after we are physiologically awake. Milton Kramer, M.D., of the University of Mississippi and his colleagues at the University of Cincinnati, found that sleepers rated themselves as more "sleepy" five minutes after awakening in the morning than five minutes before going to bed at night.

Sleep inertia usually lasts less than fifteen minutes after awakening in the morning, and is even briefer after an afternoon nap. If you've had enough sleep, you're unlikely to be bogged down by this problem.

We may need to recover from sleep as well as from wakefulness. No one knows why. The feelings of sleepiness at bedtime and sleep inertia after waking demonstrate that sleeping and waking are not as distinct as we sometimes believe.

Shuffling Sleep Around

It's rare for any of us to get the same amount of sleep every night. Most of us sleep longer on weekends or when we are not working than we do during the week or on workdays. In fact, regular sleep is an exception.

Students at the University of Florida who kept sleep diaries reported an average swing over a month of ninety-two minutes. One quarter of a group of fifty- to sixty-year-olds in another Florida survey described a usual range of three hours. People who are divorced or separated tend to go to bed not only later than average but also at a different time each night.

If we want to stay up to watch a movie, read a book, attend a party or cram for an exam, we can force ourselves to do it. If we want to get up early to catch a plane or go fishing, we can do that, too.

Observes Dr. Webb: "How fortunate this is and what a different world it would be otherwise! Suppose we were 'struck down' by sleep after sixteen or seventeen hours [of wakefulness] while we were walking home from a late show. We would have to organize 'sleep patrols' to come and gather up all those who had missed their time schedules from the sidewalks and benches and nooks and crannies where they had dropped into sleep and to deliver them to their beds.

"We would be trapped in the inexorable demands of a rigid set of boundaries in our life and much of its richness and resources would be lost."

Do changes in how much sleep we get from night to night, and when we get it, make any difference in our lives? To find out, researchers have come up with a catalog of experiments. Volunteers have slept—or tried to sleep—every two, three or four hours around the clock. People have taken naps of various lengths, at various times of day. Some have been told to go to bed and sleep as long as possible. Others have been told to go to bed and stay awake as long as possible. People have been asked to sleep more or less than they normally do, go to bed earlier or later or get up earlier or later. Some have slept in laboratories where they have been deprived of various sleep stages or states by researchers hovering over polygraph machines and dashing to the bedside as soon as it shows the prohibited type of sleep. Some people have been asked to skip sleep entirely.

The results of such studies show that even very small shifts in the timing of your usual sleep may be disruptive. Most of us have experienced jet lag after crossing several time zones, the result of trying to stay awake and to sleep at the "wrong" time of our biological day. But even the one-hour shift forward that occurs with a change to daylight-saving time in the spring may bother you. Researchers at the University of Sussex, England, found that more traffic accidents occurred the week after the spring change than the week before.

Short-sleepers suffer more than long-sleepers from acute alterations in the length and timing of sleep. John Taub, Ph.D., of the Sleep and Performance Laboratory at St. Louis University, compared two groups of ten healthy male university students, one composed of 7-hour to 8-hour sleepers, and the other of 9.5-hour to 10.5-hour sleepers. In different experiments, the students were put to bed three hours later than usual, awakened three hours earlier than usual, deprived of three hours of sleep or permitted to sleep three hours longer. On various tests the next day, the short-sleepers performed more poorly than the long-sleepers.

The timing of sleep may make a difference, even if you get the same amount of sleep. Suppose you normally sleep from midnight to seven, but an occasion arises when you have to be at a meeting at seven in the morning. If you could get seven hours of sleep, from ten o'clock to five, would you be as sharp as usual? Or suppose you stay late visiting with friends and then try to sleep from two to nine in the morning. In the first instance, you'd probably find it difficult, if not impossible, to fall asleep early. In the second, you'd be trying to sleep in the morning at a time when your body is ready to get going.

Most of us recognize that doing without two hours of sleep may hamper work, erode motivation and make us irritable the next day. However, it's less often recognized that adding on a couple of hours may not be beneficial either. Many of us deliberately sleep late on weekends to make up for lost sleep during the week. Sometimes after getting more sleep than usual, we awaken feeling terrific. But sometimes we feel worn-out and short-tempered and have trouble getting going. George Globus, M.D., of the University of California at Irvine, calls such feelings the "blah syndrome." This curious experience dashes cold water on the popular notion that "sleep is always good for us." It may be the result of trying to sleep at a time when we ordinarily are accustomed to active pursuit of daily activities. While the best way to avoid the blahs is to get enough sleep every day, the problem illustrates that both the amount and the timing of sleep need to be taken into account in our daily lives.

Taking Naps

Most of us get the bulk of our sleep in a single period, usually at night. But the very young, the very old, people living in warm climates, people confined to institutions and about half of all college students also nap during the day.

Some people claim great benefits from brief naps. Painter Salvador Dali is credited with devising a classic catnap. He puts a tin plate on the floor and sits in a chair beside it. Holding a spoon over the plate, he drifts off. As soon as he falls asleep, the spoon slips from his fingers, clangs on the plate and awakens him. He claims that he is refreshed by the sleep he gets between the time the spoon leaves his hand and the time it plunks onto the plate.

In children, napping is generally attributed to an immature central nervous system that cannot sustain sleep or wakefulness for long. In older people, naps may represent an attempt to compensate for disturbed sleep at night and reflect the availability of time free for napping. Excessive daytime napping—in the young and in the old—may interfere with sleep at night.

Napping may be a habit that is reinforced by cultural patterns. Mexican adults, for example, average more sleep than their American or English counterparts. In studying 257 residents of Hermosillo, Mexico, Dr. Taub found that four out of five took four or more naps per week during at least one season of the year. Most averaged more than nine hours of sleep per day. Their naps lasted about an hour and a half. The siesta was not simply an adaptation to heat; half of the nappers took a siesta year round despite a range in seasonal temperature from 60°F in winter to 90°F in summer. Among the nappers, older people took more and longer naps.

For those of us who experience midday drowsiness, the siesta may be more natural than the single sleep period typical of Western culture as a whole. Indeed, some of us might be better off taking afternoon nap breaks instead of coffee breaks. A regular nap might make us more alert than a simple work break.

Dr. Taub found that college students who usually napped got higher scores on skill and memory tests after napping. They also felt more cheerful and energetic after napping. When they skipped their naps, they performed and felt worse than usual. By contrast, when college students who normally did not nap slept for an hour in the afternoon, they woke up groggy and irritable, and their test scores dropped. "Like medications, naps can have side effects," says Dr. Taub.

Morning naps resemble the last part of nighttime sleep, while late-afternoon naps resemble its beginning. That's why morning naps often involve vivid dreams and late-day naps often leave us groggy after we awaken. "Naps clearly are not miniatures of the normal eight-hour sleep pattern," observes Elliot Weitzman, M.D., director of the Institute of Chronobiology at the New York Hospital-Cornell Medical Center, White Plains. The reason, he notes, is that the propensity to have one sleep stage or state rather than another varies during a twenty-four-hour period. Assuming you normally sleep at night, if you went back to sleep at ten in the morning you'd probably have a high amount of REM sleep, whereas if you did so at ten at night you'd get stage 3–4.

In sum, whether or not a person benefits from naps depends on the length of time he has been awake before napping, the time of day he naps, how long he sleeps and whether he is a regular napper.

Although a single period of sleep is customary for most of us, LaVerne Johnson, Ph.D., of the Naval Medical Research Center, San Diego, notes that there may be times when it isn't feasible. Dr. Johnson asks, "Can we space our sleep out as we do our food requirement? Will three square naps a day suffice?"

Studies of volunteers on a variety of sleeping, waking, exercising and resting schedules yielded these conclusions:

1. If you get your sleep in a single chunk, you'll probably func-

tion better than if you get the same amount of sleep in periodic naps.

2. Naps are better than no sleep at all.

3. If you cannot get as much sleep as usual, you'll probably feel and function best if you can get as much sleep as possible in a single block during your regular sleep time.

4. The next best time to sleep, if you usually sleep at night, is during the afternoon.

Giving Up Sleep

Is sleep a habit that we can kick? If we could, would we? Some of us view sleep as a waste of time, although, if pressed, we reluctantly concede that we don't feel well without it. We know that if we habitually sleep eight hours, a night in which we get only six hours is probably going to make us feel downcast the next day. The idea of being able to reduce sleep without suffering ill effects is, for most of us, a delightful fantasy.

Many of us have on occasion managed with far less sleep than usual. College students cramming for exams, soldiers on duty, hospital interns and even sleep researchers often are on restricted sleep schedules. Most quickly return to their habitual amounts of sleep as soon as the opportunity arises.

Permanently reducing the number of hours we sleep is another story. Four couples following a program of gradual sleep reduction supervised by scientists at the Naval Health Research Center, San Diego, and the University of California at Irvine, learned in four to six months to reduce their habitual sleep periods by one to two hours.

All eight volunteers were in their twenties, in good physical and mental health and had no sleep disturbances. Motivation to reduce their sleep time was one of the reasons they were selected for the study. After each partner was trained to apply electrodes to the other for sleep recordings, the couples slept in their own bedrooms at home, and portable recorders were used.

Three couples started out averaging eight hours of sleep; the other couple were already short-sleepers, averaging 6.5 hours. The eight-hour sleepers reduced their sleep to 6.5 hours by going to sleep thirty minutes later every two weeks. From 6.5 to 5.5 hours, all subjects reduced their sleep by thirty minutes every three weeks. Those who successfully reached 5.5 hours maintained this time for a month before making a further thirty-minute reduction. All were encouraged not to continue the sleep reduction beyond a level at which they felt comfortable. After completing a month at their shortest time, the study participants were allowed to increase their sleep length by thirty minutes. They stayed at this level for two more months and then were allowed to sleep as long as they wished.

Two of the eight-hour sleepers reduced their sleep to 5.5 hours, two to five hours and two to 4.5 hours. The 6.5-hour sleepers reduced their sleep to five hours.

Sleep reduction did not seem to pose a threat to anyone's health. All of the subjects continued to perform their work at the same levels as they had before the study, and none appeared to undergo major psychological changes. When the participants became too tired to continue, the study stopped.

What did the participants do with the extra time? They studied, went to the movies, exercised, read or watched television. One couple claimed the study gave them time to enrich their sex life, but another said that both partners were so sleepy and irritable that the quality and frequency of sexual intercourse suffered.

A year after the study ended, all of the eight-hour sleepers continued to sleep 1 to 2.5 hours less than they had when the study began. The couple who started out at 6.5 hours reverted to that level.

Six years later, Daniel Mullaney, M.S., of the University of California at San Diego, who was one of the original researchers, tracked down the participants. One woman, a former eight-hour sleeper, related, "I'm averaging less sleep now than before the study. I generally sleep between six and eight hours. I think I might sleep more if I had more time, but my life is very busy and I feel healthy and happy with the amount I'm getting." Her partner, with whom she was no longer living, gave this report: "I now get between zero and seven hours of sleep a night, with an average of about five hours. I'm convinced the study changed my sleep habits. I realized I could get by with less sleep without suffering ill effects. I can now tolerate total and partial sleep loss better than I could before. In sum, I'm very grateful to have been chosen as a subject." The 6.5-hour sleepers also had gone their separate ways. The male partner said he consistently averaged about 6.5 hours or slightly less. His former wife said she usually got four to five hours of sleep for five days in a row and then caught up with an eight-hour night. "I've chosen to live this way," she said. "The study showed me that this kind of flexibility was possible."

The long-term effects of sleep reduction are still not known, Mullaney cautions. "We've shown that it's possible to alter your sleep requirement, but I can't advise that anyone do it or say that it is perfectly safe," he comments.

The fact that no one in the California study was able to get by with less than 4.5 hours suggests that there may be a genetic limit below which the great majority of us cannot go. The researchers suggest that 6.5 hours may be a "bottom line" for most people.

"Perhaps, like eating, where you look and feel well and your weight stays the same on a diet that balances the amount of calories you take in with the amount of calories you burn, there also is, for any individual, an ideal sleep time that maintains effective waking behavior and maximum sleep efficiency," Mullaney says.

Find Out How Much Sleep You Need

An old folk saying on hours of sleep holds, "Nature requires five, custom takes seven, laziness nine and wickedness eleven." This saying reflects a widely held attitude toward sleep needs. But it overlooks the fact that the averages don't necessarily apply to you. Your "nature" may require five, seven, nine, eleven or a number of hours outside that range or in between.

Suppose we asked, "How much food does the average person need?" You'd say that question can't be answered. All of us are different heights and different weights and have different levels of activity and different rates of burning calories. Our individual needs for sleep are just as varied. Astonishingly, even Siamese twins require different amounts of sleep and may sleep and be awake independently, a fact confirming the individuality of the need for sleep.

The typical American adult seems to get too little sleep rather than enough or too much. That many of us are quite sleepy is illustrated by the fact that we fall asleep easily when given the opportunity to do so. In a series of "nap opportunities" offered five or six times during the day, college students and middle-aged adults fell asleep in an average of ten to twelve minutes. (People with such sleep disorders as narcolepsy and sleep apnea are even more sleepy; they fall asleep in less than five minutes.)

By contrast, when given the opportunity to sleep during the day, preadolescent children simply do not fall asleep. They are fully alert all day long. At night they fall asleep quickly and sleep solidly, with only brief and unremembered awakenings.

We recognize that it is not normal for a child to fall asleep in school. But we shrug off similar behavior in ourselves. "The fact that nearly everyone is chronically sleep-deprived has led to an acceptance of less than ideal daytime alertness as 'normal,'" says William Dement, M.D., director of the Sleep Disorders Center at Stanford University.

"It may be that if we slept more, the gain in our daytime pursuits over the long haul might more than compensate for giving up the extra hour or so of wakefulness," he adds.

Indeed, in one study, adults who slept only one hour more than usual for as few as three nights were less sleepy on the nap test and did better on tests of addition, memory, coordination and other aspects of performance.

You probably already are a good judge of how much food you need. You know how much extra you can eat without gaining weight if you're spending your vacation on the ski slopes and how much you must cut back in everyday life if the scale tips upward. In the same way, only you can figure out the proper setting of your own "sleep-stat." Throughout this book, you'll find information on factors that affect your sleep and guidelines to help you improve your sleep. Now is the time to assess your own sleep needs.

ARE YOU GETTING ENOUGH SLEEP?

- Do you need an alarm clock to awaken you? And do you have a hard time getting up in the morning? The best signs that you've had enough sleep are that you awaken spontaneously and soon feel alert.

• Do you drop off easily in front of the television, at concerts or in meetings? Such situations don't, as many people believe, cause sleepiness; they simply allow sleepiness to become apparent.

• Do you habitually "sleep in" an hour or more on weekends? That suggests that you're not getting enough sleep during the week.

• Are you trying to prove you're a superwoman or superman by getting along with less sleep than you need? Some people who claim to be short-sleepers are merely getting by with shortened sleep. (Good sleep habits are described in Chapter 15, "How to Get a Better Night's Sleep.")

• Do you have accidents or near-accidents at work or while driving because of sleepiness? Do you fall asleep while eating or conversing? This behavior is pathological and it may be a sign of sleep apnea (see Chapter 9, "The Snoring Sickness") or narcolepsy (see Chapter 10, "Too Sleepy People").

• Is feeling sleepy a way of avoiding sex or unpleasant tasks like paying bills? Are you feeling depressed? Stress and depression may cause fatigue and lack of energy. (See Chapter 14, "Troubled Minds/Troubled Sleep.")

ARE YOU TRYING TO FORCE YOURSELF TO GET MORE SLEEP THAN YOU NEED?

• Do you lie in bed long after the lights are out, wondering when sleep will come?
• Do you awaken before the alarm goes off?

HERE'S HOW TO GET THE AMOUNT OF SLEEP THAT'S RIGHT FOR YOU:

• For just one night, cut sleep back to half of your usual amount. The next day the effect that sleepiness has on you should be quite apparent. Be sensitive to sleepiness cues.
• For a month, get a fixed "dose" of sleep each night. Go to

sleep and get up at the same time seven days a week. Then adjust the dose up or down by no more than thirty minutes for two to four weeks and assess the difference in the way you feel.

• Pay attention to your daily rhythms of sleepiness and alertness. (You can chart them in the sleep/wake diary at the back of the book.)

• As an experiment, for a month or so, squeeze a regular nap into your day; for some people, a judiciously scheduled half hour of sleep is a great pepper-upper.

We might all do well, as Dr. Webb has suggested, to heed Samuel Johnson and accord sleep the respect due a "gentle tyrant." He cites Johnson's description: "To live on the best terms with a 'gentle tyrant' one must learn the rules by which he governs. Being gentle, he permits us certain freedoms to manifest our individual variations and differences; being a tyrant, he will not permit us to live in total freedom, and abuses carry their ultimate consequences."

4

THE STUFF
OF DREAMS

Every night, in the theater of the mind, you're invited to a private
showing, with previews, shorts and a full-length film. You may see
a prosaic documentary one night and a frothy comedy another.
Sometimes, you shiver through a thriller or quake at a horror film.
You might view reruns. You are both the audience and the star;
you see yourself perform the leading role. Perhaps you're not
aware that you also play the parts of your mother, your best
friends and even strangers, and that sometimes you disguise yourself as an animal or even as an object. Moreover, you concoct,
write, produce and direct your dreams. As the story unfolds, you
often watch the action, although you may step in and change it,
if you want. Afterward, you may elect still another role, that of
critic.

Some people boldly claim, "I never dream." But virtually everyone comes up with dream reports when monitored in a sleep
laboratory and awakened periodically during the night. The most
vivid, fantasylike scenarios occur roughly every ninety minutes
during the four or five periods in a normal night's sleep when our
eyes dart beneath closed lids, sometimes more rapidly than when
we are awake. But people awakened at other times during sleep also
frequently report that thoughts are going through their minds.

Reports after rapid eye movement (REM) periods usually are
more visual and storylike, while those after non-REM (NREM)
sleep tend to resemble ordinary, realistic thinking. REM reports

are the ones we relate to other family members over breakfast, the preposterous tales, the dream adventures, such as "I was out in the desert taking photographs of tigers." People who are awakened from NREM sleep and asked, "What was going through your mind just now?" may say, "I was thinking about some paperwork at my office"; they may even deny that they were asleep.

Night and day, mental activity seems to be continuous; that is, we think while we sleep as well as while we are awake. We may dredge up memories, examine our experiences and even reason in our dreams. Our REM thoughts, as reflected by our vivid and elaborately detailed dreams, may be analogous to our thoughts during wakefulness when we are concentrating. Our NREM thoughts, as reflected by brief reports and more commonplace topics, may resemble more closely the idle ideas we have while awake when our minds wander.

Some people dismiss dreams as mental graffiti, or as merely the foam on the beer of sleep. "One major obstacle to a full-fledged acceptance of dreaming as thinking is our reluctance to accept responsibility for our dreams," notes David Foulkes, Ph.D., director of the Cognition Research Laboratory at the Georgia Mental Health Institute. Dreams often seem crazy and illogical; at the same time, they may be crammed with intricate detail. "Dreams rarely are as illogical as they first seem," Dr. Foulkes points out. "But we have yet to acknowledge the full creative potential of our sleeping minds."

Viewing dreams as meaningless fantasies is like dismissing a foreign language as gibberish if we don't happen to understand it. In our waking lives, most of us rely on words. The language of dreams, however, is primarily visual. In the same way that we can grow to appreciate art, poetry or music, we can learn to decode the picture writing of dreams and use it to enlarge our understanding of our waking selves.

Dreams through History

The ancients often regarded dreams as messages from the supernatural. All cultures and religions have looked to dreams, and their interpreters, to explain the otherwise unexplainable.

The Bible attaches great importance to dreams. The Old Testament contains reports of over seventy dreams and visions; among the most familiar are those in the story of Joseph, his brothers and the Pharaoh of Egypt, which can be found in Genesis. The Gospel of Saint Matthew relates the dream of another Joseph, who has learned that Mary, his betrothed, is expecting a child. An angel appears to him in a dream and says to him, "Fear not . . . for that which is conceived in her is of the Holy Ghost." Later dreams prompt Joseph to flee with the infant Jesus to Egypt and, still later, to return to Israel.

The mother of Buddha had a dream that predicted her son's future before he was born. The prophet Muhammad is said to have received the first part of the Koran in a dream.

Ancient Egypt had temples for dream incubation whose resident priests were known as Masters of Secret Things. Dream interpretation, outlined in a four-thousand-year-old Egyptian dream book, relied on the theory of contraries—for example, if you dream of sickness, you will remain well; if you dream of losing money, you will become wealthy—an idea perpetuated today in dream guides commonly found at newsstands.

We owe our word "fantasy" to the name of the Greek god Phantasos, who, according to legend, was sometimes sent to appear in dreams by his father, Hypnos, the god of sleep.

In the fourth century B.C., Plato, in the *Republic*, observed, "Even in good men there is a lawless wild-beast nature, which peers out in sleep," a concept that is strikingly harmonious with one espoused by Sigmund Freud at the beginning of this century. Plato's student Aristotle recognized that dreams sometimes incorporate waking sensations in an exaggerated form, so that a person with a fever might dream of fire or a thirsty person might dream of rain. The way such sensations work their way into dreams has been explored by modern sleep scientists in experiments in which they have sprinkled water on the faces of sleepers, flashed lights before their closed eyes, clanged bells or raised or lowered the room temperature. In one experiment a subject was fed banana cream pie at regular intervals. This volunteer had said the pie was his favorite dessert, but after eating four pieces during the night, he dreamed he was scraping food into a garbage can.

Some 2,200 years ago, more than three hundred Greek temples

were devoted to using dreams to treat illnesses of body and mind. Pilgrims who came to these temples, which were dedicated to Aesculapius, the god of healing, would make sacrifices, pray and, often, drink a dream-inducing potion, probably made from a plant we now recognize as a hallucinogenic drug. Then they would go to sleep, hoping that Aesculapius would appear in their dreams and cure them.

In the second century A.D., a Greek soothsayer, Artemidorus, compiled an exhaustive text. His *Oneirocritica*, or *The Interpretation of Dreams*, was the first comprehensive attempt to classify and analyze dreams, and presaged later thought by addressing the concept of wish-fulfillment in dreams.

In 1900, Sigmund Freud chose the same title, *The Interpretation of Dreams*, for a book that is still held to be the single most important contribution to our understanding of dreams. Although his theories are not universally accepted, they set forth the themes that have served as catalysts for subsequent explorations. Moreover, *The Interpretation of Dreams* encompasses far more than dream psychology; it offers a comprehensive view of human nature, and it introduced the method of psychoanalysis as a way to examine that nature.

Freud saw in dreams the chance to observe what the human mind does—what it is like—when it is operating on its own, freed from external reality. As Dr. Foulkes relates, "By systematically comparing this mind with the more familiar one of waking experience, Freud saw that he not only could assimilate dream phenomena to waking psychology but that he also could, at the same time, immensely expand the scope of waking psychology."

Freud was the first to conceptualize dreams as a "royal road to the unconscious." He used the technique of free association to help the dreamer move from the actual content of the dream to the thoughts and emotions it engendered. In free association, you let your thoughts wander but pay attention to everything that comes to mind; the process attempts to re-create during waking the kind of mental activity Freud thought occurred during sleep. Freud saw that a torrent of associations could be reduced to a few common themes central to the dreamer's life.

He believed that dreams attempt to fulfill unsatisfied wishes and, by so doing, "protect" sleep and allow it to continue. He accounted for the strangeness of dreams by saying that because such wishes, involving gratification of forbidden infantile sexual impulses, are unacceptable to the dreamer and would be painful if acknowledged, they have to be disguised; hence, he distinguished between the manifest, or explicit, content of a dream and its latent, or implied, meaning.

From this viewpoint, Freud saw objects and activities that appeared in adults' dreams as having sexual connotations: Umbrellas, guns, sticks and other objects that are long or pointed or used for penetration, as well as fountains, faucets and other objects from which water flows, symbolize the penis; containers such as boxes and pockets, doorways and other entryways, and circular objects represent female genitalia. Climbing, running, flying and similar activities, according to Freud's theory, symbolize masturbation or sexual intercourse.

The concepts of wish-fulfillment and the primacy of sexual concerns aroused controversy from the very beginning. Psychologist Carl Jung termed Freud's theories "too narrow," and said, "It is true that there are dreams which embody suppressed wishes and fears, but what is there which the dream cannot on occasion embody?" The function of dreams, he wrote, "is to try to restore our psychological balance by producing dream-material that re-establishes, in a subtle way, the total psychic equilibrium." Jung suggested that the dream could "have the value of a positive, guiding idea," and that all the figures in the dream are "personified features of the dreamer's own personality."

In clinical psychiatry and psychology today, dreams are frequently used as tools to obtain access to the dreamer's thoughts and feelings. If, for example, a person is having trouble sorting out and confronting his feelings about his father, the task of relating and analyzing a dream about his father may help focus his thoughts and hence be useful as a point of departure. Therapists of various persuasions sometimes emphasize different—although not necessarily contradictory—aspects of the same dream content.

Dream Research Today

Discoveries made in the sleep laboratory offer the potential for productive new explorations into both the content of dreams and the nature of dreaming sleep.

"Dream recall, as a rule, is terrible," notes Rosalind Cartwright, Ph.D., director of the Sleep Disorders Service and Research Center at the Rush-Presbyterian-St. Luke's Medical Center, Chicago. "When we awaken, we ordinarily shift our focus quickly to the outside world. Unless dreams are unusually exciting, we need to make a special effort to remember them," she adds. "The sleep laboratory, however, lets us sample a far greater volume of dream material than is generally remembered the morning after."

Using the electroencephalograph (EEG) to determine when REM periods are in progress, scientists awaken sleepers and ask what is going through their minds. There are, of course, some practical limits to using the sleep laboratory to study dreams. Relatively few sleepers can be monitored there. Awakening a sleeper to "catch" his dream may alter its content, or that of the next dream. Even the relationship between the dreamer and the dream recorder can alter the nature of the report, since people sometimes choose not to reveal intimate or embarrassing thoughts.

The discovery of a biological marker for dreaming—rapid eye movements—has also raised questions about the function of the REM state. REM sleep—and perhaps dreaming as well—may serve a "sentinel" purpose. It's crucial for our own self-protection to be able to respond quickly during the night, in case of fire, for example. We might not be able to do so if we were totally oblivious to the world for seven or eight hours, but REM sleep brings us up out of deep sleep periodically during the night. Laboratory studies have shown that we respond to sounds when in REM sleep much as we do during the light sleep of NREM stage 2, and in both cases more easily than we do during the deep sleep of stage 3–4.

Some scientists believe that dreaming may aid learning and memory by helping us to consolidate the memories of the day just past with all that went before. They point to the progressive development of a theme in the dreams of a given night as evidence of the orderly, nonrandom nature of dreams. Studies of the changes in the content of an individual's dreams over time support the concept that dreams have problem-solving functions and reflect day-to-day events in our lives.

Dreams may serve as an "emotional thermostat" that helps us to regulate our daily moods, suggests Milton Kramer, M.D., director of the Division of Somnology at the University of Mississippi. Your emotional state influences what you dream, and what you dream influences your mood the next day. When you're in good shape emotionally, you tend not to remember your dreams, just as you don't ordinarily pay attention to your stomach unless it aches, he notes. If something is troubling you, you may continue to mull it over in sleep. Unresolved problems may stimulate unpleasant, often repetitive, dreams.

Researchers have been trying to uncover the physiological concomitants of dreaming. Some recent physiological research, understandably controversial, challenges the widely held concept that dreams are meaningful. It suggests that dream content reflects random activity of the brain during REM periods.

In the part of the brain that is critical for sleep, the brain stem (the lowest sector of the brain), certain large cells, appropriately called giant cells, have projections that go both up toward higher brain centers and down toward the rest of the body. These giant cells increase their activity just before a REM period and peak during it, according to J. Allan Hobson, M.D., and Robert McCarley, M.D., co-directors of the Laboratory of Neurophysiology at the Massachusetts Mental Health Center in Boston. They suggest that the giant cells trigger the specific type of eye movements associated with dreaming sleep and, as a result, initiate visual sensations. At the same time, they set off the brain waves characteristic of REM sleep and turn off large muscle movement. Dreams, Drs. Hobson and McCarley suggest, represent the efforts of the brain to make sense out of the various random discharge signals of the giant cells.

During dreaming our brains are as active as they are when we are awake, and in some ways more active. The brain sends messages out to the body—for instance, to walk, hop, climb, run or kick. These messages are, of course, blocked; otherwise, we would jump out of bed and act out our dreams. But Drs. Hobson and McCarley suggest that these messages may influence the contents of our dreams. Activities involving movements of the legs and feet are reported in four out of five dreams.

Their theory offers a possible explanation for the bizarreness of dreams, too, ascribing it to random intense brain activity. By contrast, psychological theories suggest that the oddness in dreams stems from the metaphoric language of dreaming thought. Further, the "then suddenly" statement is a frequent part of dream reports; "I dreamed I went to the bank; then suddenly, I was at a birthday party." The physiological researchers believe such scene shifts can be accounted for by the fact that cells don't discharge evenly but rather are set off in runs of activity and in patterns that are different from those characteristic of waking.

Nonetheless, Drs. Hobson and McCarley concede that dream reports represent a unique individual response to brain stimuli. "You put together a picture in terms of the kind of person you are," says Dr. McCarley. "Dreams provide useful windows into what's going on in the mind of the dreamer. Dreams reflect the conceptual baggage we usually carry."

The concept of a dream-state generator in the brain stem has prompted another theory of the function of REM sleep. Nobel laureate Francis Crick, Ph.D., of the Salk Institute in La Jolla, California, and British mathematician Graeme Mitchison, Ph.D., of the Medical Research Council Laboratory of Molecular Biology in Cambridge, propose that REM sleep reduces the irrelevant, bizarre or repetitive memories we accumulate each day and makes it easier for us to manage our waking lives unburdened by such unneeded thoughts. Hence, they say, "We dream in order to forget." Moreover, they suggest that "attempting to remember one's dreams should perhaps not be encouraged, because such remembering may help to retain patterns of thought which are better forgotten," a view quite contrary to that held by psychologically minded theorists and one certain to spark renewed debate.

The search for the reasons why we dream and the relationship that dreams have to waking life is viewed by some scientists as a curious odyssey. "What's the function of waking thought?" asks Allan Rechtschaffen, Ph.D., director of the Sleep Research Laboratory at the University of Chicago. "We try to solve problems, we amuse ourselves or perhaps we indulge in mental idling. Like waking thought, dreaming may have a similar range of functions."

What Dreams Are Like

Dreams, though seemingly ephemeral, can be subjected to scientific measurements. Several different scoring systems have been developed to assess such factors as the number of characters in a dream, their relationship to the dreamer, the emotions expressed and the activities and settings portrayed.

The "typical" dream contains two characters in addition to the dreamer, takes place in a building, has more passive than active behavior, is more hostile than friendly and more unpleasant than pleasant, reported Calvin Hall, Ph.D., of the University of California, Santa Cruz, after studying thousands of dreams.

The dream experience most frequently reported as unpleasant has to do with falling; the next most unpleasant experience involves being attacked. Other common dream themes include seeing a loved one in danger or dead, sexual activity, accomplishing something important, flying or floating, being paralyzed or unable to cry out for help, preparing for and taking an exam, missing a plane, train or appointment and being naked in public.

Sexual dreams may have manifest sex content, such as explicit sexual acts; symbolic content, such as telephone poles or snakes; or latent content, in which the sexual meaning becomes clear only by the exploration of the dreamer's life and his associations to his dream. "The sexual concern or metaphor expressed in the sexual dream is inevitably a vehicle for the expression of attributes or problems of the dreamer which permeate much, if not all, of his life," Dr. Kramer observes. Frank sexual dreams may be a consequence of increased sexual interest and activity as well as of abstinence. Men sometimes ejaculate during sexual dreams, a phenomenon often referred to as a wet dream. Women also sometimes reach orgasm during dreams.

Guilt is a prominent dream theme for people aged twenty-one to thirty-four, while death anxiety shows up more frequently in dreams of people over sixty-five. Families are more prominent in the dreams of men aged thirty-five to fifty-five than in the dreams of older men. Divorced and widowed people dream about death more often than do married people or those who have never married. Depressed people dream frequently about family members, while schizophrenics dream more often about strangers. Women report more dreams than men, and more characters and emotions in their dreams. Men are more likely than women to have dreams involving aggression or striving for success.

Animals in dreams frequently represent uncontrollable, unacceptable urges that we fear in ourselves or others. This observation is supported by a study that investigated what else happens in dreams in which animals appear. Dreams with animals are shorter, reports Robert Van de Castle, Ph.D., director of the Sleep and Dream Laboratory at the University of Virginia. That may be because such dreams engender anxiety. The more animals in the dream, the more aggressive acts it is likely to contain, and the more likely it is to involve death, illness, tornadoes or other calamities. Apprehension is the main emotion expressed. Animals almost always attack the dreamer, even when the dreamer tries to be friendly. Children dream of wild, threatening animals far more than do adults, who most frequently dream of domesticated or pet animals—another indication that as we grow up, we learn to bring our "savage" impulses under greater control.

Although dreams may involve scenes and actions that would be incredible in real life, we accept them at the time as entirely real. This fact explains why primitive peoples thought the soul left the body during sleep. "We may talk to people we know to be dead, visit places we know not to exist, fly without any mechanical help, and while transcending all these laws of time and space, of cause and effect, only occasionally do we note, in passing, our own cleverness in so doing," notes Dr. Cartwright.

Dreams seem to happen to us; that's why many of us are incredulous about the notion that we program our own dreams. During dreams, we seem to draw on a logic different from the logic we ordinarily use during waking. We might make associations, for example, based on the sounds of words rather than on their meaning; a rabbit in a dream might represent our friend Robert.

Cats, dogs and other animals have REM sleep. Newborn babies spend about half of their time in REM periods and have the same

types of eye movements as adults do. Precocious talkers just cele-
brating their first birthday have reported on awakening words that
suggest that they were dreaming. Indeed, young children often
have trouble distinguishing dreams from reality. When Ryan
wakes up crying, "There's a monster in my closet," it's a real
monster to him.

Dreams change with increasing emotional maturity, and children's dreams are quite different from those of adults. Dr. Foulkes,
who has studied children's dreams extensively, has found that in
children aged three to five, movement and activity are seldom
reported. Their dreams contain more animal than human characters and focus more on hunger, sleep and other body states than
on social interaction. Unlike adults, young children seldom claim
to have experienced feelings in their dreams.

People think about the same things during the night that they
think about during the day. Students dream about tests; people
with anorexia nervosa, the starvation sickness, dream about food.
"Dream content is most concerned with and influenced by the
activities of the day that have the greatest emotional impact on the
dreamer," notes Dr. Kramer. In one study in his laboratory, ten
patients and their therapists slept in the laboratory the night before
each therapist was scheduled to present his patient to his supervi-
sors at a conference. The patients dreamed about the therapists,
but the therapists dreamed about the conference and the experimental situation.

A group of women undergoing divorce who were studied by
Dr. Cartwright reported dreams with a more negative mood than
did married women who were not contemplating divorce. Dreams
of the women in the divorce group tended to involve past, present
and future, while dreams of married women took place mostly in
the present. Divorcing women who were not depressed often
dreamed of themselves as "wife," "separated or ex-wife," or
"alone," reflecting their waking concerns with these issues. By
contrast, depressed, divorcing women avoided the whole marital
issue and seldom dreamed of themselves in these roles until
months later, when their depression had lifted.

In studies in which vision was changed during the day, dreams
changed, too. Volunteers who spent their waking hours wearing
red-tinted goggles reported a reddish tint in many of their dreams,

Howard Roffwarg, M.D., and John Herman, Ph.D., of the University of Texas Health Science Center, and their colleagues found. They saw less blue and green in their dreams. The "goggle effect" did not seem to alter dream content, but it did indeed color it. In a later study volunteers wore tunnel-vision goggles for five days, limiting their field of vision and making things look smaller, an effect similar to watching the world through the wrong end of a telescope. To compensate for the small eye movements experienced during wakefulness, the subjects had larger and more frequent eye movements during REM sleep. Although they were not awakened during the night, the dreams they reported in the morning often concerned small, distant objects, such as a small boat on a lake and a "teeny" swimming pool.

Dreams in progress can be altered when emotionally significant material is introduced. Many dreamers who were exposed just once to the name of a family member or friend played on a tape recorder during REM sleep dreamed about the person named, whereas unfamiliar names seldom were incorporated into dreams.

Myths and Facts about Dreams

Laboratory studies of dreams make it possible to answer authoritatively many questions people ask sleep researchers about dreams. These are among the most common ones:

WILL WE GO CRAZY IF WE DON'T DREAM?

Early studies that succeeded in depriving people of REM sleep seemed to indicate that this notion was plausible. People became extremely irritable and moody and some even developed hallucinations. But later it was realized that in these experiments people were being deprived of both REM and NREM sleep. The less REM sleep people got, the quicker they entered the REM state when they fell back asleep. A sleep researcher trying to keep someone from REM sleep eventually had to awaken him every few minutes. Hence, the effects seen were in fact the results of loss of sleep in general. Today it is felt that the effects, if any, of going without REM sleep are slight and subtle. In fact, depriving people with depression of REM sleep seems to help them toward recovery. (See Chapter 14, "Troubled Minds/Troubled Sleep.")

HOW LONG DO DREAMS LAST?

It has been postulated that dreams may last but an instant and develop in the seconds while, or just after, you awaken from sleep, not before. A dream often cited to illustrate this theory was reported by André Maury in 1861. He dreamed that he was brought before the French revolutionary tribunal in Paris during the Reign of Terror. Condemned to die, he was taken to the guillotine. The blade fell. He felt his head being severed from his body. He woke in a sweat, to find that the top of his bed had fallen down, striking his neck just where the blade would have come. He assumed that he had fabricated the dream rapidly to account for his rude awakening.

Brain-wave records show that REM periods grow progressively longer as sleep continues; the first of the four or five REM periods that occur in a normal seven- or eight-hour sleep period usually runs about ten minutes, while the last runs for about an hour. But how long are dreams? A study at the University of Chicago in the early days of sleep-laboratory research showed that the longer the REM period, the more words a sleeper used to describe the dream. Moreover, people were able to tell correctly how long they had been dreaming whether they were awakened five or fifteen minutes after the beginning of a REM period. These findings suggest that dreams may last as long as the REM period lasts.

DO WE WATCH OUR DREAMS UNFOLD?

A man whose eyes had been moving from side to side as he slept reported, "I dreamed I was watching a Ping-Pong match." A woman who described walking up five steps in her dream had moved her eyes upward vertically five times just before she was awakened. These and other reports in which dream activity seemed to correlate with the direction and type of eye movements led William Dement, M.D., of Stanford University, and Howard Roffwarg, M.D., of the University of Texas Health Science Center, to develop the "scanning hypothesis" in the early 1960s. The activity of the eyes was thought to help explain why dreams seem real.

Later experiments by other researchers challenged these findings, however, and the scanning hypothesis remains controversial. For one reason, people often report uninterrupted dream imagery during quiet periods between eye movements. Moreover, people who are blind from birth may have rapid eye movements during sleep, but they do not describe visual dreams. Studies of the way people look at things while awake show that eye movements are not completely predictable. Some researchers suggest that eye movements that occur in sleep are not related to vision in dreams at all but rather may be related to the intensity of the dream experience or perhaps may simply be one of the curious ways in which the brain runs a "self-test" on the rest of the body to see that "all systems are go."

The relationship between actual eye movements and dream activity may be clarified by further study of "lucid dreams," in which people are aware while they sleep that they are dreaming (discussed later in this chapter). Lucid dreamers have been able to signal when they are dreaming by making eye movements in a prearranged sequence, such as left, left, right.

WHAT DO BLIND PEOPLE DREAM ABOUT?
While people who are blind from birth do not dream with sight, they use their other senses to generate dream images. For the congenitally blind, "life can be dreamed just as it is experienced in wakefulness," reports Nancy Kerr, Ph.D., of the Cognition Research Laboratory at Emory University, Atlanta. "Dream happenings fuse into events, and events into narratives. One simply can 'know' where one is or what is happening," she adds.

A young woman who had been blind from birth said she had dreamed of a machine like an "instant banker" with a screen and a keyboard with buttons. "You could look through the screen," she explained, adding, "I guess I imagined it. It's not that I could really see it with my eyes, but I know what it looks like through touch."

People who become blind later in life do have visual dreams, in which they see with normal vision. The blind are no more restricted than others to dreaming only about what they have actually seen. However, they do tend to dream about familiar settings more than people with normal vision. Blind dreamers also tend to make greater use in their dreams of their senses of hearing, smell and touch, just as they do in real life.

DO WE DREAM IN COLOR?

Certainly we do; that's the way the world is. But we probably don't pay any more attention to color in our dreams than we do in waking life. Do you recall right now what color clothing your spouse was wearing this morning? If the sky is blue and the grass is green in your dreams, you probably won't give it much thought. But if the opposite is true, you may well remember it. You are more likely to remember colors, as well as other details, of dreams that occur later in the night, because these dreams are closer to the time you arise.

WHY DON'T WE REMEMBER MOST OF OUR DREAMS?

Although you may have four or five dreams and spend some ninety minutes dreaming each night, seven days a week, you probably remember few dreams. That's undoubtedly because most of them are dull accounts of mundane waking experiences, no more memorable than a visit to the filling station or the ride home from work. We don't pay attention to such trivial information and discard such dreams within a few seconds or minutes of awakening. You can, of course, increase your ability to remember your dreams by lying in bed quietly and making a deliberate effort to do so.

Sometimes, during the day, we have a flash of recognition when some experience dredges up a previously unrecalled dream. This phenomenon is referred to as a déjà vu ("already seen") experience, and it illustrates how full indeed is the largely unexamined store of memories in our brain.

CAN DREAMS FORETELL THE FUTURE?

Jung suggests that a dream can be like a preliminary exercise or sketch, a plan roughed out in advance. By directing our attention to some aspect of our lives that we might not otherwise notice, a dream may suggest possible consequences of certain behaviors. In this way, the dream may offer a prediction, which we can choose to heed or to ignore. Dr. Dement relates a dream that occurred at a time when he was smoking two packs of cigarettes a day. "One night I dreamed I had inoperable cancer of the lung. I remember the ominous shadow in my chest X-ray and the subsequent examination, in which a colleague found that the cancer was widespread. I experienced the incredible anguish of knowing my life was soon to end, that I would never see my children grow up, and that none of this would have happened if I had quit smoking when I first learned it could cause cancer." He adds, "I will never forget the surprise, joy, and exquisite relief of waking up." He never smoked again.

Can You Solve Problems in Your Dreams?

Dream language may give us a different way of looking at something that we've been worrying about while awake. Dreams often follow a predictable sequence through the night, with the first dream posing the problem, the second to the fourth progressively resolving it, and the fifth allowing you to review your night's "work" and relax. The narrative doesn't necessarily follow from one dream to the next like a television serial, but certain images or themes tend to recur through the night. We may deal with the same issues over and over in our dreams. Some people get literal "reruns," a cogent indication of unresolved problems.

Dr. Cartwright cites a personal example of problem-solving in dreams that occurred while she was trying to make a decision about whether to accept her present position as head of a medical school department. She relates, "I had a secure place at the university. I knew that Ph.D.'s have lower status than M.D.'s in a medical school, and I wasn't sure I wanted to be an administrator. I dreamed that it was a dark, stormy night; I was being tossed high by winds, and I wanted to get out of the storm. Looking down I saw an English moor, and a church with open arches. I thought if only I could get under the arches, I would be out of the wind. As I did, I saw a coronation ceremony in progress. It was for me. I accepted the crown and sat on the chair. "This is a nice dream solution, with no ambivalence. The coronation dream draws on my childhood experiences growing up in Canada; like many dreams, it integrates the past with the present. The dream doesn't deal with such issues as problems that face the person who wields power, but I saw it as a positive dream and it helped influence me to take the job."

Samuel Coleridge awakened from an hour-long nap with two or three hundred lines of the poem "Kubla Khan" clearly in mind. Robert Louis Stevenson said the plots of *Doctor Jekyll and Mister Hyde* and other works came to him in dreams. Friedrich Kekule, a German chemist, saw in a dream six snakes biting each other's tails and whirling in a circle; on arising, he visualized the ring structure of the benzene molecule, a discovery that revolutionized organic chemistry.

The trick, of course, is to recognize that the dream image offers a solution to a waking problem. Perhaps only the most creative of us can make that connection. Solutions in dreams may be presented in intriguing metaphors that we have to work to decode. Moreover, we don't necessarily solve problems in our dreams any better than we do while awake. How many of us have awakened during the night with a brilliant inspiration, turned on a light and recorded the thought, only to discover in the morning that we have written down gibberish, or at best a trivial idea not worth preserving!

Akin to the idea of problem-solving is the notion that we can learn while we sleep. While it's true that we are able to pay attention during sleep to meaningful noises, such as our baby's cough or the ringing of the phone, the way we respond to such noises is to awaken. We learn best when we are fully alert and attentive. Hence, you're not likely to master a foreign language or to memorize a poem that's played on a tape recorder near your pillow unless you spend a good part of your night awake.

Take Charge of Your Dreams

A divorced woman frequently dreamed that she was waiting for her former husband in a restaurant. Just as he was about to kiss her and bring about a reconciliation she would wake up. With the help of Dr. Cartwright, she, like more than fifty other divorced women, has learned to change the endings of her dreams. She spent a night in the sleep laboratory with a small buzzer taped to her hand so that she could signal when she was having "that dream." In return, the therapist signaled back, "Now is the time to change the dream." Having discussed alternative solutions, the woman now chooses one. When her former husband appears in her dream, she introduces her new husband.

"We've helped her to consider a forward-looking and possible solution," Dr. Cartwright says. "A repetitive dream is like a record that's stuck. This approach offers a way to lift the needle." Now that the woman knows she can solve her dream problem, she is better able to manage her waking life without her former husband.

The phenomenon known as lucid dreaming also demonstrates how people can control their own dreams. In such dreams, people are aware, while they sleep, that they are dreaming. To demonstrate that he could tell when he was dreaming, sleep researcher Steven LaBerge, Ph.D., of Stanford University had himself wired for the night in a sleep laboratory; he signaled his initials in Morse code with eye movements at times when the brain-wave tracings and eye movements confirmed he was in a period of REM sleep.

Many of us have occasionally been aware, while dreaming, that we were dreaming. Some people say they have such experiences almost every night. Some are content to observe their dreams, much as they would watch a movie. But others like to step in and shape the action. One psychologist suggests that a way to demonstrate to yourself both that you are dreaming and that you can control the dream is to make yourself do something unusual as you dream, something you could not do while awake, such as float in midair or fly.

If you could become skillful at directing your dreams, you might be able to tap more effectively some cognitive abilities that you don't normally use, both to help solve your waking problems and to explore your creative potential. "The statistical evidence indicates that most dreams are unpleasant," Dr. LaBerge notes, adding, "This suggests to me that there's a lot of work that we could be doing in our dreams that we presently are not doing."

Dr. LaBerge finds he can increase the frequency of lucid dreams by concentrating, just as he is falling asleep, on telling himself, "Next time I'm dreaming, I want to remember I'm dreaming." He visualizes himself asleep in bed, dreaming and realizing that he's dreaming.

How to Remember Your Dreams

The key is to record them, right away, when you awaken.

- Keep a pen and paper, or a tape recorder, by your bed.
- As you fall asleep, concentrate on dreaming. If you want to collect dreams from an entire night, tell yourself you want to awaken at the end of a dream. Everyone has the potential to exert this kind of influence over the mind during sleep; most of us simply do not tap it, or choose not to do it frequently because the process does, after all, interfere with sleep. If you don't succeed in recalling dreams at first, set your alarm to go off about thirty minutes earlier than usual in the morning; dream periods are longer late in sleep and the odds are higher then that you will be able to interrupt a dream.
- On awakening, lie in bed quietly. Even if your mind seems blank, lie still and wait until the dream comes back. Then, "interview" yourself. What was just going through your mind? Was all or part of the setting familiar, or was it fantasy? Were other people present? Were they familiar or strangers? What were they wearing and doing? Were the events taking place now or in the past or future? Was the setting a scene from the past, present or future? How old were you in your dream? How old were other people? Were you an active participant or a passive observer? What emotions were involved, and how intense were they? Was your experience pleasant or not? Did you feel the events were going on in your mind or really taking place?
- Fix your thoughts in your mind. Then, sit up and record them. If you use a notebook, give each dream a separate page. Later, you may find you have additional material to record about a particular dream, or you may want to jot down your thoughts about it.

How to Interpret Your Dreams

You don't need a dream-symbol handbook to gain insight from your own dreams. As Sigmund Freud himself noted, the dictionary to decode dreams is not found on a bookshelf but in the mind of the dreamer. Hence, the interpretations in the books that you can buy at a newsstand are unlikely to have specific applicability to your life. Does a dream of taking an exam mean that you're afraid of failing at some task or that you actually can do what you're worried about doing? You can figure out for yourself the meanings that your dreams may have. While a single dream symbol may suggest many meanings to you, numerous symbols are likely to reinforce a single meaning.

People who grow up in the same culture do have certain symbols in common, but few symbols are universal. The ancient Greeks, for example, thought snakes in dreams predicted sickness, while the Egyptians saw the same symbol as an omen of good luck.

An examination of a single dream may raise your consciousness of your feelings at a particular moment, but if you look at a series of dreams, you'll probably find greater illumination of your continuing concerns. For most of us, specific images and themes tend to recur. When trying to solve problems, Cookie frequently searches in her dreams for a missing treasure. In times of distress, Ralph dreams his wallet has disappeared. In Marilyn's dreams, the telephone serves as a symbol either of communication or of failure to get through.

The fact that a dream concerns a mundane subject does not necessarily mean its meaning is trivial. The dream "I was riding my bike" at first seemed commonplace to one man. On reflection, he realized, "My son, with whom I ordinarily ride my bike, is leaving for college soon. My father used to ride an exercise bike, but he died young from heart disease." It quickly became obvious that he was feeling sadness over the departure of his son and worry about his own mortality. The dream seemed prophetic too, in that it warned him to pay more attention to his health.

Dr. Kramer proposes a method of dream "translation" as a step toward dream interpretation. You systematically go through the dream from beginning to end, making associations to one sentence at a time. You look at the characters in your dream, the setting, the nature of the action and the emotions that are being expressed. Suppose there's some symbol in your dream that resists interpretation—a strange cat, for example, although you don't own a cat or haven't had anything to do with cats? Dr. Kramer suggests, "If the symbol remains elusive, you're just not working hard enough." However, Freud himself observed, "Sometimes a cigar in a dream is just a cigar."

If your dreams wake you from sleep or bother you when you think about them during the day, you may want to discuss them with a psychiatrist, psychologist or other mental health counselor.

Nightmares

We all have nightmares occasionally, rousing us abruptly from sleep, often drenched with perspiration and with head and heart throbbing. Nightmares are more likely than ordinary dreams to portray catastrophes and violence and to involve us in a flight or fight situation. We're about to crash the car, or be caught by a knife-wielding robber, attacked by a ferocious dog or buried under an avalanche. Although muscles are paralyzed during REM periods, we may be so frightened that we break out of sleep and, in the act of waking up, flail our arms, kick with all our might, tumble to the floor or entangle ourselves in bedclothes.

Nightmares occur most often in the second half of the night, as you might expect, since dreams are longer and more intense then. Because such experiences awaken us from REM sleep or sometimes light NREM sleep, sleep clinicians prefer to describe them as "dream anxiety attacks." They distinguish these dream disturbances from "sleep terror" or "night terror" attacks, which usually occur during the deep states of NREM sleep.

In terror attacks, the sleeper awakens with a sense of overwhelming fear. He can't breathe; it's as if something heavy were sitting on his chest. Panic!! Finally his terror erupts as a scream. A child in this state may be inconsolable for five or ten minutes but, as a rule, he remembers nothing in the morning. Even adults who describe their sense of dread and helplessness seldom recall the frightening dream that triggered it. (For more on sleep terrors, see Chapter 12, "Things That Go Bump in the Night.")

Disturbing dreams that occur as we drift off for a nap are thought to be continuations of the previous night's dreams. You're more likely to have a particularly vivid dream if you get up briefly, to send the children off to school, for instance, and then go back to sleep. If you nap in the late afternoon, you're more likely to start your normal ninety-minute sleep cycle and to awaken from your nap before you enter a REM period.

Lifelong nightmare sufferers may tread a thin line between being creative, artistic people and suffering from personality disorders, suggests Ernest Hartmann, M.D., of the Lemuel Shattuck Hospital, Boston. After studying over fifty people who have nightmares at least once a week, he suggests that frequent nightmares may be a marker for vulnerability to schizophrenia, even in people in whom clinical illness has not become apparent.

When the development and clinical course of the nightmares and personality patterns of thirty adults were charted by Anthony Kales, M.D., and his colleagues at the Sleep Research and Treatment Center of Pennsylvania State University College of Medicine, they found that the nightmares usually began in childhood or adolescence and did not go away. Nightmares often started after major life events and worsened with stress. Nightmare sufferers in general were distrustful, alienated and emotionally estranged.

People with nightmares may benefit from psychotherapy that helps them to better understand and deal with their emotions, particularly anger, the Pennsylvania State researchers say. When they are able to express their emotions more efficiently, they are less likely to become excessively frustrated and to discharge their resentments during sleep in the form of nightmares.

POST-TRAUMATIC STRESS

Anxious dreams sometimes first appear after a severe shock.

The majority of the twenty-six children kidnapped as they were riding home on a school bus in Chowchilla, California, in 1976 still had repetitive traumatic dreams five to thirteen months later, when they were interviewed by child psychiatrist Lenore Terr,

M.D., of the University of California. The children had been confined for sixteen hours in a buried truck trailer, which the kidnappers had covered with earth. Many of the children dreamed of death; five had particularly horrifying dreams in which they allowed themselves to die. Barbara, age nine, dreamed of being killed and put in a hole. She relates, "We were at the cemetery where my grandma is buried. We don't go there much." Louis, eight, recalled two dreams; he said, "A dinosaur stabbed me, and a wolfman got me and ate me."

Four years after the kidnapping Dr. Terr found that the children continued to have nightmares related to the event. Fourteen of the children at this time reported dreaming of their own death. Such dreams apparently were triggered by the experience of being utterly helpless, as happened during the kidnapping, says Dr. Terr. In a separate study of twenty-five other children, she found that most of those who had dreamed of dying also had suffered unexpected fright or episodes in which they had been suddenly rendered unconscious.

Combat veterans seem particularly prone to the post-traumatic stress syndrome, a constellation of symptoms that includes day-time flashbacks to combat scenes and blunting of emotion. Ten years or longer after leaving the service, some Vietnam veterans are plagued by repetitive nightmares in which they re-experience actual war events. Their wives often report that their husbands wake in the middle of the night, screaming or flailing about. The experience makes some men fearful of falling asleep, thus contributing to insomnia and daytime irritability.

Bessel van der Kolk, M.D., and his colleagues at the Veterans Administration Hospital and Tufts Medical School, Boston, found that veterans who suffer frequent nightmares usually were younger when they served in Vietnam than those who also served in combat but did not develop such nightmares. They were more likely to have formed an intense attachment to their combat unit. "Veterans who developed nightmares felt they were in charge of their lives until they went to Vietnam," Dr. van der Kolk reports. "Then they lost the sense of control over their destiny." The problem is not limited to Vietnam veterans; the researchers found that some men who saw action in World War II still suffer nightmares more than once a month.

Using Our Dreams

Some of us still dismiss each nightly adventure as "only a dream." But the feelings we have in our dreams and about our dreams are real. Dreams present a fascinating opportunity to examine our inner lives. If we are able to integrate our dreaming with our waking thoughts, we may come to know ourselves better. It's sometimes said that a dream not explained is like a letter not read. How many of us would be willing to casually discard any other "personal and confidential" communication?

5

THE
GROWING YEARS

All children undergo occasional bouts of disturbed sleep. Indeed, children encounter many of the same problems adults do, with one conspicuous distinction: The child with a sleep problem rarely suffers alone. Parents, sometimes sisters and brothers and even neighbors, find their sleep disrupted by a child's unrest.

Trouble sleeping may manifest itself in different ways at different ages. A baby may be colicky and difficult to soothe; a toddler may invent ruses to keep from meeting the tigers that creep through the cracks in his ceiling when he's alone at night.

Psychological and social stresses may undermine a child's sleep. A move to a new house or teasing at nursery school can turn a three-year-old into an insomniac. An adolescent may stay up late on weeknights to do homework and later still on weekends to party with friends, despite chronic sleepiness that blunts his ability to learn.

Other maladies are associated with a delay in maturation of the central nervous system. About 7 percent of all nine-year-olds wet their beds occasionally. About 15 percent of all children sleepwalk at least once.

Some problems can be traced to physical disorders. Enlarged tonsils and adenoids that partially block the air passages and cause repeated interruptions in breathing during sleep may make a child sluggish during the day. Mental retardation or other brain damage may make sleep fragmented. Even a cold or a mild stomach upset can turn sleep askew. Chronic illnesses such as epilepsy or narcolepsy may impair the quality of sleep.

If your child has difficulty sleeping, you are called on to do *something*, but deciding what is no easy task. You may get conflicting advice from in-laws and friends. One bonus of sleep-laboratory studies has been the development of practical ways for parents to handle some age-old problems. Moreover, physicians can now distinguish between behavior that is merely part of growing up and behavior that requires medical intervention. Following is information and advice based on the latest research findings.

The First Year

In the early months of life, a baby rules the household with seemingly incessant demands. Yet a baby soon begins to establish a predictable schedule of rest and activity. Most newborns accumulate sixteen to eighteen hours of sleep a day, although some perfectly healthy babies sleep more or less than that. Studies show a sleep range for newborns from about eleven to twenty-one hours.

When the baby no longer wakes at two in the morning, that is a major milestone, although it is seldom reached as soon as weary parents wish. The ability to sleep five or six hours in one stretch and to get that sleep from about midnight on are both signs of maturity, explains Thomas Anders, M.D., head of the division of child psychiatry and child development at the Stanford University School of Medicine. In a household where parents are awake during the day and asleep at night, parents want the baby to become "entrained" to their schedule.

Breast-fed babies are sometimes slightly slower to evolve a long sleep pattern than bottle-fed babies, but many parents feel that the other advantages of nursing outweigh this temporary inconvenience. Premature babies and full-term babies who are small may also lag behind in early sleep development, although they do catch up within a few months.

New parents expect to be bleary-eyed for the first few months of their child's life. Yet the distress triggered by persistent sleepiness prompts the oft-repeated question for the doctor, "Will the baby *ever* sleep through the night?"

Getting an accurate picture of infants' sleep challenged researchers. Even the most attentive parent cannot observe every minute of a baby's sleep. Sleep-laboratory studies show that the application of electrodes and the unfamiliar surroundings distort sleep patterns, even in newborns.

Time-lapse photography solved the problem. Dr. Anders and his colleagues filmed children for a night at periodic intervals during their first year in their own cribs at home. A camera designed for low-level light was focused on the crib for twelve hours; a microphone made it possible to record the baby's sounds. The infant's parents also kept a log for the week in which the night's recording was done and verified that their child's sleep during the filmed night was typical.

The parents' records showed, as one example, that nearly half of the two-month-old children and three quarters of the nine-month-olds fulfilled the definition of "sleeping through the night." However, the videotapes revealed that only one in seven two-month-old infants and one in three nine-month-olds truly slept without awakening.

Some children signal their parents by crying when they awake, but others do not. Sleeping and waking behavior, as the videotape studies attest, is highly complex, even in the youngest infants.

The 10 percent of babies who do not sleep or stay quietly in bed for at least five hours during the night by their first birthday "can tax the capacities of even the most caring and concerned parents," observes Richard Ferber, M.D., director of the sleep clinic at Boston Children's Hospital. The ill effects of sleep loss on parents should not be forgotten; parents who themselves are cranky have a harder time coping with the minor aggravations of parenthood.

Some babies sleep easily. Others are colicky, hard to comfort, cry a good deal and have more than the usual difficulty in establishing a predictable sleep pattern. What accounts for such differences? One key factor seems to be the success of parent-child, particularly mother-child, bonding, asserts psychiatrist Cotter Hirschberg, M.D., clinical director of the Menninger Clinic. When a newborn baby looks at his mother and responds to her cuddling by relaxing, the mother is pleased to know her presence is comforting and she relaxes also. This nice circle reinforces itself, and the baby sleeps more easily and longer, Dr. Hirschberg says.

Waking your baby occasionally to show him or her to visiting relatives is no cause for worry. Nor is changing mealtimes or bedtimes now and then. But inconsistency in daily care can foster erratic sleep rhythms in the baby, points out Dr. Ferber. Reasonable, not rigid, attention to regularity of nighttime sleep, as well as of nap and play times, feeding, bathing, outdoor strolls and other activities, will help teach your baby the ways of the world. If you are nursing, limit your intake of coffee, tea and cola drinks; these contain caffeine, which may be passed on to the baby and disturb his sleep.

In the latter half of the first year, strangers, including babysitters and perhaps even a grandmother, provoke a torrent of tears. This distress heralds the baby's recognition of the important distinction between parents, particularly his mother, and other people. The baby develops a fear of losing his mother. Yet at bedtime, she walks away and seems to disappear. It's no surprise that the baby cries! Daytime games such as peekaboo can help reassure your baby that you will be there in the morning and make it easier for your baby to fall asleep and stay asleep, Dr. Ferber suggests.

A favorite blanket or teddy bear provides comfort, too, substituting to some extent for the presence of the baby's mother. Just as the baby prefers his mother to a babysitter, he will be better satisfied by his own blanket with its special corner or the teddy whose ear has been nuzzled bare than by an unfamiliar object. Although you can buy a battery-run teddy bear that makes a sound mimicking the maternal heartbeat, music boxes or the like, the best objects, in terms of teaching the baby to be responsible for himself, are those that he can find by himself if he awakens in the middle of the night, says Dr. Ferber.

In a young baby, trouble falling asleep and middle-of-the-night awakenings may go hand in hand. A baby who wakes often during the night seldom goes to sleep without a struggle. "When a baby cries, there's a reason," notes Dr. Anders. A baby who cries at bedtime and wakes one or more times crying in the night usually is protesting being alone.

You can help your child fall asleep easily by creating a bedtime ritual. You might stay in the room a minute or two after you tuck him in and turn off the lights. Or sing a lullaby—no matter how off-key your voice, your baby probably will find it comforting.

But it's wise not to prolong your departure. You don't need to stay in the room until the baby is asleep; in fact, if you do so, the baby is likely to cry if he wakes in the middle of the night and discovers that you're not there.

When you leave the room, it's not necessary to shut the door and insist on silence from the rest of the family. The sense of isolation may produce anxiety in the child. A night-light will show your baby that familiar things don't disappear at night. Extra cues, such as sounds or lights, may help a child who is blind or deaf to maintain contact.

The notion that babies should sleep alone is, incidentally, a Western notion, and one only a century old. It's curiously out of kilter with the recognition that most adults in our society prefer to sleep with someone else. Why should babies be any different?

In less-industrialized cultures, babies generally sleep in close physical contact with their mothers, at least until the birth of the next child. Even then, the older child may continue to sleep in the same room. In Japan, children usually sleep in a room with others throughout their childhood.

If a mother is breast-feeding, as more than half of all mothers in the United States now do, it is certainly easier not to have to get up during the night to go to the baby. A mother need barely rouse herself, yet can nurse successfully. If the baby is being bottle-fed, the mother or father can get up to get the bottle, then return quickly to the baby, without the need for either parent to be disturbed again when feeding is done. The concept that a parent might smother a baby by "overlaying" has no basis in fact. Smothering does not account for cases of the Sudden Infant Death Syndrome (SIDS), also known as crib death (discussed later in this chapter).

In *The Family Bed, An Age-Old Concept in Child Rearing*, Tine Thevenin writes from a mother's perspective on the advantages of "co-sleeping" for both child and parents. The parents' closeness provides the child with attention and security and helps strengthen ties between the child and both parents, she says. She suggests that parents find a time other than bedtime for marital relations.

One child who slept in her parents' bed for the first few months of her life has been filmed periodically during the night by Dr.

Anders and his colleagues. They also have assessed her psychological well-being. She has always had perfectly normal sleep patterns and normal daytime development. "At four years of age she is a charming and delightful little girl, with no sleep or other problems," Dr. Anders reports.

Thevenin asserts, "The healthy child will wean himself in time from the parental bed." Although parents she surveyed said this time was variable, Dr. Anders suggests that the second half of the first year, when the process of separation begins, would be reasonable. He tells parents, "It's important to maintain some semblance of community norms, so that, by the time your child goes to nursery school or visits a friend's house, he doesn't feel that there's something odd about his own home."

Some experts express reservations about co-sleeping. Dr. Hirschberg says, "It's a genuine freedom for a child to have his own bed, not to be bothered by the movements of other people during sleep. One of the ways parents can nurture the independence that is necessary for the development of the child is to let him sleep by himself." And Dr. Ferber worries that co-sleeping may result from, or contribute to, strained marital relations.

Most parents seem to permit their children to come into their bed to sleep at least occasionally. A survey of 415 middle-class families with children aged two to ten revealed that virtually all did so when the child awakened ill or frightened during the night. Younger children came to their parents' bed as often as once a week but older children came only once or twice a year, Stanford University psychiatrist Alvin Rosenfeld, M.D., and his colleagues found. Children of single parents came to their beds more frequently and stayed longer than those of married parents. However, most children stayed only a few minutes before returning to their own beds.

The researchers note that the context of co-sleeping is key to its impact. An ill or frightened child might benefit from the security of being taken into his parents' bed, while a son taken into his recently separated mother's bed because she is frightened of the dark is being used to serve the mother's interest and may be adversely affected. As with other aspects of child rearing, parents need to keep in mind what is best for the child.

Ages One to Three

Even after their first birthdays, some children continue to cry at bedtime and repeatedly awaken crying in the middle of the night. To eliminate this behavior, some arbiters of child care, including Benjamin Spock, M.D., have long counseled letting the child cry it out for at least three nights. Other authorities worry that ignoring the child induces in parents an attitude of insensitivity to the child's needs.

The lengthy crying, understandably, is stressful for both parents and child. The child wails, trembles and may even vomit. At three in the morning a child's shrieks seem penetratingly loud; a parent may be concerned about protecting the sleep of other members of the household or of neighbors. Most often the mother or father gives in and provides food, a story or simply company. Unfortunately, this surrender reinforces the child's behavior and sets the stage for a repeat performance the following night.

Parents of a two-year-old who still wakes several times a night are likely to be frantic. Dr. Ferber says, "The sleep clinic phone will ring, and the caller immediately will say, 'I'm at my wit's end.' That alone tells me I'm talking to the parent of an infant or toddler who can't sleep or won't sleep. This is the only childhood sleep problem that causes such extreme parental agitation." Parents may think the child's sleep problems reflect poorly on their ability as parents.

"Every night at Brad's bedtime, we have a family feud around here," explains the mother of a thirty-month-old boy. "He hates to go upstairs for bed. As soon as I put him down, I hear 'More water, more stories, open the door, close the door, find my teddy.' My husband and I don't get to sit still long enough to read the newspaper or watch a television show. We're worn out by the time Brad falls asleep. Even when we go to bed, we know Brad is likely to wake us by screaming during the night. My mother says, 'You're spoiling him. Put him in his bed and shut the door.' Steve's mother says, 'Let him come in your bed.' We've tried it both ways. Neither works."

For this type of problem, Dr. Anders, a psychiatrist, makes

house calls. He tells the story of one eighteen-month-old baby who, for over ten months, had not been able to fall asleep without direct physical contact from a parent lying in bed next to him for at least fifteen minutes. The child would sleep for about two hours, then wake and not go back to sleep without more lengthy cuddling. Dr. Anders advised the parents to put the baby in his own crib—where they couldn't go. They were, however, to sit by the crib, together, and both put their hands through the crib bars on the baby until he fell asleep. The first night the baby slept through without awakening. Within a week, he also fell asleep easily at the beginning of the night.

The problem here was that the child was in control. The parents were at their baby's mercy. "The child needed to have control taken away but in a supportive manner, not in a punitive or rejecting way," Dr. Anders explains. Both parents, sitting together, helped get the message across more strongly than one alone could have done.

Rigorously charting a child's sleep/wake cycle can alert you to patterns, such as an overlong afternoon nap, that can be interrupted to encourage longer nighttime sleep. It also helps parents, who may feel as if they have been up the entire night, to put their usually modest sleep loss in perspective.

Sometimes you may unwittingly trigger middle-of-the night awakenings by providing your child with copious amounts of fluids at bedtime. One result is that your child is likely to drench his diaper; the wetness becomes a stimulus for waking, and, once awake, he expects to be fed. When your child cries, you think, understandably, that he's hungry; you may not realize that your willingness to respond is itself prompting the waking, says Dr. Ferber.

The common practice of letting a child fall asleep in the living room or in your lap on a rocking chair sometimes causes middle-of-the-night problems, too, Dr. Ferber adds. When your child has a normal—and usually brief—awakening during the night and finds he's in the "wrong" place, that is, not the place where he fell asleep, he awakens fully. You can imagine how you would feel if you fell asleep in front of the television and woke up in your bed with no memory of how you got there.

Similarly, if you let your child go to sleep with a room light or a hall light on, and then turn it off, you may cause fretting in a child who wakes during the night. Allowing a child to fall asleep with a bottle or a pacifier may have the same result; your child may "need" these objects to return to sleep during the night.

The best approach is to teach your child from the very first to fall asleep in the bed in which he will be spending the night; this will enable him to return to sleep easily, should he awaken at any time. Let your child help create simple rituals whose performance makes it easier to fall asleep; for example, he can help pull down the shades, turn on his night-light and turn off the room light. The techniques a child develops to comfort himself at this age, such as falling asleep on one side or another, favoring a special pillow or blanket, or arranging his bed or room in a certain way, often carry over into adulthood.

In contrast to the child who won't sleep is the one who can't sleep. Delayed sleep patterns can occur even in toddlers. A typical example is the child who is put to bed at eight but doesn't fall asleep until eleven. Once asleep, he stays asleep. Often parents become concerned that the child won't get enough sleep, and they let him sleep later than usual the next morning. Predictably, that night, there are fights at the customary bedtime.

The remedy for this problem is straightforward. Start by putting the child to bed at eleven, to reinforce the concept of a hassle-free bedtime, but if he formerly was permitted to sleep until ten in the morning, wake him at nine forty-five the first day or two, then nine-thirty, and so on. Since your child will be a little sleepy on this routine, it soon will be possible to schedule bedtime earlier in the evening. You have to be firm, waking the child at the predetermined time every morning, regardless of when he falls asleep at night. This approach works best in younger children who can't tell time.

Some children are natural short-sleepers. The child who resists falling asleep at the bedtime you set but awakens cheerfully by himself in the morning may be among them. A modification of bedtime is in order.

Some children, like some adults, can stay up later and sleep later on weekends than during the week with no adverse effects, but others require regular times for going to bed and arising throughout the week.

During the years between one and three, children develop increased control over their bodies and establish independence from their parents. The struggle to master toilet skills, walking, talking, feeding themselves, dressing themselves and similar tasks produces anxieties in children about their ability to succeed on their own. As a result, children may devise ingenious excuses to keep parents close by. Susan says a witch whispers bad words unless Mommy is in the room, in which case the witch is afraid to talk. Darren insists a ghost hides in the light switch. The ghost wakes up when the light is turned off.

A bedtime ritual, which might include a snack, a bath, toothbrushing, a bedtime story or prayers, will ease your child's transition to sleep. Nicki wants her favorite blanket, and Jordy, his teddy bear. Rocking, thumbsucking and touching the genitals are normal bedtime activities in toddlers; doctors advise parents not to interrupt such activities.

Ages Three to Five

"It is rare to find a child in the three-to-five age group who is not experiencing some difficulty over sleep," Dr. Anders observes. Such problems as tardiness in falling asleep, night waking, nightmares, fears of ghosts and wild animals, inability to sleep alone or in the dark, and ritualistic presleep behavior are common in this age group. Most of these disturbances last only a short time and respond well to practical support.

Fretting about monsters, Ryan, age four, goes to bed more willingly with his baseball bat tucked in beside him, "for safety." Now he has a way to ward the creatures off. Todd's parents gave him a powerful flashlight to help him cope with nighttime fears. Brian likes the door propped securely open.

Children in this age range continue to have concerns about their growing independence from their parents and mastery over their own bodies. When sleep disturbances occur, children may need to return to "outgrown" symbols of safe passage into the night, including favorite blankets and toys.

One common reason a preschool child can't sleep or won't sleep, Dr. Ferber says, is that parents fail to set a regular bedtime.

If a mother or father isn't insistent enough at bedtime that the child go to bed and stay in bed, the child keeps testing the parent's authority. Try to be firm, but remember that flexibility is also important; a child needs to know that he'll be permitted to stay up late on special occasions such as a birthday, the Fourth of July, a visit by grandparents or even to see a special television show. He also needs to feel that it's all right to go to bed early if he wants to do so.

Some parents find it difficult to be firm because they feel they were treated too harshly as children. Others are overly concerned about a child who may have been born prematurely or had a serious illness early in life. Parents of a handicapped child sometimes blame themselves for causing the child's problem and try to compensate by giving in to all the child's demands, even at the expense of the child's real well-being and their own needs.

Other parents simply lack knowledge about ways to ensure good sleep in a child, Dr. Ferber says. They may think, for example, that it's all right to let the child stay up until the child wants to go to sleep. Unfortunately, the child usually isn't the best judge of an appropriate bedtime. You may not realize that signs of sleepiness are more subtle in a child than in an adult; in younger children, crankiness can indicate the need for sleep well before the yawning starts.

Young children may have trouble distinguishing dreams from reality, an issue Maurice Sendak, author and illustrator of children's books, often explores poetically. A child may fear going to sleep because bad dreams may appear. By talking to your child about his or her dreams, you can help relieve anxieties. (See also Chapter 4, "The Stuff of Dreams.")

If concerns about dying during sleep develop, children need to be taught the distinction between sleep and death. Dr. Ferber recalls a child whose parents took him to the wake of a favorite uncle and tried to ease the experience by saying, "Uncle Bill will look just like he's sleeping." The child's bedtime troubles began that very night.

Parental behavior that is disturbing, like other stresses, can undermine the sleep of a child. If a child's bedtime occurs while his or her parents are quarreling, the child may fear for their safety and request attention in order to interrupt the fight. A child who sees or hears parents' sexual relations may also devise ways to interrupt what is perceived as fighting.

Punishing a child by sending him to bed may backfire; the child may come to view all bedtimes in a negative way, and parents may have a hard time undoing this perception.

Ages Six to Twelve

If there were a Sleep Olympics, children from age six until puberty, at around twelve to fourteen, would carry off all the medals. They are the champion sleepers and the champion wakers, as well. They fall asleep easily, sleep solidly through the night and are on the go, without signs of sleepiness, through the entire day. During these years, sleep disturbances are much less frequent than they are earlier in life. Children of these ages tend to follow the maxim "Early to bed, early to rise," going to sleep between eight and ten at night and getting up between six and eight in the morning weekdays and weekends.

Many parents report that the major problem during these years has more to do with bedtime than with sleep; some children seem to hate to go to bed. Nearly every night there's a cry of "I forgot some homework," "I lost my pencil," or "I have to take a bath." Many children develop the habit of reading before sleep or listening to music in bed as a replacement for the rituals of early childhood.

During these years children take increasingly frequent steps toward independence, by sleeping at a friend's house or going away to summer camp. Such activities may produce anxieties, such as homesickness, that may disturb sleep. To forestall them, parents can stress the fun of being with friends.

In the school years, exams, athletic competitions and demanding homework assignments occasionally interfere with sleep. Stresses such as a move, the birth of a sibling, illness (particularly one requiring hospitalization), parents' divorce or classroom pressures can produce regular disturbances of sleep, including trouble falling asleep, frequent awakenings and bad dreams. Usually sleep returns to normal within about six weeks of the resolution of the stressful situation. Children with attention-deficit disorders (popularly called hyperactivity), depression or other emotional disturbances seem more prone to insomnia. Hyperactive children, for example, move around more than other children when they are asleep as well as when they are awake.

The Teenage Years

Around the time they enter puberty, many children develop a pattern of sleeping roughly an hour more on weekends than on weekdays, apparently to recover from losing sleep during the week. Few of the more than two hundred children aged ten to thirteen surveyed by Dr. Anders and his colleagues complained of daytime sleepiness and falling asleep in the classroom. But when youngsters of high school and college age are queried, half say they are sleepy during the day. Many admit to sleeping in class.

While cumulative sleep loss may eventually exact a toll, it's not the only factor that causes sleepiness. Even when permitted to sleep as long as they can every night, adolescents are sleepy during the day, reports Mary Carskadon, Ph.D., of Stanford University. Although many parents hold the view that sleeping late on weekends is "immoral" or a sign of laziness, sleepiness may be related to hormonal changes that occur during puberty. Since growth hormone is secreted during sleep, and the teenage years are a time of rapid growth, increased sleep may well serve a biological need. Parents' recognition and acceptance of their youngsters' increased need for sleep during puberty often eliminates a major source of household contention.

Adolescents' sleep habits may complicate the picture of what is normal sleepiness and what is not. Teenagers may be engaged in so many interesting activities that they regularly do not get enough sleep. Sandy can't tear himself away from his computer; Nancy loves romance novels. Furthermore, dramatic disparities— sometimes as much as five or six hours—between weekday and weekend bed and waking times may push adolescents' biological clocks out of sync with the world in which they're expected to function. High school teachers complain heatedly of the "Monday morning daze."

For adolescents who don't fall asleep until three or four in the morning, rigorous awakenings at seven every day, with no naps permitted, may have the desired effect of helping them to fall asleep earlier at night. However, this schedule is so difficult to adhere to that success may be more reliably obtained by progressively delaying bedtime by three hours for several days running until the youngster has been rotated to a more desirable bedtime. This remedy is admittedly drastic, but it can be accomplished within a week. The youngster should then try to stick to a regular schedule for going to bed and getting up, seven days a week. (For more on this type of treatment, see Chapter 11, "The Time of Our Lives.")

Many teens like to move out of their old bedrooms, finding a new place in basement or attic, farther away from parents. Although parents sometimes view this move as a rejection of family ties, Dr. Hirschberg explains that it's more appropriately understood as a healthy expression of the wish for independence. "It's important for teenagers to feel they have space of their own," he adds.

In adolescence, sleep disturbances may appear as a result of the use of drugs, including alcohol. Disturbed sleep may also be the first sign of serious mental illness, such as depression or schizophrenia. An adolescent who is troubled by insomnia may benefit from exercise, relaxation training and following guidelines recommended for adults with this problem. (See Chapter 15, "How to Get a Better Night's Sleep," and Chapter 16, "What to Do If You Can't Sleep—or Can't Stay Awake.") Finally, some sleep disorders first become apparent in the teenage years. A teenager with narcolepsy, for example, may complain of falling asleep in class, lack of energy for social activities and bouts of occasional muscle weakness in moments of excitement. (Narcolepsy is discussed later in this chapter, as well as in Chapter 10, "Too Sleepy People.")

Nighttime "Happenings"

Bed-wetting, walking, talking and frantic crying during sleep have long been blamed on bad dreams, acting-out of dreams, possession by evil spirits (in contemporary parlance, psychological disturbance) or physical illness. Sleep-lab studies largely refute such notions.

Children who occasionally experience these problems are, as a rule, no different psychologically from children who don't, except to the degree that the disorders themselves, particularly bed-wetting, contribute to feelings of shame and guilt or cause isolation from peers.

Only rarely are illnesses, such as epilepsy, present. Most often nothing seriously wrong can be found. Bed-wetting, sleepwalking and attacks of sleep terrors may reflect some immaturity in the central nervous system, but they seldom require treatment and usually disappear by themselves before adolescence.

These common disorders often recur, singly or together, at different ages in a person's life. They are far more frequent in boys than in girls, and the constellation of these disorders often runs in families. Both hereditary and environmental factors may play a role. The problems may show up early in life, but they're not usually recognized until a child is several years old. A nine-year-old brought to a sleep clinic because of concern about his sleepwalking was described by his parents as walking around in his crib at night when just a toddler.

The disorders have certain common characteristics. Frequently they are triggered by an outside stimulus, such as a noise; it's possible that some internal stimulus ordinarily sets them off. Except for bed-wetting, episodes usually last a few minutes, although in very young children they may last up to about half an hour. During these episodes the child is difficult to arouse. Afterward, he usually cannot remember the event.

Even though these problems may occur only occasionally, parents can benefit from knowing the best ways to cope. We offer guidelines in Chapter 12, "Things That Go Bump in the Night." If your child has such episodes nightly, or even several times a week, and particularly if they influence his or her ability to function during the day, talk to your doctor. Some underlying medical or psychological cause might be present.

Bed-wetting, or *nocturnal enuresis,* is the most common of this group of childhood sleep disorders. Many parents view wetting at night as a problem when it continues past age three. Nonetheless, at age four, 40 percent of boys and 30 percent of girls still wet at night at least once a week. At age nine, 7 percent of both boys and girls continue to do so; at age twelve, it's still a problem for about 3 percent. That means there's probably at least one child with a bed-wetting problem in the typical sixth-grade classroom. United States military statistics, compiled at a time of universal draft, show that between 1 and 2 percent of new male recruits still wet their beds occasionally.

Several comprehensive studies of large numbers of children may ease many common parental worries. These studies conclude that bed-wetting is not caused by too early toilet training and is not associated with such behavioral habits as thumb-sucking and nail-biting. It is not more common in children who have been circumcised. It does, however, tend to run in families, a fact that most grandparents can affirm and that should reassure parents that their child, too, will eventually outgrow the problem.

If you view bed-wetting as a normal, acceptable part of the growing-up process, you can help your child form a positive self-image. Most child-care specialists advise parents to try not to place much emphasis on the wetting, particularly before the child's fifth birthday.

Should a child begin to show emotional distress (as is more likely in a child five or older), you may want to consider some simple behavioral techniques. If your child has wet his bed, don't let him come into your dry one in the middle of the night. Instead, give him the responsibility for washing himself, changing pajamas and sheets and throwing the soiled ones into a laundry hamper. Don't resort to diapers; they may make your child unduly embarrassed and possibly cause skin irritation.

If your child hates to leave his warm bed, a robe and slippers by the bedside or a bedroom urinal may help, as may night-lights placed along the way to the bathroom and in it. Some children like a calendar chart where stars are "rewards" for dry nights; some parents offer a special treat at the completion of a dry week.

You may also be able to cut down on bed-wetting by waking your child at your bedtime and walking him to the bathroom. Few experts believe that withholding fluids from as early as four in the afternoon makes any difference, unless the child has been drinking truly copious amounts—that is, a quart or more at bedtime.

Because some children who wet at night appear to have smaller-than-usual bladder capacity, Barbara Starfield, M.D., and her colleagues in the department of pediatrics at the Johns Hopkins University School of Medicine devised a program of "stretching" exercises. They explain to the child and his family that the bladder can be stretched like a rubber balloon at a faucet. They then encourage the child to drink freely during the day, to practice holding urine as long as possible before going to the bathroom and to try stopping and starting the urinary stream as a way of learning better control. The child also learns to urinate into, or pour the urine into, a measured container and to try to beat his own former record. Star charts and family praise for dry nights reinforce the child's sense of control.

A single day of intensive training starts a highly successful bed-wetting treatment program developed by Nathan Azrin, Ph.D., professor of psychology at Nova University, Fort Lauderdale, and his colleagues. The children are taught urine retention, with practice sessions every half hour. The child rehearses appropriate nighttime action, such as jumping out of bed and dashing to the bathroom. That night, parents awaken the child hourly for the first few hours, to show the child that he can control his own urination. In one study involving fifty-five children, twenty below age six, the average child had four accidents before achieving fourteen consecutive dry nights. Only one in five later started wetting again, and most of these improved with a second training session.

Some families get good results by combining bladder training with the use of a "wetness alarm" device—a pad of electrode-lined foil that is placed beneath the child's bedsheet; when wet, the pad activates a buzzer or bell or turns on a lamp, thus awakening the child.

If a child can be conditioned to awaken just at the time of wetting, proponents claim, he soon will awaken in response to internal signals of the need to urinate. Use of this system usually requires, however, that parents get up when the alarm sounds to make sure the child is awake, to help change the bed linens and to reset the alarm. The training generally requires several weeks, even months. Foil pads and alarms are available in major department stores and through mail-order catalogs. There is, incidentally, no danger of electric shock with these devices.

In a few instances, bed-wetting is caused by a defect or a dysfunction of the genital and urinary organs, and in such cases, it can often be corrected by surgery or successfully treated with medication.

If your child dribbles urine in the daytime, urinates frequently or appears to experience pain when urinating, he or she needs to see a doctor promptly. The doctor can readily determine whether medical problems exist, by means of a physical exam, a urine culture or, occasionally, more elaborate tests.

For children whose bed-wetting begins after a specific event—the most frequently reported is loss of a parent through death or divorce—psychotherapy may be helpful. It may be recommended also if your child is having behavioral problems in addition to the nighttime wetting.

If your child has begun wetting after regular dryness has been achieved, take him to the doctor. Sometimes, medical problems have developed.

When bed-wetting continues to occur nightly, or nearly so, even after behavioral conditioning, and particularly in an older child for whom emotional distress has added a heavy burden, drug treatment is sometimes recommended.

The drug that many doctors prescribe is the antidepressant imipramine. Judith Rapoport, M.D., chief of the unit on childhood mental illness at the National Institute of Mental Health, comments, "Although antidepressants take weeks to work in adults, they may be effective in children the very first night. Hence, imipramine may be useful for the child who wants to spend the night at the house of a friend or a fussy grandmother. It can also provide relief to a child who wants to go away to summer camp."

Looking at the way imipramine works, Anthony Kales, M.D., and his colleagues at Pennsylvania State University suggest that it produces a decrease in bladder excitability and/or an increase in bladder capacity, thus markedly reducing the number of bed-wetting events that occur early in the night when sleep is deepest. Hence, the child can sleep uninterruptedly through the night, or at least be more aware of a full bladder later in the night, when sleep is lighter.

Doctors generally agree that the drug should not be prescribed for longer than one to three months. One concern, which goes beyond the drug's potential unwanted side effects, is that long-term drug therapy may predispose children to rely more heavily on drugs in general later in life. Both parents and the child, assuming he is responsible for taking the medication himself, need to be aware that increasing the dosage will not make the problem go away faster.

Too Little or Too Much Sleep

While parents quickly heed a child who can't sleep or won't sleep, they sometimes overlook a "sleepy" child. Indeed, rather than reporting that the child is sleepy, they may describe him or her as lazy, inattentive, forgetful, uninterested, falling behind in school or even hyperactive.

Persistent excessive daytime sleepiness in children, especially in adolescents, most frequently results from either the sleep apnea syndrome, a disorder of breathing during sleep, or narcolepsy, a disorder in mechanisms that control sleeping and waking.

The *sleep apnea syndrome,* which is more common in children who are extremely overweight than in children of normal weight, and more common in boys than in girls, involves repeated pauses in the flow of air at nose and mouth, despite continued efforts to breathe. Each time the child struggles for air, he awakens briefly, gasping as breathing restarts. Not surprisingly, his numerous arousals during the night leave him sleepy during the day.

Since some babies snort and gurgle from the very start, parents may not be aware that their youngster's nighttime breathing is abnormal. One child was brought to the sleep clinic only when the staff at the day-care center he attended told his parents they could no longer assume responsibility for him. Whenever he napped, he seemed to gasp for every breath. During a night in the sleep laboratory, this child stopped breathing more than eight hundred times; a healthy child would have only a few such interruptions.

Be suspicious of loud snoring, squeaking or other nighttime respiratory noises, particularly if your child seems to be having trouble breathing. Many youngsters with sleep apnea habitually breathe through their mouths and seem to sleep fitfully, although they are seldom as restless as adults with this problem. As a rule, these children fall asleep quickly at night and are hard to awaken in the morning.

Some children with sleep apnea complain of morning headaches. Many are sluggish during the day and function poorly in school. Some are considered by their teachers to be of below-normal intelligence. But some have no symptom other than sleepiness, yet they may be just as severely affected as those with several symptoms.

Enlarged tonsils and adenoids may also interfere with breathing during sleep. While awake, the child may breathe adequately; a physician who examines him may not detect a problem. During sleep, the position of the tongue and the structure of nose and throat may obstruct the airway. When tonsils and adenoids are implicated, the appropriate treatment often is to remove them. Relief can be dramatic. After surgery, some youngsters appear alert during the day for the first time in their lives. Occasionally, as in adults, a permanent opening in the airway, known as a tracheostomy, is required to ease breathing during sleep; a valve closure permits the child to breathe and talk normally during the day. (For more on sleep apnea, see Chapter 9, "The Snoring Sickness.")

Children with *narcolepsy* sometimes are viewed as natural long-sleepers. They nap frequently and may fall asleep during class. Yet the symptom of sleepiness is so subtle that the diagnosis of narcolepsy seldom is made until adolescence or early adulthood.

The sleepiness is usually apparent before other symptoms associated with narcolepsy appear. These include sudden muscular weakness, known as cataplexy, hallucinations and an inability to move just before falling asleep. All of these sensations are normally associated with the REM stage of sleep; they are troublesome only when they occur while we are still awake, as happens in people with narcolepsy.

A child with narcolepsy may justifiably fear going to bed. Just as he is about to drift off, he may hear strange noises, such as voices or a door opening near his bed. He may see shadows without real form, or vague white or gray shapes. If he tries to move and run away from these specters, he may discover that he is paralyzed. He can't even call out for help. Yet he may not be able to describe these experiences to his parents except as "bad dreams."

Because the problem is still seldom recognized in young children, treatment guidelines are just now being developed. As in the
treatment of adults, drugs such as stimulants to combat daytime
sleepiness and tricyclics for the muscular weakness of cataplexy
are most likely to be prescribed. Regulating daytime behavior can
be helpful, and periodic naps are often advised. (For a more complete discussion of narcolepsy, see Chapter 10, "Too Sleepy People.")

The Sudden Infant Death Syndrome (Crib Death)

The Sudden Infant Death Syndrome (SIDS) kills eight thousand
to ten thousand infants in the United States every year and is the
leading cause of death of children one week to one year old in this
country. In nearly every instance of this disorder, also known as
crib death, an apparently healthy baby is tucked into bed for the
night or set down for a nap. Hours—sometimes only minutes—
later, the baby is found dead. No one hears the child make a sound.
Usually there is no indication that he or she struggled or smothered in the bedclothes, or vomited and choked, and no reason for
the death is found at an autopsy performed on the child's body.

Although it has never been proved that all such deaths actually
occur during sleep, nearly all occur when the child presumably is
sleeping. Hence, researchers are trying to determine the role, if
any, that sleep plays.

Dozens of possible clues to the cause of SIDS have been examined, leading researchers to conclude that many factors interact to
produce the fatal sequence of events. Recent studies confirm the
suspicion that babies affected are not as healthy as was once
thought, although doctors still have not been able to pinpoint the
specific abnormalities that figure in SIDS, reports Christian Guilleminault, M.D., of Stanford University.

Autopsies of some SIDS victims show damage to lung, brain
and fat tissues that could have been caused by low levels of blood
oxygen for long periods. The important question, still unresolved,
is whether frequent pauses in breathing during sleep, or the sleep
apnea syndrome, may have this effect.

Sometimes a sleeping child is discovered not breathing and is pale, limp and unconscious; a parent or babysitter shakes the baby or provides mouth-to-mouth resuscitation that restarts breathing. Such children often are termed SIDS near-misses, even though it is possible that they might have started breathing again on their own. When observed in a sleep laboratory, many of these children are found to have sleep apnea. In others, the muscles that normally assist in breathing during sleep fail to work properly. Some children have gastroesophageal reflux, a disorder that causes them to regurgitate stomach contents during sleep. In their waking hours, some prove to have trouble breathing while being fed. Others have seizures, metabolic disorders or infections. One or all of these disorders may account for SIDS.

At the Sudden Infant Death Syndrome Institute at the University of Maryland, the SIDS research team has been evaluating the status of about one thousand babies a year since 1978.

"We are investigating simultaneously as many reasonable theories as we can by following the same babies," explains Alfred Steinschneider, M.D., director of the institute. When the babies are one week old, and again when they are four weeks old, they undergo a number of studies, none of which causes any pain. Their sleep is monitored, using conventional sleep-study techniques, in one of the hospital's seven infant sleep labs. The way the heart and lungs work during feeding is studied with the aid of a nursing-bottle nipple equipped with a sucking gauge. Neurological development is also assessed. The aim of the research is to identify factors that might place the baby at increased risk for SIDS.

If evidence shows that a baby is having heart trouble or breathing difficulty, or if a brother or sister has died from SIDS, the baby goes home with an electronic monitor designed to alert parents by sounding an alarm if breathing stops for twenty seconds or if the child's heart rate slows to a serious degree during sleep. Parents are taught how to perform cardiopulmonary resuscitation, should it prove necessary. The monitor unit also includes a twenty-four-hour tape cassette. If the alarm goes off, it puts a signal on the tape that in turn makes a mark on the printout when the record is analyzed at the hospital.

There, babies' records are stacked floor to ceiling. Here is a child who stopped breathing for intervals of thirty-one, thirty-seven and thirty-two seconds. Here is one who never set off the alarm but had hundreds of brief pauses in breathing accompanied by a slowing of heart activity. The researchers are trying to assess the relevance of these distinctive patterns to the babies' health and, further, to identify the causes. Babies are kept on the monitors until a month has gone by without the alarm's sounding. Most babies are taken off the monitors by their first birthday.

It is important to recognize that the use of a monitor is unfortunately no guarantee that any trouble that might develop is correctable, and the monitors are not without drawbacks. The standard models use a belt wrapped around the baby to measure the movement of the chest, but this is not a completely reliable indicator. It is possible for the chest to move even though a blockage in or close to the nose and mouth prevents air from entering the lungs. Also, false alarms can occur, if, for example, breathing is shallow. And although some parents find the bleeping protective and reassuring, enabling them to get their own rest more easily, others find they are worn down with anxiety from the constant reminders that their baby's life is precarious.

Because of such problems, monitors are not an item to be added to the layette shopping list, along with booties and diapers. Even though the monitors can be purchased without a doctor's prescription, the American Academy of Pediatrics advises that they "should be used only under medical supervision."

Summing Up

Laboratory studies of sleep have added considerably to our present understanding of children's sleep problems. Specific illnesses can be distinguished from normal variations in emotional and physical development. You can help your child develop good sleep habits, starting in the first months of his life.

Here are a few key points to keep in mind:

- Sleep disturbances in early childhood can usually be resolved by paying attention to daily habits that might interfere with sleep and establishing bedtime rituals.
- If your child's sleep problem affects the way he or she behaves

or feels during the day, it demands a comprehensive medical and psychological evaluation.

• Treatment of a sleep problem should be tailored to your child.

• Most sleep disorders of childhood fade with time.

6

THE LATER YEARS

The evolution of sleep over a lifetime is gradual. Signs of aging show up in sleep, just as hair slowly grays, wrinkles appear and eyesight becomes less sharp. "Like our ability to run the one-hundred-yard dash, the sleep process becomes less athletic," asserts Wilse Webb, Ph.D., of the University of Florida.

Beginning in our forties or fifties, most of us realize that we do not sleep quite as soundly as we used to. As we grow older, we wake more often during the night, and we stay awake longer. We also doze more easily during the day—while riding the bus or watching television, for example.

Even though these changes are subtle, the fact that they occur at all sometimes delays the recognition of true disorders of sleep. *Vastly disturbed, unrefreshing sleep is not an inevitable part of aging.* Some sleep problems do occur more often as we grow older, but once they are identified, they can frequently be treated successfully.

Once it was thought that people needed less sleep in their older, presumably less active, years than they did in their twenties and thirties. That's not true. Our need for a specific number of hours of sleep seems to remain fairly constant throughout adulthood. Aging does, however, reduce the amount of sleep that we are able to get at any one time. It also alters the timing of sleep. We sleep less at night because we do not sustain sleep in long, unbroken stretches as easily as we did when we were younger. But we sleep more during the day, supplementing nighttime sleep with daytime naps.

Regrettably, many of us do not seem to get enough sleep to feel fully alert at all times. Although this problem appears to be shared by adults of all ages in the United States, it becomes more acute as we grow older. The common stereotyped portrayal of elderly people dozing on a park bench affirms that chronic sleepiness is a well-recognized sign of advanced age.

A sleep-laboratory study at Stanford University demonstrates the magnitude of the problem. Healthy volunteers over the age of sixty-five who had no complaints about their sleep slept as long as they wished at night. When given several opportunities to nap during the day, some averaged only five minutes to fall asleep. Falling asleep so quickly represents pathological sleepiness, Mary Carskadon, Ph.D., and her colleagues assert. Healthy young and middle-aged adults tested in the same way typically fell asleep in an average of ten minutes, revealing that their sleepiness was less severe. But by comparison, preteen children tested under the same circumstances didn't fall asleep at all; they showed the optimum state of alertness.

This chapter explores the impact of changes in sleep as we grow older and offers practical guidelines to help foster good sleep all life long.

The Aging of Sleep

As we grow older, we spend a greater proportion of sleep in the lighter stages 1 and 2 and a smaller proportion in the deeper sleep of stage 3–4. In fact, by the time we reach sixty-five the proportion of deep sleep is half what it was in our twenties. These changes make sleep seem less restful. (For more information on sleep stages, see Chapter 2, "What Is Normal Sleep?")

Although the sleep of men and women in young adulthood is quite similar, as people get older, women sleep "younger" than men—that is, later in life women have more deep sleep than men do. Women take longer to fall asleep than men but they wake less often and for shorter periods during the night.

The proportion of time spent in REM sleep, the state in which most dreaming occurs, remains at about one fifth of the night in most people well into extreme old age and then declines slightly.

The proportion of REM sleep we have may be a biological marker showing how sharp we are mentally. Older people who continue to experience a normal percentage of REM sleep prove faster and more accurate on tests of memory and addition than those who show a fall in REM sleep, according to studies by Patricia Prinz, Ph.D., of the University of Washington, Seattle.

Healthy people well into their nineties continue to experience physiological responses of sexual organs during REM sleep. Men continue to have erections of the penis, and women, vaginal lubrication. As people get older, the frequency of this response during sleep seems to be linked more strongly than in earlier years with regular sexual activity and enjoyment. Older men who suffer impotence are likely to write it off as a sign of aging; in fact, the persistence of normal erections during REM sleep in healthy older men demonstrates that aging may not be the cause at all. Unrecognized illnesses, such as diabetes, often prove to be at fault. (For more on impotence, see Chapter 13, "In Sickness and Health.")

Older people spend more time in bed than younger people. Between lights out and getting up in the morning, young adults spend 94 percent of the time actually asleep. But older people are not equally efficient sleepers. They spend one fifth of the time awake, an astounding one to two hours every night. In early adulthood, awakenings during the night are usually so brief that we have no memory of them in the morning. Later in life, we are more aware of awakening and we stay awake longer.

Many older people also have dozens, sometimes hundreds, of partial awakenings that last fifteen seconds or less. Sometimes these brief arousals fuse in the memory to create the impression that we have been awake all night, one of those curious tricks the body plays. Recognizing what has happened may help make this distressing feeling more bearable.

Faulty Clocks

Suppose you tried to run your life with a watch that didn't keep proper time. When it was fast, you'd be arriving at dinner parties while the hostess was still in the shower. When it was slow, you'd miss the bus. As we get older, many of us develop faulty inner clocks. For most of our lives, we have a single sleep period and a single waking period every twenty-four hours. In later years this daily rhythm seems to break down. Our daily cycle lacks the "high" of full wakefulness and the "low" of solid sleep. Sleep interrupts wakefulness and wakefulness interrupts sleep.

Since changes in the timing of sleeping and waking also occur in persons of all ages who participate in experiments cut off from time cues, it may be that aging "isolates" us in the real world. Aging may make us less able to respond to time cues in a variety of ways. Body temperature, known to be one of the most stable biological rhythms and intimately tied to the timing of sleep, becomes more erratic as we grow older. If eyesight dims, we may not pay as much attention to changes in light and dark. If hearing fades, the thud of the morning paper on the door step or the shriek of the noon whistle may lose their power to be pacesetters in our lives. If appetite dulls, whether or not meals are served on time may lose importance.

Generally, as we grow older, we tend to become larks; we are "early to bed and early to rise." But if we go to bed at nine, it is quite likely that we will be awake at three in the morning, when there probably are fewer interesting things to do and fewer people around to do them with. Hence, we have to be careful not to let this pattern become extreme.

If confined to hospitals or long-term nursing homes, we may have to turn out the lights at night and get out of bed in the morning at hours that are not of our choosing. However, rigid schedules may help some elderly people to stabilize their times of sleeping and waking. Bed rest by itself seems to lead to more frequent awakenings and, hence, to less restful sleep. Relating to the world primarily while lying down seems to disrupt circadian rhythms, including temperature rhythms. These abnormalities in inner clocks develop even if people are not isolated from contacts with others, time cues or light and dark and are permitted to exercise, according to a study of young people confined to bed for nearly two months conducted at the NASA-Ames Research Center at Moffett Field, California, by Carolyn Winget, Ph.D., and her colleagues. (For more on inner clocks, see Chapter 11, "The Time of Our Lives.")

But you need not despair that as you grow older you will be condemned to suffer poor sleep at night and the resulting miserable days. You can compensate for an unreliable inner clock in later years by applying some commonsense rules to your daily life.

- Follow a regular schedule. If you go to sleep and get up at approximately the same times each day, you'll sleep more soundly at night and feel less drowsy during the day.
- Make firm plans to be with other people. It's easier to get up, even if you've had a sleepless night, if you promised to be at your neighborhood school at nine to help children with reading, or at a nearby hospital to staff the information desk. If you lack a compelling reason to get up in the morning, you may decide after a bad night to linger in bed. While sleeping late generally is regarded as one of the pluses of retirement, it's a mistake for troubled sleepers to do so. This practice makes it harder to sleep the next night and thus may perpetuate a vicious circle.
- Organize your day. Eat at specific times, with someone else if possible. If you are to take medications at regular intervals, do so at the same hour each day. Let the end of the eleven o'clock television news or a regular nighttime entertainment show be a signal that it's time for bed.
- If you find it takes hours to fall asleep, you may be going to bed too early. Just go to bed later. You'll probably fall asleep at about the same time as before.
- If you feel better after a nap, take one regularly at the same time each day. But don't use naps now and then to make up for poor sleep at night. If you can stay up all day after a bad night, you are likely to sleep much better that night.

Interruptions in Breathing

The older we get, the more likely we are to have interruptions in breathing during sleep. It's possible for a person to have vastly disturbed breathing during sleep, yet breathe normally while awake, because the regulation of breathing differs at these times.

Pauses that are prolonged and frequent characterize sleep apnea. Some people with this disorder complain of excessive daytime sleepiness but do not realize that they awaken repeatedly during their sleep in order to breathe. Others complain that they awaken frequently but don't know why.

Snoring almost always indicates that breathing during sleep is not normal. By the age of sixty-five, three of every five men and two of every five women customarily snore. Habitual snorers are two times as likely as nonsnorers to have high blood pressure, a risk factor for heart disease and stroke. Both snoring and high blood pressure are more common in older people than in younger people. A recurrent pattern of persistent raucously loud snoring is frequently associated with sleep apnea; however, even people who do not snore may have the disorder. (For more information, see Chapter 9, "The Snoring Sickness.")

Sleep apnea is predominantly a male disease in earlier life, but in old age the gap between the sexes narrows. Severe sleep apnea is potentially fatal and is suspected of causing many cases of sudden and unexpected death during sleep, the most common time of death for the elderly.

Healthy elderly volunteers were selected for a study at Stanford University because they had no complaint about their sleep. In this study of elderly people believed to be the most likely to have undisturbed sleep and normal breathing, the worrisome finding was that two in five stopped breathing five or more times per hour. Five interruptions is generally held to be the dividing line between normal and abnormal breathing. The possible impact of these pauses on daytime functioning and health is currently the focus of intense investigation. This study showed that people who had breathing problems during the night proved to be sleepier during the day (even if they didn't see themselves as "sleepy") than those whose breathing was normal. They fell asleep faster when given the opportunity to nap. They also did worse on tests of thinking ability.

"Severe cases of sleep apnea in older people might be mistaken for senility," notes Dr. Carskadon. "Such tragic results are all the more lamentable because sleep apnea often can be remedied," she adds. If you suspect you or someone close to you may have apnea, don't put off a visit to the doctor.

Muscle Twitches and Restless Legs

As you're sitting here reading, try flexing your knee, your hip and your foot at the ankle. At the same time extend your big toe. Do it rapidly. Stop and relax for thirty seconds. Do it again. You can probably now appreciate how disruptive this would be during sleep.

Such movements may occur for an hour or two at a time and trigger a hundred or more arousals during the night, involving a lightening of sleep and sometimes a complete awakening. Curiously, many people who have these periodic leg movements do not realize what it is that is waking them up; they are aware only of frequent awakenings and fitful sleep. Others do not remember waking; they complain only of being sleepy in the daytime. Even people who have no complaints at all may have this problem, although their cases are usually mild. Often the clue to the nature of the disorder comes from a bed partner. Doctors hear the lament, "He literally kicks me out of bed."

The older we get, the more likely we are to develop these periodic movements. Sleep studies of a random sample of people aged sixty-five and over by researchers at the Veterans' Administration Medical Center, San Diego, showed that one in three experienced this disorder.

Some people who experience periodic movements during sleep also have "restless legs" while awake, particularly while sitting or lying down. Disagreeable "deep creeping" sensations run through the calves, triggering the urge to move the legs repeatedly. If you feel you have restless legs or have been told you move repeatedly during sleep, see your doctor. Drugs, most notably those used for seizure disorders, including clonazepam or valproic acid, may be prescribed to help you sleep better.

Depression and Other Mental Illnesses

Depression: Feelings of sadness are intimately related to poor sleep. People with depression tend to awaken frequently during the night, and the continued loss of sleep may worsen the depression.

Although depression can often be successfully remedied with medications, in older people it frequently goes unrecognized. The emotional inertia is often chalked up to "just getting old." Furthermore, older people are more likely than younger people to deny feeling sad or down in the dumps. Instead, they may insist, "If only I could get a good night's sleep, I'd be fine," or they may dwell on a multitude of aches and pains. Poor hearing or failing memory may make it harder for an older person to respond to questions or communicate feelings.

Poor sleep, loss of appetite and lack of interest in the events of daily life should alert you to the possibility of depression. If you suspect this disorder exists in someone who is close to you, see that he or she is examined by a physician. (For more about depression, see Chapter 14, "Troubled Minds/Troubled Sleep.")

Dementia: People with degenerative brain disease sometimes awaken during the night highly confused; they may experience hallucinations and may wander around their homes and even outside. Because vigilance is required to protect someone with this "sundown syndrome" from injury, it is often necessary for the person to live in a nursing home or other institution rather than at home.

Side Effects of Medications

In view of the increase in illnesses of all kinds as we get older, it's no surprise to find that, on average, each person sixty-five and older in the United States receives twelve prescriptions for medications annually, compared with only four for younger adults. Some 30 percent of the nation's prescription drugs and 40 percent of all sleeping pills are used by the elderly, even though, at this writing, they represent only 11 percent of the population.

An estimated 7 to 8 percent of people aged sixty to seventy-four use sleeping pills every night or frequently, while only 1 to 3 percent of people aged eighteen to thirty-four do so. Most elderly patients in institutions receive sleeping pills every night, a practice brought to light by a recent United States Public Health Service survey of physicians' prescriptions for nearly one hundred thousand patients in skilled-nursing facilities.

Yet few tests of sleeping pills have been done on older people. One reason is that elderly people frequently have illnesses or are taking other drugs that might alter the results. Another is that the people most likely to use sleeping pills may not be well enough to spend every night for two to four weeks in a sleep laboratory. There is an urgent need, however, to assess the effects of sleeping pills on older people.

Sleeping pills, for example, are designed to promote drowsiness, and because an older body is less efficient than a younger one in metabolizing drugs and excreting them, the possibility that drowsiness may be carried over into the next day increases as we get older. Yet measuring daytime carry-over has only recently been incorporated into the evaluation of sleeping pills. It is of vital importance because a sleeping pill tonight may make you a less attentive driver tomorrow, and at the same time make you less aware that you are not as alert as you should be.

The effect of sleeping pills on the ability to awaken at any time during the night is another pressing issue. What happens if a fire alarm sounds? If you are in your sixties or older and have taken a sleeping pill, are you more likely to stumble and fall if you have to get out of bed during the night? The older we get, the more likely it is that falls will cause fractures and other injuries.

One of the most worrisome aspects of the use of sleeping pills by older people arises from the pills' potential to depress breathing. This may pose a serious threat to people who, because of their age, are at high risk of having breathing problems during sleep. One seventy-two-year-old man with severe sleep apnea volunteered to take a standard dose of a widely used sleeping pill. Previously his pauses in breathing lasted about one minute. Now some lasted three minutes. One episode lasted five minutes, so long that the experimenter feared for his life and awakened him.

Because older people take more drugs than younger people, they are also at higher risk of experiencing a harmful drug interaction. One particularly dangerous combination is that of sleeping pills and alcohol, which may give a knock-out punch.

Confusion and hallucinations are among other side effects of sleeping pills that are more common in the elderly. The dose of sleeping pills that will prove fatal is lower for an older person than for a younger one.

If you regularly take sleeping pills, whether purchased without a prescription or ordered by your doctor, discuss with your doctor the advisability of continuing them. Since most sleeping pills lose their ability to promote sleep after as little as two weeks, the odds are high that the pills are not doing you any good and may be doing some harm. But don't stop taking the pills before talking to your doctor. Doctors often advise that sleeping pills be discontinued gradually, to make it easier for your body to adjust. (For more on sleeping pills, see Chapter 8, "Sleeping Pills and Other Drugs for Insomnia.")

Better Ways to Cope

Many problems that have been blamed on "just getting old" now are known to arise from sleep disorders or from other physical and mental illnesses. However, sleep problems are both more frequent and more serious as we get older. Fortunately, better understanding of these problems has led to more effective treatment.

If you recognize any of the symptoms or problems discussed in this chapter in yourself or in someone close to you, see your doctor or urge your friend or relative to do so. After talking with you and conducting an exam, the doctor may want you to visit a specialist in sleep disorders to find out more about your problems.

These are the questions your doctor may ask: Do you have trouble falling asleep at night? Do you wake up during the night? Are you waking "too early" and then finding yourself unable to fall back to sleep? Are you sleepy or drowsy during the day or early evening? Does discomfort or pain disturb your sleep? Have you been told that you snore loudly or breathe unusually during sleep? Are you aware of abnormal movements or excessive restlessness during sleep? Do you take medication to help you sleep at night or to help you stay awake during the day? Does your bed partner or anyone who has observed your sleep tell you that your sleep seems unusual in any way?

"Yes" answers to these questions mean your sleep needs to be carefully assessed.

There are steps you can take in your daily life to enhance both the way you sleep at night and the way you feel during the day.

Those listed here apply specifically to persons in their later years; for more guidelines for good sleep for people of all ages, see Chapter 15, "How to Get a Better Night's Sleep."

- Look for ways to keep your inner clock running smoothly. Regular times for going to bed, getting up, eating, taking medications, meeting friends and fulfilling obligations to others all help.
- Don't overdo the alcohol; several drinks actually may worsen sleep. A drink at bedtime may pose a problem for people who experience gastric reflux, since it stimulates acid secretion. (This disorder is described further in Chapter 13, "In Sickness and Health.")
- To drink warm milk is a soothing bedtime ritual and helps keep you from waking with hunger pangs during the night. Milk may help prevent pain if you have ulcers, but if you have heartburn and choking caused by gastric reflux, you will probably sleep better if you avoid food and drink for several hours before you go to sleep.
- You probably find that noise, such as that from street traffic or airplane flyovers, bothers you more now than when you were younger. Even if you have slept in the same bedroom for many years, now may be the time to install heavy draperies or to mask outside noises with a fan or air conditioner. If you live alone, however, earplugs aren't advisable; they may block protective noises, such as the telephone or smoke alarms.
- Your body's temperature-regulating mechanisms probably are less efficient than they were when you were younger. If you wake up during the night feeling chilly, try using an electric blanket.
- If you have a bad back or arthritis, ask your doctor if a special mattress or a bed board would help. If you have gastric reflux or breathing or heart problems, you may sleep better if the head of your bed is elevated on six-inch to eight-inch blocks or if you prop yourself up with pillows.
- Even if you've been a coffee, tea or cola drinker all your life, consuming these drinks after about four in the afternoon may make sleep restless. Sensitivity to caffeine increases with age.
- If you are taking diuretics, you may wake frequently to uri-

KVCC KALAMAZOO VALLEY
COMMUNITY COLLEGE
LIBRARY

nate. You may be able to minimize this problem by cutting down on fluids from dinner time on.

• If you take sleeping pills every night or frequently, you may not be doing yourself a favor. Doctors generally advise reducing such medications gradually, but be sure to talk with your own doctor about the best way to proceed.

• If you live alone, secure locks, a smoke and fire alarm and perhaps even a burglar alarm will help give you peace of mind. Use a night-light to help avoid confusion or stumbling in the dark if you awaken and wish to get out of bed.

• Many people, old and young, report that it is comforting to have other people sleeping close by, but if you live with your children or others, you may have to make special efforts to adjust to the lack of privacy. Here's where earplugs and an eye shield may be helpful.

• Does a pet share your bedroom at night? A restless dog or cat may be interfering with your sleep more than you might suspect.

• If you are having trouble sleeping in your bedroom, but find you can fall asleep easily on the living room couch, stay there for the night. A break in your routine may be worthwhile.

• Anticipate occasional sleeping problems. Plan ways to keep your mind occupied so that you don't worry about not being able to sleep. Mentally rearrange closets or make shopping lists. Buy pillow speakers for your radio to help you pass the time without disturbing anyone else. (See also Chapter 16, "What to Do If You Can't Sleep—or Can't Stay Awake.")

• If you and your bed partner go to bed or get up at different times, or if he or she snores loudly, kicks or flails about and wakes you, consider separate beds or even separate rooms. Urge him or her to see the doctor, too.

Summing Up

Many of us find that sleep "frays" as we get older. Most of us adjust good-naturedly to such changes, just as we learn to tolerate our wrinkles and creaky joints. At the same time, we need to be sensitive to changes in how we sleep at night and how we feel during the day. We might question whether certain habits of daily life are having an impact, for better or worse, upon our nighttime sleep.

All around the country, scientists are working to identify changes that are part of the evolution of sleep over a lifetime and to distinguish them from problems that are potentially correctable. Such research is important to people of all ages, for we all are growing older.

PART II

TROUBLED SLEEP

7

INSOMNIA

Insomnia is not just a disorder of sleep. It is a twenty-four-hour illness.

Inwardly churning, you plump your pillow, tuck the covers around your shoulders or hurl them to the floor, smooth out hills and valleys in the sheets. You curl up on your right side, switch to your left side, flop on your back. Staring out into the dark, you try the tricks you've read about in magazines, such as concentrating on painting an entire wall with a tiny brush. Soon bored with that, you self-consciously conjure up a passel of fluffy sheep and start counting. You're distracted by the ticking of your clock, the wind rattling the window, a horn honking down the street.

Frustrated, you go to the bathroom, flip through a magazine, or trudge to the kitchen to nibble on leftover chicken. More often you just lie there, wishing that wakefulness would evaporate. Beside you, your spouse is breathing rhythmically, oblivious to your agony. Bitterly you reflect, The whole world is asleep. I'm all alone in my misery.

In the morning you dress wearily. On the street you stare gloomily at other people, thinking, All of them slept better than I did. You plod through your work, trying to ignore your burning eyes and to rein in your wandering mind. Someone makes a simple request, to which you snap a rude reply. Your co-workers bristle at your brusqueness. In a meeting, your chin slowly sinks to your chest; then, as your head suddenly jerks up, you hear someone titter.

That evening you can't muster up the energy to go out or even to do household chores. Instead, you settle down in front of the television, newspaper in hand. Dozing off, you decide you are ready for bed. You wash your face, brush your teeth, lie down, plump the pillow, tuck the covers around your shoulders . . . and wait. Where did that overwhelming urge for sleep go? Another sleepless night is just beginning. And another day of feeling washed out is in the offing.

Total insomnia, that is, "no sleep," even for a few nights, is very rare. The real complaint of the insomniac is "poor sleep"—trouble falling asleep or staying asleep, or awakening too early. Virtually all of us have at least occasional bad nights in which we experience one or more of these problems; the older we get, the more frequently we do so. But for one in six American adults, the battle of the bed is a "most nights" or an "every night" event.

The notion that insomnia can be "cured" simply by getting more sleep still drives many people to the drugstore or doctor's office. Although sleeping pills' long-term ineffectiveness and dangers have been widely publicized over the past decade, leading to a dramatic decline in their use, Americans still gobble up twenty-one million prescriptions for sleeping pills annually.

The ancient Egyptians held that one of the world's "worst things" is "to be in bed and sleep not." Millions of us would agree. Friends and colleagues, who may be titillated by our bizarre dreams, have no patience for a minute-by-minute playback of a restless night. There's no National Insomnia Foundation sponsoring all-night radio talkathons to raise funds for research, although many weary souls feel there should be. No one wears a T-shirt saying, "I'm proud to be an insomniac." There are no bumper stickers reading, "Honk if you can't sleep." Even people who suffer from insomnia sometimes joke about it. The insomniac humorist Richard Armour suggests that lost hours of sleep ought to be tax deductible. And in the catalog of human miseries, insomnia long has been held to be about as serious as hiccups. Perhaps insomnia is trivialized because, when you're in the throes of it, there's usually no one around to notice and sympathize. And even though its effects the next day may be devastating to you, they are largely invisible to others.

Some people are embarrassed by their insomnia. They assume —quite erroneously—that insomnia is "all in the mind" and feel that not being able to sleep "right" stamps them as woefully incompetent. To add to their feelings of frustration, the complaint "I didn't sleep a wink last night" is frequently challenged by a spouse who insists, "But you did. I saw you." In fact, both sides of such an argument have validity, for there's often a wide discrepancy between how an insomniac perceives his sleep and what objective measures of his sleep show.

Most of us define insomnia as poor sleep at night that has unpleasant consequences during the day. Indeed, about two thirds of all insomniacs say their insomnia colors their entire lives. The color is gray, insipid gray, for lack of sleep typically brings lack of stamina, lack of motivation and lack of pleasure. But astonishingly, as many as one third of all people who insist that their sleep is poor claim that their waking lives do not suffer. They say they only have trouble sleeping, a problem that is disturbing all by itself and one that they would like to remedy. Sleep-laboratory tests, such as the Multiple Sleep Latency Test, which measures the speed with which a person falls asleep at several different times of the day, affirm that these insomniacs are no sleepier in the daytime than people who have no complaints about their sleep; however, scientists acknowledge that they need better ways to assess the impact of troubled sleep on daytime functioning.

Until recently, the notion that a person may be healthy even if he sleeps poorly was widely accepted. But sleep-laboratory studies dispute this assumption. Today, poor sleep is increasingly recognized as a warning that something's wrong. Both satisfying sleep at night and alertness during the day should be taken for granted, just like the normal functioning of the gastrointestinal system. We should pay attention to disorders of sleep and waking, just as we do to diarrhea or vomiting. If you got sick every time you ate, you'd most likely seek help soon. Yet many people tolerate insomnia for years. Some treat themselves with medications and try other insomnia "remedies," usually without gaining relief. To postpone seeking medical help is a mistake. Today, many causes of insomnia can be identified and corrected.

Waking and sleeping may be viewed as opposite ends of a seesaw. When arousal pushes up, it causes sleep to go down, and vice versa. Peter Hauri, Ph.D., director of the Sleep Disorders Center at the Dartmouth Medical School, suggests that insomnia may involve an arousal system that is chronically overactive, or a sleep system that is chronically underactive, or both. The insomnia that many of us develop the night before an important meeting at work may originate in an overly excited waking system, while the insomnia that some of us have suffered from virtually every night for years may represent an underactive or malfunctioning sleep system. The distinction is more than semantic, because what you view as the cause of a problem usually influences what you do about it.

Insomnia is *not* a disease. Rather, it is a symptom, like a backache or chest pain. It has not one but many possible causes. The surest way to get rid of it is to find out what accounts for it and to remedy that. In this chapter, we'll explore the most frequent reasons for insomnia.

What's Wrong in Insomnia?

The insomniac's most common complaint is that it takes "too long" to fall asleep. Other, and often more disturbing, problems include waking "too often" during the night, waking "too early" in the morning or sensing that sleep is "too light." Most insomniacs feel they do not get "enough" sleep or "good" sleep. They say sleep varies considerably from one night to the next. Most feel sleepy during the day. Here's what these laments mean.

HOW LONG IS "TOO LONG" TO FALL ASLEEP?

Even in the unfamiliar confines of a sleep lab, tethered to a bundle of wires, 95 percent of normal sleepers under age seventy fall asleep within half an hour of lights out. Hence, taking thirty minutes or more to fall asleep at the usual bedtime is sometimes cited as an indication of insomnia.

But judging when sleep begins is tricky. The standards used in sleep labs are based on the appearance of certain brain wave patterns in the polysomnographic record. But some people don't feel they are asleep until they have been asleep according to the usual criteria for a solid fifteen minutes, reports Allan Rechtschaffen, Ph.D., director of the Sleep Research Laboratory at the University of Chicago. Awakenings or partial awakenings as brief as thirty seconds in this early part of sleep may make a person insist, "I wasn't sleeping at all, merely lying here thinking."

HOW MUCH WAKING IS "TOO MUCH"?

The average adult awakens fifteen or twenty times during the night. Such arousals usually last less than fifteen seconds and thus are not remembered in the morning. Some people, however, wake dozens, even hundreds, of times during sleep. Even if these numerous awakenings are brief, the sleeper may groan in the morning, "What a terrible, restless night!" If the awakenings are long enough to be remembered, and if they are frequent, he may feel in the morning that he lay awake all night. In part, that's because we remember time spent awake better than time spent asleep. (In extreme cases, sleep may be vastly disturbed but the person may not even recognize that his sleep is troubled and he may not complain of insomnia. Instead, he reports excessive sleepiness during the daytime.)

The line between normal sleep and disturbed sleep depends a great deal upon the sleeper's age. Younger people have fewer and briefer awakenings, while older people have more and longer ones. Many sleep specialists would describe as "insomnia" more than five remembered awakenings and thirty minutes or more of wakefulness after the person first falls asleep.

HOW EARLY AN AWAKENING IS "TOO EARLY"? HOW MUCH SLEEP IS "ENOUGH"?

Waking earlier than you desire may or may not mean that your sleep is ending prematurely. Some people who stay asleep only three, four or five hours worry that they have a sleep problem even though they awaken refreshed and alert. These rare people are natural short-sleepers who are victims of myths about how much sleep they "ought" to get. We all differ in the amount of sleep we need to satisfy our inner criterion of "enough." If you get eight hours of sleep but long for ten, you may feel as frustrated as someone who gets four hours but wants six. Eight out of ten healthy adults aged twenty to eighty are able to sleep six hours or more. While less than six hours of sleep was once regarded as a measure of insomnia, today the emphasis is not on the amount of sleep you get but rather on whether or not you feel that your sleep is sufficient, and whether or not you sense that a lack of sleep makes you feel out of sorts and function poorly.

WHAT MAKES SLEEP "TOO LIGHT"?

The same amount of broken sleep or lost sleep will bother some people more than others. Uncomfortable beds, noises and other environmental factors also are more disturbing to some people than to others. Remember the folktale about the princess and the pea? Only the "real" princess squirmed all night in agony because a pea had been placed beneath her twenty down-filled mattresses. By contrast, other maidens who had spent previous nights in the same bed had slumbered blissfully.

As we get older, we get less of the deeper stages of sleep and more of the lighter ones. As we reach our forties or fifties, most of us recognize that we don't sleep quite as soundly as we did in our twenties. Nonetheless, such changes ordinarily develop gradually, and we probably don't complain about our sleep unless it varies considerably from night to night or has suddenly deteriorated.

WHAT MAKES SLEEP "GOOD OR BAD"?

Again, the answer is subjective. What matters the most to you? Is it how easily you fall asleep, whether or not you awaken during the night or how you feel when you awaken in the morning?

The answer may be different at different times of your life. When Wilse Webb, Ph.D., and his colleagues at the University of Florida, Gainesville, surveyed different age groups, they found that high school students rated their sleep as poor when they didn't get enough sleep, woke up tired and had a hard time waking up. College students were bothered most when they had many worries on going to bed, woke up during the night and had many dreams. People over fifty thought that sleep was poor if they did not feel "exhausted" when they went to bed, had physical complaints during the night or had unpleasant dreams both during the night and on awakening. If none of these conditions existed, people thought their sleep was "good."

Because insomniacs do tend to sleep more erratically than satisfied sleepers, their torment may be magnified by their inability to predict whether they'll have a good night or a bad night. If you wake several times a night to urinate, for example, you probably have learned to go back to sleep quickly without fretting, and you don't worry about how you'll feel in the morning. But the insomniac is chronically dissatisfied with his sleep and frequently anticipates feeling bad the next day.

What Triggers Insomnia?

We're really talking about insomnias, plural. Many different and circuitous roads may lead to difficulty falling asleep or staying asleep.

The list of possible causes is a long one. It includes anxiety, depression, poor sleep habits, living in noisy surroundings, poor scheduling of sleeping and waking, dependency on drugs or alcohol, periodic leg movements during sleep and restless legs, interruptions in breathing during sleep, arthritis, ulcers and other illnesses. Some people have more than one of these problems.

Sleep loss due to many of these problems may masquerade as insomnia caused by "worries and stress." After all, it's understandable that you might feel upset and concerned when you're not sleeping well and mistake these effects for the cause of your problem. If relatively simple measures, such as those described in Chapter 15, "How to Get a Better Night's Sleep," don't relieve your insomnia, you need an evaluation by your doctor or at a sleep disorders center to tell what's really wrong. Here's what research studies reveal about the most common reasons for insomnia.

Transient Insomnia

Perhaps you recall from childhood the anticipation of the days before Christmas, as hints were dropped and boxes arrived and were hidden in closets and under beds, then wrapped with great attempts at secrecy. Finally came the night of Santa's journey! You giggled and squirmed and strained to hear the grate of a sled on the roof. Christmas Eve insomnia overwhelms all of us now and then, when we are gliding on an emotional high or our excitement mingles with anxiety. Remember the fidgety sleep of the night before you left for college or started your first job?

In times of stress, disturbed sleep is so frequent, even in good sleepers, that its absence is remarked upon. Exam periods, impending work deadlines and marital spats commonly provoke restless nights.

Even sleeping away from home in a strange bed bothers many of us, a phenomenon known as the "first night" effect. Vacationers may choose to make up for lost sleep by "sleeping in" or napping the next day, but business travelers on the road may be worn down by night after night of "first nights" in unfamiliar surroundings. One Baltimore salesman combats this drain by taking along his own pillow.

Crossing many time zones disrupts the body's internal clocks, often causing both trouble sleeping at night and trouble staying awake during the day.

When we are ill, with anything from a sore throat to arthritis —any problem that causes aches and pains while we are awake— we are likely to sleep poorly. If we are hospitalized, we must contend with anxiety over our well-being and, possibly, with pain. And though rest may be just what the doctor ordered, a hospital, with its unfamiliar surroundings and schedules, usually is no place to get it.

As most of us know from experience, a single night of insomnia that's triggered by a specific event, an illness or new surroundings is easy to take in stride. We've learned that even if insomnia continues for a few nights, it usually fades as things calm down or as we adapt to the troubling situation. Most of us are able to reassure ourselves that "this, too, shall pass."

Some of us are, however, particularly susceptible to trouble sleeping when emotions are churning. In the same circumstances, someone else might develop an upset stomach or erupt with hives. If certain situations predictably give you restless nights, discuss this problem with your doctor. Exploring the reasons for your difficulty may help you identify ways to cope better or to better tolerate the loss of sleep. Some doctors believe that the occasional use of sleep-promoting medications is warranted, especially if a stressful situation can be anticipated or is likely to last only a few days. Sleeping pills may also be indicated if you're ill or hospitalized. (For guidelines on the appropriate use of sleeping pills, see Chapter 8.)

Short-term Insomnia

All of us occasionally face problems that can't be resolved quickly. Often these involve our work or family life or serious medical illness. Having to deal with the illness or death of a close relative or friend will wreck nearly everyone's sleep. Here is a typical case: Joan's widowed father, although seemingly in good health, was grounded by back pain one weekend. His doctor sent him to the hospital, where X-rays showed inoperable liver cancer. For the next month, until he died, Joan, an only child, rarely left him alone. Although achy, fatigued and "washed out," she could not sleep well at night or nap easily during the day. Loose ends had to be tied up at her father's business, and relatives had to be called. After the funeral, the house was full of visitors. It wasn't until weeks later, waking one morning with the startled realization that she had "slept like a log," that Joan acknowledged to herself the strain of the previous weeks.

"The fact that insomnia is virtually universal in times of stress suggests it may be an important mechanism for coping," says Charles Pollak, M.D., director of the Sleep-Wake Disorders Center at the New York Hospital-Cornell Medical Center. "It forces us to pay attention to the problem. The process of mourning, for example, shouldn't be cut short. It's the way people repair themselves."

At such times, it helps to pay particular attention to factors that foster good sleep, such as going to bed and arising at regular times and not consuming large amounts of caffeine or alcohol. In addition, some doctors believe sleeping pills may be useful for a few weeks when a person is under continuing stress.

Insomnia That Won't Go Away

Most of us know someone who says, "I haven't had a good night's sleep in thirty years." Following are some of the most common reasons for this complaint.

PROBLEMS OF EVERYDAY LIFE

Tension, anxiety, poor sleep habits and negative expectations about sleep are often at the root of insomnia. It may be caused by stress or become worse under stress, and it may persist after the stressful situation has subsided. Perhaps it begins in the cradle. When Dr. Hauri asks adult insomniacs, "When did your problem start?," he finds that some had difficulty sleeping even as children. "Insomnia may be around from day one," he suggests. "Some babies seem alert all the time and cry all night." In such cases, insomnia may reflect a disorder of the neurological centers that control sleeping and waking, he notes.

Psychological factors may keep insomnia going. Some insomniacs turn concerns about bad sleep into a self-fulfilling prophecy. They fret: I am an insomniac, and I may never ever get another good night's sleep! Their fear of being unable to sleep keeps them awake.

Some of us may be "more awake" at all times than others are, observes Quentin Regestein, M.D., of the Boston Hospital for Women. "Super-alert people make terrific stockbrokers, salespeople, lawyers, athletes, surgeons or editors," he says. "They pay attention to details and set high standards for themselves. They're great during the day. But at night, some find it hard to turn off." Such people are described as hypervigilant.

Bob is an advertising account executive, with a knack for finding offbeat but sales-producing aspects of his clients' products. He has a hard time separating criticism of his work from criticism of him as a person. When he flips off the lights at night, thoughts about how he might have or should have handled a particular presentation race around in his mind. An hour or two after getting into bed, he might still be drumming his fingers against the sheets.

People like Bob often sleep better on Friday nights than on

Sundays, at the beginning rather than the end of a work or school break, when pressures are down. They often sleep better away from home, too, having left everyday stresses behind. Yet they may be reluctant to go on trips for fear of worsening their sleep. Some are rigid people who are unwilling to make changes. They worry more than most about the possible adverse effects on the next day of even a single hour of lost sleep.

But, as Dr. Hauri observes, "Not all of us are going to sleep soundly every night. Some of us are faster runners, some are smarter, some can play the piano, some have eyes of a deeper blue. The way to enjoy life most fully may be to acknowledge, 'I'll never be a champion sleeper.' "

Some of us blame lack of sleep for one unsatisfactory situation after another in our lives. It's tempting to think, My job would go better if only I could get more sleep, or better sleep, or enough sleep. We may go to bed earlier than usual in the hope of "catching up," or try to nap during the day, but typically we can't fall asleep or we awaken unrefreshed.

Some troubled sleepers find that their bedrooms or their bedtime habits, such as taking a shower or brushing teeth, create a barrier to sleep instead of fostering it, Dr. Hauri says. If you're among them, you may find you can nod off in front of the television or doze contentedly on the living room sofa. Unlike most people, you probably sleep better while traveling. But once you get into your own bed, you find yourself awake. You watch the clock and worry, Will I ever get to sleep? Unfortunately, trying to sleep is counterproductive. You can force yourself to stay awake if you want to, but you can't force yourself to sleep.

No one wants to be a slave to the clock, but some of us unwittingly abuse the body's inner clock that regulates sleeping and waking. Gary, for example, went to bed some nights at two in the morning, other nights at eleven o'clock. He frequently had trouble falling asleep. He kept a daily log for two weeks, recording when he went to bed and when he got up. The log showed him that he had been giving his body clock confusing instructions, expecting it to shift automatically from twenty-three-hour to twenty-seven-hour days. Sleep comes more easily now that he makes an effort to be in bed as close as possible to midnight seven days a week and gets up at seven every morning.

The results that emerge from sleep laboratory studies of chronic insomniacs underscore the baffling complexity of the disorder. People with one type of chronic insomnia, for example, actually take longer to fall asleep, wake more often and sleep less than good sleepers. These people have more of the lighter sleep stages and less of the deeper ones, as well as less of the REM state in which most dreaming occurs; they shift between stages more often, too. Their brain-wave recordings sometimes show the peculiar appearance of brief periods of wakefulness during deep sleep. These poor sleepers move around more and have a higher temperature and a faster heart rate than good sleepers do. Lawrence Monroe, Ph.D., of Ohio State University describes them as "more awakelike" during the night, an observation that may explain why some insomniacs feel they spend much of the night awake and why their sleep seems nonrestful.

On the other hand, the sleep of some people who complain of chronic insomnia is no different from that of people who have no complaints about their sleep, at least according to the usual criteria by which sleep is currently assessed. When 122 people whose insomnia could not be attributed to physical illness were studied by Mary Carskadon, Ph.D., and her colleagues at Stanford University, half proved no different from satisfied sleepers in the time it took them to fall asleep or in their total time asleep. These insomniacs may overestimate their difficulties. Sixty people in the study thought it took more than fifteen minutes longer than it actually did for them to fall asleep. They averaged more than six hours of sleep, but they thought they got less. Over one third of the group consistently underestimated their sleep time by more than an hour a night.

Each of us estimates time differently at different times of the day. For most normal sleepers, time moves quickly at midnight; for many insomniacs, it drags. In a study at the University of Cincinnati, insomniac and normal sleepers both were awakened after the first "spindle" appeared on the polygraph tracing, a marker that sleep had begun. When asked, "How long did it take you to fall asleep?," a normal sleeper may say, "Fifteen minutes," although twenty minutes have actually elapsed; after the same amount of time, an insomniac may reply, "Thirty minutes." An attempt is now in progress to improve insomniacs' skills in estimating time during the day, with the hope of producing more realistic appraisals of time at night.

Many insomniacs are convinced that their sleep is different from and generally inferior to that of most people, reports Thomas Roth, Ph.D., of Henry Ford Hospital, Detroit. These insomniacs believe most people get two more hours of sleep a night than they do, and that most people fall asleep much faster and more easily, are better sleepers, are more rested in the morning and enjoy their sleep more. Such negative feelings may reinforce and help perpetuate their poor sleep.

While it has never been proved that there is an "insomniac personality," some studies suggest that insomniacs may be more depressed, anxious, worrisome and likely to have hypochondriacal complaints than satisfied sleepers. People who describe themselves as light sleepers, for example, report tension headaches, palpitations and low back pain more frequently than satisfied sleepers do. "Type A" people, who are troubled by a sense of time urgency, are more likely to sleep poorly than are those of the more relaxed "Type B." But many people who sleep poorly show no signs of psychological distress.

What do insomniacs do, think and feel during the day? Some poor sleepers prove to be less active and less involved with their work and with other people than good sleepers, studies suggest. Evelyn Marchini, Ph.D., of the Pacific Graduate School of Psychology in Palo Alto, and her colleagues gave good and poor sleepers electronic paging devices and buzzed them at random intervals for several days; at these times, the subjects described what they were thinking and doing. The insomniacs spent more time relaxing and thinking about relaxing, while good sleepers spent more time talking to other people, working, studying and thinking about their daily activities. This study implies that some poor sleepers might be able to improve their sleep if they could be motivated to become more active and more involved with other people.

If you suspect that psychological factors contribute to your insomnia, be reassured that our improved understanding of their role has yielded practical ways to overcome them. You'll find these detailed in Chapter 16, "What to Do If You Can't Sleep—or Can't Stay Awake." You also may find it helpful to have sleeping pills on hand, for occasional use, if you should have a period of particularly troubled sleep.

MENTAL ILLNESS

Manic-depressive disease, schizophrenia, anxiety, obsessive-compulsive disorders and other mental illnesses are frequently accompanied by disturbed sleep. Indeed, it is often the symptom that prompts a visit to the doctor's office. In people with a particular form of depression, early morning awakenings are so common that they are viewed as a hallmark of the disorder. Nonetheless, distinguishing the fatigue caused by disturbed sleep from alterations in mood and behavior triggered by depression often proves a difficult task. Often a person who is depressed pays more attention to sleeping poorly than to feeling "sad."

The sleeping disturbances of the mentally ill are usually both more severe than, and different in character from, those of insomniacs who do not have such illnesses. When depressed people were compared with chronic insomniacs, for instance, researchers at the National Institute of Mental Health found that the depressed patients spent more time awake in the early morning and entered the first REM period of the night much sooner after they fell asleep. They were less likely to have trouble falling asleep, the most common problem for the chronic insomniac.

Of thousands of patients who were referred to sleep disorders centers and whose records were studied by the Association of Sleep Disorders Centers, about one in six with insomnia was diagnosed as having depression. Some researchers think the percentage of insomniacs with depression is even higher. One problem with such speculation is that disturbed sleep may cause, as well as result from, feelings of depression. Nonetheless, if you have insomnia, you should explore with your doctor the possibility that depression may be a factor; medications that are highly effective in relieving depression also frequently relieve insomnia.

For more information on sleep disturbances in depression and other mental illnesses, turn to Chapter 14, "Troubled Minds/ Troubled Sleep."

ALCOHOL AND DRUGS

Alcohol: Until quite recently, alcohol in modest amounts was often recommended as a sleep-promoter. It's quite true that a glass of wine or beer downed during the evening may help you unwind and make it easier for you to fall asleep. But today it's recognized that this benefit is far outweighed by alcohol's adverse effects. As the alcohol is metabolized by the body, a mini-withdrawal occurs, making you awaken. In the morning, you are likely to feel more irritable and less refreshed than you would if no alcohol had been present in your system. Further, because alcohol is a sedative drug, it may disturb breathing.

Sleeping pills: Medications used to induce or sustain sleep are known to be effective only for a few weeks. With long-term use, tolerance is likely to develop; as the drugs stop working, any improvements in sleep that they brought also disappear. When someone who is unaware of this possibility finds that his sleep is worsening, he may be even more convinced that he "needs" pills to sleep and may try to convince his doctor to increase the dosage.

When people who have been taking sleeping medications for many months stop abruptly, they often find that sleep is severely disturbed, an effect related to the time it takes for the body to readjust to the absence of the drugs. If you want to cut back your use of sleeping pills or alcohol, it's best to do it gradually, under your doctor's supervision.

Smoking: Smoking can disturb sleep, too. Nicotine is a stimulant, and smokers do not seem to develop tolerance to it. When eight men who had consistently smoked between one and a half and three packs of cigarettes a day for at least two years were persuaded to stop abruptly, they fell asleep faster and woke less during the night, reports Constantin Soldatos, M.D., and his colleagues at Pennsylvania State University. These improvements occurred despite unpleasant daytime effects of cigarette withdrawal, including depression, lack of concentration, irritation, anxiety, tension, restlessness and drowsiness.

Caffeine: While it is widely recognized that the caffeine in coffee, tea or cola drinks, if consumed near bedtime, often makes it harder to get to sleep, that is not its only effect. Indeed, caffeine's peak impact as a stimulant comes two to four hours after it is consumed; hence, it may trigger frequent awakenings during the night. Tolerance for caffeine decreases with age.

Ed had consumed four or five cups of coffee daily since his teens, and did not avoid it even late at night. Because he continued to fall asleep easily, he never suspected caffeine as the culprit when, in his thirties, he started waking during the night. His "insomnia" continued for the next fifteen years and might have gone on indefinitely if a family emergency had not taken him away from home. Staying with a relative who did not drink coffee, he went without it every evening. His sleep improved so dramatically that he decided to continue the "experiment" at home. Today, he says he seldom awakens during the night and feels better than he has in years.

Ed was lucky. Many people who cut way back on caffeine all at once experience withdrawal symptoms for two to three days. During this time, they feel tense and sleep poorly. Cutting back gradually can help you to keep such problems to a minimum.

Other medications: Insomnia may be caused by prescription or nonprescription drugs, including medications for asthma, thyroid disorders, weight reduction and depression, for example. If you seek help from your doctor for insomnia, be sure he or she knows about all the drugs you are taking. (More detailed information about alcohol and other drugs that affect sleep, along with guidelines for using sleeping pills, appears in Chapter 8, "Sleeping Pills and Other Drugs for Insomnia.")

PERIODIC LEG MOVEMENTS, RESTLESS LEGS AND NIGHT LEG CRAMPS

Periodic leg movements: Restless nights may be caused by leg jerks that occur during sleep. These movements last a second or two and recur approximately every thirty seconds, sometimes for several hours. The sleeper may be partially or completely awakened dozens of times during the night; yet he is often unaware of the trigger for these awakenings. Millions of people have this problem. Like many other disorders, it becomes more frequent and more severe as we grow older. (For more information, see Chapter 6, "The Later Years.") The cause remains unknown.

A videotape, speeded up, showing a night's sleep of a fifty-four-year-old man with this problem at the Baltimore Regional Sleep Disorders Center, conveys the frenetic routine. The man kicks the blankets off, lunges, twists, turns, half sits up, rolls around, all night long. The sleep recording shows hundreds of these leg twitches. The patient is startled when he views the tape, but his wife is not; she, like many spouses, had provided the clue to the diagnosis. When the doctor first asked her to describe her husband's sleep, she admitted hesitantly, "We no longer sleep together." Pressed to elaborate, she explained, "He's kicked me out of bed so many times, I prefer to spend the night on the couch."

Since periodic leg movements occur only during sleep, this disorder can be confirmed only by an evaluation in a sleep laboratory. Please note that periodic leg movements are quite distinct from the sudden twitch of a leg, arm or even the whole body that most of us experience occasionally, just as we are falling asleep. This curious sensation, known as a hypnagogic (or sleep) startle, may give you the sense that you are falling, but it is no reason for concern.

When periodic leg movements are severe, drugs used for seizure disorders, such as clonazepam or valproic acid, may be prescribed. Although they don't eliminate the twitches, the drugs seem to keep them from interrupting sleep, thus giving a person a better night.

Restless legs: While awake, some people who have periodic leg movements during sleep also have disagreeable "deep creeping" sensations in the calves, and often in the thighs, that occur unpredictably when they sit or lie down. One woman likens the sensation to "current going through my legs." Referred to as restless legs, the problem (which often is worse at night) produces the urge to move the legs repeatedly; activity often relieves the feeling. The problem often seems to run in families and may be related to poor circulation.

Like periodic leg movements, restless legs may interfere with sleep. Virtually everyone with restless legs also suffers from periodic leg movements, but not everyone with periodic leg movements has restless legs. Drugs frequently prescribed for restless legs include oxycodone and carbamazepine.

Leg cramps: Nocturnal leg cramps, too, may disrupt sleep, although, unlike periodic leg movements, their presence is no secret to the sleeper. The muscles in the calf and the sole of the foot are most commonly involved. The cramps typically occur when a person is lying in bed, often causing exquisite pain. Again, they are more common in later years.

A simple exercise program developed by Harry Daniell, M.D., of Redding, California, is said to give dramatic results. If you are troubled by these pesky leg cramps, give it a try. Stand facing a wall two or three feet away. Place your hands on the wall and lean forward, keeping your heels on the floor and your legs straight, until you feel a moderately intense but not painful pulling sensation in the calves. Hold this position for ten seconds, stand up straight and relax for five seconds, then repeat the exercise. Do the routine three times a day until you no longer experience nocturnal cramps and then do it as often as necessary to maintain a cramp-free state. You may also find it helpful to keep blankets loose and off your feet when you sleep. If you sleep on your stomach, let your feet hang over the edge of the mattress.

PAUSES IN BREATHING

The common complaint "I don't have any trouble falling asleep, but I wake frequently during the night" may stem from disordered breathing during sleep. People who breathe quite normally while awake may prove, when monitored in a sleep laboratory, to stop breathing dozens, even hundreds, of times during the night. The pauses, known as apneas, cause numerous awakenings, which may be so brief that they are not remembered in the morning; the sleeper simply recalls "light" and "restless" sleep.

The condition most often associated with the complaint of insomnia is central sleep apnea. Here, failure of the diaphragm and chest muscles during sleep sets off an alarm in the brain; the person partially awakens and breathing resumes. The other, more common, form of sleep apnea, which involves an obstruction of the upper airway, causes longer—although seldom remembered—awakenings and greater loss of sleep. Someone with obstructive apnea is more likely than someone with central apnea to complain of sleepiness during the day.

Problems with the control of breathing during sleep become

more common as we get older. As many as one out of three people aged sixty-five and older may have apneas during the night, although the impact of such pauses in terms of daytime alertness and general health still aren't known.

The danger is that people may try alcohol or sleeping pills to reduce the anxiety that they blame for waking them up and to maintain sleep, but as both of these substances are depressants, they may further disrupt breathing. Today, as doctors are becoming more aware of sleep apnea, they are less likely to prescribe sleeping pills without first investigating the patient's sleep. (See Chapter 6, "The Later Years," and Chapter 9, "The Snoring Sickness.")

BAD DREAMS

Most of us have nightmares that wake us now and then. Some people apparently find their dreams so disturbing that they awaken themselves early in dream periods repeatedly through the night. Ramon Greenberg, M.D., of Boston University Hospital, calls the resulting complaint "dream interruption insomnia." Many people with this problem don't remember disturbing dreams each time they awaken and don't have such regular REM periods that the timing of their awakenings by itself can provide the diagnosis. Hence, certain identification of this problem usually requires that sleep be evaluated in a laboratory. (See also Chapter 4, "The Stuff of Dreams.")

A CASE OF MISTAKEN IDENTITY

Some people who call themselves insomniacs prove, when evaluated in the sleep lab, to have quite normal sleep.

Some are natural short-sleepers who happen to live in a household of longer-sleepers. They may hold misconceptions about how much sleep people need. Debbie was determined to get her "proper" sleep, all eight hours of it. She set her alarm for seven in the morning and jumped into bed at ten-thirty at night. When she found herself still awake at eleven-thirty, she decided to move her bedtime forward. Soon she was going to bed at nine. Now her complaint was, "It takes me three hours to fall asleep." Once she accepted the idea that six or seven hours apparently was all she needed, she started going to bed at midnight. Her "problem" evaporated.

Other people simply have locked their sleep into unusual time slots. Some find ways to cope with their "insomnia." Phil, for example, never fell asleep before half past three, no matter when he went to bed. He needed two alarm clocks at opposite sides of the room to get him going at seven the next morning. During the day, he napped whenever he could. Once he completed his surgical residency, he decided to structure his life around his desire to sleep until ten-thirty or eleven in the morning. His habit has made him popular with the other surgeons, who fight to get on the operating-room schedule at six. Phil doesn't take his first case until noon.

But others seek help. Diane would be content with a schedule similar to Phil's, but as the mother of two young children, she has to start her day early. She came to a sleep center complaining that thoughts raced through her mind and kept her from sleeping. In fact, she was having such thoughts merely because she was lying in bed awake. Once, such people might have been considered hypervigilant. Now it is recognized that some of them may have problems with the scheduling of their sleep. Distinguishing the two problems often requires a careful sleep/wake diary, psychological testing and sometimes laboratory monitoring of the individual's sleep.

When timing of sleep is the problem, a person can often be helped to "reset" his or her biological clock with chronotherapy ("time therapy"). The person is scheduled to stay up three hours later and sleep three hours later each day until a more suitable bedtime is reached. (This and other problems of scheduling of sleeping and waking are discussed in Chapter 11, "The Time Of Our Lives.")

The Mystery Remains

Complaints about sleep sometimes resist scrutiny. In one in ten insomniacs, sleep in the laboratory appears normal in all respects, but the sleeper nonetheless insists his or her sleep is inadequate. Until quite recently, such people sometimes were branded pseudoinsomniacs, with the implication that they were sleep hypochondriacs who blatantly exaggerated their symptoms, or malingerers who claimed to sleep poorly in order to receive drugs and, perhaps, attention.

Today, most sleep clinicians acknowledge that the polysomnographic record, although a marvelous tool, may not reveal all of the factors that are critical for sleep. Or perhaps the information is already on the sleep record but it is too subtle to be recognized at present (this is a puzzle that the increasing use of computers to analyze the data may soon solve). Additionally, better ways of assessing distortions in the way people perceive or think about their sleep might help more of us to enjoy the sweet and private pleasure of a good night's sleep.

8

SLEEPING PILLS AND OTHER DRUGS FOR INSOMNIA: WHEN THEY WORK, WHEN THEY DON'T

The "ideal" sleeping pill does not exist. But if it did, it would:

- help you fall asleep quickly and sleep soundly,
- make you feel more alert the next day than you would if you hadn't taken it,
- not leave you with a "hangover" the next day,
- not interfere with or interact with other drugs,
- be safe even when consumed in large quantities,
- bring your sleep stages and patterns closer to normal,
- continue to improve sleep over a long period without an increase in dose, and
- not be addicting.

Even though no sleeping pill yet developed meets these criteria, millions of Americans reach for such pills every night. They are trying to combat trouble falling asleep or staying asleep, problems often referred to simply as insomnia.

Sleeping pills do induce sleep and help sustain it; otherwise, people would have stopped using them long ago. However, there is a growing realization that the drawbacks of these drugs, when they are taken nightly for long periods, far outweigh their benefits. When a person stops using them, his sleep may be more disturbed than before he began. Daytime mood and ability to work prove no better after one has started taking sleeping pills and often are worse than before starting them.

These facts, which have emerged just in the past decade, have prompted physicians to prescribe pills less often and for shorter periods. There were twenty-one million prescriptions for sleeping pills in the United States in 1981, a dramatic fall from the all-time peak of forty-two million in 1971. But sleeping pills remain among the most widely used of all drugs, reports Mitchell Balter, Ph.D., chief of the applied therapeutics program of the National Institute of Mental Health.

About half of all patients in hospitals receive sleeping medications sometime during their stay. Often, sleeping pills are ordered on an "as needed" basis, meaning that the person has only to request a sleeping medication in order to get it. Many people who take sleeping pills regularly say the habit began while they were in the hospital. In many nursing homes, most patients get a sleeping pill every night. Millions of sleeping pills also are sold without a prescription in pharmacies, supermarkets and other stores; these are referred to as over-the-counter (OTC) sleep aids.

Drugs that induce sleep are taken in other guises, too. Drugs prescribed for anxiety and depression are often given at bedtime in order to capitalize on their sleep-inducing effects; other drugs, including antihistamines used for hay fever, other allergies or colds, and many pain-relieving drugs and muscle relaxants, also are given at night to avoid drowsiness during waking hours. Finally, many drugs that are abused or used illegally, including marijuana and heroin, also induce drowsiness.

An estimated 4 percent of all adults in the United States—some six million people—use a drug prescribed to help them sleep on at least one occasion every year, Dr. Balter says. Even more use OTC sleep aids or rely on an alcoholic nightcap. Although it has long been known that alcohol speeds falling asleep, only recently has it been shown that even small amounts of alcohol may interfere with sleep later in the night, by causing more frequent awakenings.

The use of drugs to restore troubled sleep dates back to ancient times. Our term for such drugs, "hypnotics," comes from the name of the Greek god of sleep, Hypnos. According to legend, Hypnos carried a horn, from which he poured his slumber potion, and a poppy stalk, the source of that potion.

The poppy and its chemical cousins were once viewed as the best, indeed, often the *only*, remedy for insomnia complaints. But since it has become obvious that insomnia is a symptom of many disorders, not a disease for which sleeping pills are a "cure," the focus of medical attention has shifted from attempts at symptomatic relief to efforts to identify the reasons for the insomnia. A panel of health-care specialists, convened in 1983 by the National Institutes of Health and National Institute of Mental Health to develop a consensus on the use of medications to promote sleep, concluded, "Treatment of insomnia should start with the assessment and necessary correction of sleep hygiene and habits." Hence, treatment today is better tailored to the needs of the individual. The panel recommended that sleeping pills or other drugs, when indicated, be part of a comprehensive treatment plan, which may also involve instruction concerning good sleep habits, relaxation skills and other behavioral techniques or psychotherapy. (For details on drug-free ways to prevent or alleviate trouble sleeping, see Chapters 15 and 16.)

This chapter aims to help you understand when sleeping pills may be appropriate, what precautions to take if you use sleeping pills and when to avoid them. Following are the facts you need to know.

When You Might Take Sleeping Pills

If you've ever suffered a string of near-sleepless nights, you know how fervent the desire for a good night's rest can be. You expect you would be able to cope better during the day if you could sleep better. Today, doctors most often prescribe sleeping pills as a temporary measure, for adults only, and in specific situations, such as those listed here.

IF YOU ARE FREQUENTLY TROUBLED BY INSOMNIA BUT ARE
OTHERWISE HEALTHY

There are several important "ifs" here. *If* you've put rules of good
sleep hygiene to work in your life, *if* you've seen your doctor or
visited a sleep center and do not have sleep-related breathing
problems, periodic leg movements or other disorders, and *if*
you've explored relaxation or other strategies without sufficient
relief, *then* sleeping pills may be appropriate. In this case, the pills
would be an adjunct to your continuing efforts to employ psychological or behavioral techniques. Your doctor may recommend
that you keep the pills "on reserve" and take them intermittently,
only after a night or two of severely disturbed sleep. Some of us
worry so much about not sleeping that the worry itself interferes
with sleep. "An occasional sleeping pill, taken no more than once
or twice a week, may help a chronic insomniac escape the panic
of feeling that he will never be able to sleep again," says Peter
Hauri, Ph.D., of the Dartmouth Medical School. "Even simply
knowing that pills are in the medicine cabinet may ease worries
and foster sleep," he adds.

IF YOU'RE UNDER UNUSUAL STRESS

Perhaps you just lost your job or learned your child is flunking out
of school. Or suppose noisy truck traffic is being detoured right
under your bedroom window for a few weeks. Maybe you're
trying to quit smoking. After several bad nights, you may feel like
a zombie. The longer you go without sleep, the more miserable
you're likely to be. Again, pills may be useful for a few nights just
to keep you going. They usually are not prescribed for more than
three weeks; even if the stress continues, your sleep is likely to
have improved by then. While using sleeping pills, you also need
to minimize your use of caffeine and alcohol, avoid daytime naps
and keep regular hours, all habits shown to benefit nighttime sleep.

IF YOU EXPECT TO CROSS SEVERAL TIME ZONES

Jet lag lasts for a few days, until your inner clocks reset themselves.
While you can minimize it with advance planning (see Chapter
11, "The Time of Our Lives"), you may not be able to escape it

entirely. If you must give a lecture or negotiate business matters soon after your arrival, pills may help you go to sleep at the local bedtime, although you are still likely to be more sleepy than usual at the time when you ordinarily sleep. Don't take a sleeping pill on the plane; it might interfere with your alertness in an emergency situation.

IF YOU'RE GOING IN THE HOSPITAL

Sleeping in an unfamiliar place, particularly when you're anxious about your health, disrupts nearly everyone's sleep. Discomfort from surgery or illness may be more obvious during the night than during the day, when people are around to distract you and there are things to do. Sleeping pills may give you respite for a few nights and enable you to benefit from sleep's restorative effects. Of course, in this situation, you'd be carefully observed by doctors and nurses to prevent problems from any interaction between your sleeping medication and other drugs you might be taking.

IF YOU HAVE PERIODIC LEG MOVEMENTS THAT REPEATEDLY DISTURB YOUR SLEEP

Sleeping pills do not reduce the muscle movements, but sometimes they are given in addition to other medications specifically prescribed for this problem. They may help you to sleep more soundly and, as a result, to feel better in the morning.

Take Pills with Care

Your doctor may advise you to take sleeping pills intermittently, skipping a dose after one or two nights of good sleep. This practice, recommended by the federal consensus panel on drugs and insomnia, allows you to see if your sleep has improved and to gradually taper off your use of drugs.

A sleeping pill is designed to be taken about thirty minutes before bedtime. If taken any earlier, it might interfere with your evening's activities. Certainly, after you have taken a sleeping pill, you should not drive. On the other hand, on nights you are to take a pill, don't gamble on having a good night and wait to take the pill until you've tossed restlessly for an hour or more. If you've taken the prescribed amount, don't take more, even if you still have trouble falling asleep or if you awaken in the middle of the night. Taking a pill late or increasing your dosage might give you a pill "hangover" the next day.

If you feel dizzy, lightheaded, clumsy, unsteady, less alert or more sleepy during the day after using sleeping pills, call your doctor.

When You Should Not Use Sleeping Pills

IF YOU KNOW OR SUSPECT YOU HAVE A BREATHING PROBLEM OR LUNG DISEASE

If you are a habitual loud snorer, you are more likely than a nonsnorer to have breathing problems. (See Chapter 9, "The Snoring Sickness.") These problems are also more common among older people. (See Chapter 6, "The Later Years.") If you have sleep apnea, a disorder that involves many interruptions in breathing during the night, both sleeping pills and alcohol may make the pauses occur more often and last longer. Longer pauses may trigger both a drop in blood pressure and irregular heartbeats. Hence, they may be life-threatening.

A thirty-eight-year-old man with long-standing insomnia, known to be a loud snorer, volunteered to take a commonly used sleeping pill and to have his sleep monitored in the laboratory. On nights when he did not take a pill, he had eighteen or fewer interruptions in breathing. On nights when he did, the number of pauses soared to one hundred, and he was extremely sleepy the following day. "This study suggests that the daytime sleepiness often associated with sleeping pill use sometimes is a consequence of pill-induced sleep apnea," notes Wallace Mendelson, M.D., of the National Institute of Mental Health.

IF YOU ARE—OR MIGHT BE—PREGNANT

Since no drug has been proven completely safe for an unborn child, and since a woman may not know that she is pregnant in the early months, when the child's organ systems are developing, all women of childbearing age should be cautious about drug use.

When sleeping medications are used during pregnancy, the baby may become dependent on them and experience withdrawal side effects after birth. Moreover, certain sleeping pills have been linked to specific birth defects. Some babies of mothers who took the sleeping pill thalidomide during pregnancy were born without arms or legs; this drug was used mainly in Europe in the 1960s and was never approved for use in the United States.

IF YOU ARE BREAST-FEEDING YOUR CHILD

Sleeping medications may be transferred to the baby through your milk. Even though the amounts transferred may be small, the possibility that the drugs may cause problems prompts caution.

IF YOU MUST GET UP AND BE ALERT DURING THE NIGHT

If you have young children who sometimes need comforting, or if you usually wake during the night to go to the bathroom, it's not a good idea to take a sleeping pill. Pills may make you harder to arouse. Being zonked by a sleeping pill may be dangerous if, for example, you are unable to respond to an emergency.

IF YOU CONSUME ALCOHOL

Both alcohol and sleeping pills are depressant drugs. The combination can be dangerous and is potentially fatal.

When You Should Be Extra Cautious about Sleeping Pills

IF YOU ARE MIDDLE-AGED OR OLDER

The older you are, the more likely you are to have interruptions in breathing, or apneas, during sleep. An estimated one in three persons over the age of sixty-five has this problem, and sleeping pills may aggravate it. (See Chapter 6, "The Later Years.")

Older people who use sleeping pills are more likely than nonusers to stumble and fall when they get out of bed and, as a result, to fracture a bone or suffer other harm.

Furthermore, the older we get, the longer sleeping pills stay in the body. That's because an older liver takes longer to break drugs down and older kidneys are slower to excrete them. And since Americans over the age of sixty-five average twelve drug prescriptions a year, compared with only four for younger people, older people are more likely to experience harmful interactions between sleeping pills and other drugs they take. For all of these reasons, if sleeping pills are prescribed for older people, they often are given in doses lower than those used for younger people.

IF YOU HAVE A LIVER OR KIDNEY DISORDER

Poor function of these organs may occur with illness as well as with aging and affect your body's ability to deal with sleeping pills.

IF YOU ARE TAKING DRUGS FOR ANY ILLNESS

The more drugs you take, the more likely you are to suffer a drug interaction. Even though you may have trouble sleeping if you are ill, you should be particularly careful about using sleeping pills at such times. Consult your doctor before adding sleeping pills to your other medications, and whenever you receive a new prescription, be sure your doctor knows about all the other drugs you are taking. The body's metabolism of most drugs in the benzodiazepine category, which include the most commonly prescribed sleeping pills, is slowed by cimetidine, a drug commonly prescribed for people with duodenal ulcers and some conditions in which the stomach produces excess acid. Sleeping pills in the barbiturate category reduce the effectiveness of the anticoagulant warfarin (Coumadin), often used in the treatment of heart disease. If you were taking both drugs, you would need more warfarin; if you were to stop taking the barbiturate, you might experience internal bleeding unless the warfarin dose were adjusted too. Barbiturates also lower the effectiveness of tetracyclines, corticosteroids and tricyclic antidepressants.

IF YOU HAVE PREVIOUSLY TAKEN SLEEPING PILLS AND FOUND THAT THEY DIDN'T WORK

Sleeping pills are quite similar in their ability to aid troubled sleep. If one doesn't work, another is unlikely to do so. (However, if you have taken a pill that worked for a week or two and then stopped helping you, you may have developed tolerance to the drug; it, or another drug, may work for you at a later date.)

IF YOU WILL BE DRIVING LONG DISTANCES, OPERATING
MACHINERY OR INVOLVED IN OTHER TASKS THAT REQUIRE
ALERTNESS AND COORDINATION

Daytime grogginess sometimes comes from use of sleeping pills and may pose a danger to you and others. Even if you feel fully alert the morning after taking a pill, you may not be. The situation is comparable to that of the person who has had too much to drink and is staggering, all the while insisting he is toeing a straight line.

What Sleeping Pills Do

The typical sleeping pill will reduce the time you take to fall asleep by ten to twenty minutes and let you sleep twenty to forty minutes longer. This minimal effect would not be much of a plus were it not that the pills also give the sense that sleep is "better." This benefit comes from the pills' ability to reduce the frequency of awakenings during the night; in general, the fewer the awakenings, the more satisfying your sleep. Further, most of us expect that better sleep at night will make us feel better the next day.

Sleeping pills do not produce normal sleep. On the contrary, they generally suppress to some degree either the deep sleep of stage 3-4 or the REM state in which most vivid dreaming occurs. While the significance of the various types of sleep remains a matter of conjecture and no harm has been shown to come from getting less of any particular stage or state of sleep, common sense suggests that changes from the normal are probably undesirable.

The power of a sleeping pill to make you drowsy is a liability if you have to get up during the night (to respond to a fire alarm, for example), and it becomes a major drawback if the effect continues after you get up in the morning. Drugs don't have on-off switches; they wear off gradually. Sleeping pills that work for different lengths of time are now available. A drug that stays effective for just three or four hours might be more appropriate if you have trouble falling asleep, whereas one that works seven or eight hours or longer might be more helpful if your main problem is staying asleep. The longer-acting the drug, the more likely it is that its effects will carry over into the next day and lower your ability to drive or concentrate.

If you use sleeping pills, keep clearly in mind that you may be paying for better sleep at night with sleepiness during the day. Of course, the diminished alertness resulting from sleeping pills has to be weighed against the diminished alertness caused by lack of sleep; someone who tosses restlessly all night may feel the next day just as bad as, if not worse than, someone who has taken a long-acting sleeping pill.

A study at Stanford University compared long-acting and short-acting drugs. People who took the long-acting drug got more sleep at night, but they were more sleepy in the daytime, because of the carry-over effect. Those who took the short-acting drug got less sleep at night but were more alert in the daytime. This study suggests that if the benefit sought from the drug is greater alertness during waking hours, as is the case in most people with transient or short-term insomnia, a short-acting drug is probably more appropriate. On the other hand, for someone in a highly stressful situation, experiencing considerable anxiety during the day as well as disturbed sleep at night, a long-acting drug may be more helpful.

All sleeping pills, at some doses, worsen the ability to function during the day, according to a comprehensive review of fifty-two studies of "day after" effects. People were asked to add numbers, play video games, copy drawings, steer and brake driving simulators, remember lists of words and try their skill at other measures of thought and action. *In no case did people who took sleeping pills handle tasks better the next day than they did when not taking the pills,* report Laverne Johnson, Ph.D., of the Naval Health Research Center, San Diego, and Doris Chernik, Ph.D., of Hoffmann-La Roche, Inc. They conclude, "Sedative-hypnotics generally improve the quality of sleep, but not the quality of daytime performance."

Most "day after" tests have been done with normal sleepers rather than with insomniacs. Insomniacs are such erratic sleepers that it is hard to interpret the effects of drugs on their sleep. It's possible that insomniacs who take sleeping pills do better during the day than insomniacs who don't, but this question is just beginning to be studied.

Scientists use the term "elimination half-life" to describe the time needed for half of a drug to leave the bloodstream. "Half-life" is a mathematical concept that permits comparisons of various drugs; it does not, strictly speaking, tell how long the drug will continue to work. However, the longer the half-life, the more likely the drug is to accumulate excessively in your body and to make you sleepy during the day. Some sleeping pills have an elimination half-life of one hundred hours or more.

Many sleeping pills cease to benefit sleep after as few as two weeks of nightly use. None has been proven in sleep-laboratory studies to work longer than a month. The user soon develops a tolerance for the drug—that is, he or she takes longer to fall asleep and wakes up more and more frequently during the night. A higher and higher dose would be required to produce the desired effect, but that, of course, could be dangerous. The development of tolerance explains why sleeping pills are not recommended for continued nightly use.

At the same time that the drugs are losing their power to help you sleep, you may be becoming dependent upon them. Emotionally, you may "need" that pill to sleep, and your body may be physically dependent as well. Should you try to stop using them, you may develop withdrawal symptoms. For example, you may develop "rebound insomnia"—right away if the drug has a short-half-life, or several nights later if it has a long half-life. Then, for a few nights, your sleep may actually be more disturbed than before you started taking the pills.

Safety is a key concern when sleeping pills are used. A drug that can put you to sleep for a night has the potential, if taken in large enough quantities, to keep you from ever waking up. The greater the difference between the amount of the drug that aids sleep and the amount that could be lethal, the safer the drug. Safety is lowered when sleeping pills are taken with other depressant drugs, such as antihistamines or alcohol. The combination produces more of a knock-out effect than either would have alone.

The most ominous aspect of sleeping-pill use is the association of these drugs with a higher death rate. When the American Cancer Society looked at personal habits and life-style in over one million men and women in a study that began in 1959, seemingly healthy people who "often" took sleeping pills were 50 percent more likely to die in the next six years than people who did not. The dangers that sleeping pills pose to people with sleep apnea, many of whom are unaware that they have it, may in part account for this finding, suggests the head of the study, Daniel Kripke, M.D., director of the Sleep Disorders Center at the Veterans Administration Medical Center, San Diego.

All of these recently discovered drawbacks of sleeping pills explain why medical authorities now recommend pills for *temporary* use only.

Prescription Sleeping Pills

The drugs most commonly prescribed for insomnia are divided into two main categories, those in the chemical family known as benzodiazepines, and others, which are referred to as nonbenzodiazepines. The latter group of drugs includes barbiturates. Your doctor's choice of one type of drug over another for you will depend upon your particular problem and needs. The information in the following section conforms to *AMA Drug Evaluations* (fifth edition), the standard state-of-the-art reference book.

BENZODIAZEPINES

Two out of every three sleeping-pill prescriptions in the United States are for the benzodiazepine drug flurazepam (Dalmane). Introduced in 1970, it was the only benzodiazepine marketed in this country for insomnia until 1982, when temazepam (Restoril) and triazolam (Halcion) became available. However, other benzodiazepines are among the most widely prescribed drugs in the United States. They include diazepam (Valium), chlordiazepoxide (Libritabs, Librium), clorazepate (Tranxene) and lorazepam (Ativan). These drugs, prescribed for the treatment of anxiety, are quite similar in chemical structure and action to drugs prescribed as sleeping pills. In fact, they are often given at bedtime to anxious people who have trouble falling asleep.

Benzodiazepines are popular because they are effective, when used properly, and the safest of all sleeping medications. The federal consensus panel on drugs and insomnia, meeting in 1983, concluded that when drugs are indicated in the treatment of insomnia, "benzodiazepines are preferable." These drugs are less likely than nonbenzodiazepine drugs to cause adverse reactions, development of tolerance, drug dependence, drug interactions and death, if taken in overdose.

However, the 1979 report, *Sleeping Pills, Insomnia, and Medical Practice,* issued by the National Academy of Sciences, adds certain caveats. It notes that nightly reliance, as distinguished from physical dependence, is just as likely with benzodiazepines as with barbiturates. Benzodiazepines also may depress breathing.

Flurazepam has a half-life of forty-seven to a hundred hours. Hence, you have more of it in your body the second night you take it than the first, and more the third night than the second. You may not notice that it has begun to work for several days, and it takes about two weeks before a "steady-state" concentration is reached. Fortunately, you do not become sleepier and sleepier each day because at the same time you are acquiring tolerance to the drug. Some people, of course, are more sensitive to its effects, most notably the elderly, who are also more likely to keep it in the body longer. By contrast, temazepam has a half-life of about eight to twelve hours, and triazolam, of about three to four hours. These shorter-acting drugs do not accumulate in the body.

Benzodiazepines have a high margin of safety. If someone consumed them in excess, he would sleep for a long time but probably would not die. Nonetheless, when taken in combination with alcohol, these drugs pose a greater danger and may be fatal.

A benzodiazepine, when taken in conjunction with alcohol, alters behavior and mood more than any other sleeping pill. In one study using driving simulators, drivers who took a small amount of either the benzodiazepine diazepam or alcohol had more collisions and ignored more traffic rules than they did when they did not consume either substance. When they took both drugs, they became even worse drivers.

NONBENZODIAZEPINES

The use of barbiturates has declined in recent years as the use of benzodiazepines has risen. Safety is the key reason. In the United States annually there are about sixteen hundred deaths from barbiturate overdose, nearly as many as from heroin and morphine use. In 1971 nearly half of all sleeping pill prescriptions were for barbiturates, but by 1981, the number had fallen to only one in ten. The barbiturates most often used for insomnia include secobarbital (Seconal), amobarbital (Amytal), pentobarbital (Nembutal), and a combination of secobarbital and amobarbital (Tuinal).

Barbiturates as a group have shorter half-lives than the long-acting benzodiazepines; hence, they have less of a carry-over effect into the next day. This advantage, however, is being whittled away by the development of shorter-acting benzodiazepines. When barbiturates are taken night after night, they stimulate the liver to produce enzymes that not only break down the barbiturates faster but often have a similar effect on other drugs. As a result, the other drugs may not stay in the body as long or work as well as intended.

Barbiturates produce both sedation and a partial withdrawal syndrome each night. The withdrawal may cause frequent awakenings and disturbing dreams. If you are not aware of this problem, you may ask your doctor to increase your medication and end up with even more trouble sleeping. If you have this problem, your doctor may want to prescribe a different type of drug.

People quickly develop tolerance to barbiturates and become dependent upon them. They may then be tempted to increase the dose without talking to the doctor. As little as ten times the dose that helps you sleep can kill you. If you take barbiturates on an evening when you have been drinking alcohol, a much lower dose may be fatal (a mixture of barbiturates and alcohol was implicated in the death of film actress Marilyn Monroe).

Chloral derivatives, such as chloral hydrate (Noctec), have also lost ground to the benzodiazepines. However, the fact that chloral hydrate promotes drowsiness soon after it is taken and has a half-life of just six to eight hours makes it particularly useful for people whose main complaint is trouble falling asleep. It may, however, irritate the stomach.

Other nonbenzodiazepine compounds include ethinamate (Valmid), ethchlorvynol (Placidyl), glutethimide (Doriden) and methyprylon (Noludar). Like chloral hydrate, many of these act rapidly and do not stay in the body long. Their overall safety is thought to be comparable to that of the barbiturates and some have a high potential for abuse; hence, they are seldom prescribed today.

Nonprescription Sleep Aids

OTC DRUGS

Drugstore remedies for sleep are used in greater volume than doctors' prescriptions. Not surprisingly, over-the-counter (OTC) drugs are more popular with people under the age of forty-five, who as a group tend to be healthier and thus see the doctor less often, notes Dr. Balter.

The active ingredient in virtually all OTC "nighttime sleep aids" is an antihistamine. This type of drug, as its name suggests, counters histamine, a chemical whose release triggers allergic reactions such as itching, swelling, hay fever and asthma. In people with allergies, drowsiness is usually an unwelcome side effect of antihistamines, but in nonallergic people, drowsiness may be the major effect. That is why antihistamines are used as sleep aids. As you might expect, the amount in OTC drugs is generally lower than that frequently ordered by prescription.

Antihistamines go to work quickly and have a short half-life. Because even low doses of antihistamines are not innocuous, the question remains as to whether their potential hazards outweigh their possible benefits. Among the most worrisome of their unwanted effects are disorientation and confusion, particularly in elderly people. Other side effects include dizziness, ringing in the ears, lassitude, poor coordination, blurred or double vision and irritability.

Currently, pyrilamine maleate is the antihistamine most used as an OTC sleep aid; it's in Nervine, Nytol, Sleep-Eze and Sominex, for example. A chemically similar compound, methapryline, was taken off the market a few years ago after animal studies suggested that it had the potential to cause cancer; as a result, studies of pyrilamine's cancer-causing potential are in progress.

Another antihistamine, doxylamine succinate, is marketed by a single manufacturer as Unisom. The antihistamine diphenhydramine received approval as an ingredient in OTC sleep aids in 1982;

previously, this substance had been available only by prescription. It is in Compoz and Sominex Formula 2, for example.

ALCOHOL

Alcohol is often said to be the most widely used of all drugs, even though most of us seldom think of it as medicine. Until recently, a drink at bedtime often was "just what the doctor ordered." Alcohol may help you to relax and may make it easier to fall asleep, but the trade-off may not be worth it.

"Alcohol in any dose disturbs sleep," notes Thomas Roth, Ph.D., director of the Sleep Disorders and Research Center at the Henry Ford Hospital, Detroit. "Anyone who has troubled sleep probably will sleep better if he avoids liquor in the evening." Keep in mind that it takes the body about an hour to burn every half-ounce of alcohol you drink. A glass of wine at dinner probably won't be around long enough to harm your sleep, but a nightcap just before you turn in will.

Alcohol initially depresses REM sleep, the state in which most vivid dreams occur. As it is burned, the body goes through a miniwithdrawal, stimulating a surge of REM activity. As a result, particularly in the latter part of the night, when you normally have your greatest amount of REM sleep, you are likely to have anxious and disturbing dreams or to awaken and then have trouble falling back to sleep. You end up getting less sleep during the night and, because of the frequent awakenings, you'll feel less rested.

Even more worrisome, a mere two ounces of alcohol taken shortly before bedtime is enough to markedly worsen obstructive sleep apnea. Interruptions in breathing occur more often and last longer. Twenty healthy men volunteered for a two night study at the University of Florida conducted by Jay Block, M.D., and his colleagues. Nine of the men drank orange juice containing about two ounces of hundred-proof vodka the first night and plain orange juice the second night, and eleven had the same drinks in opposite order. Eighteen of the twenty had at least one episode of disturbed breathing during sleep after drinking alcohol; only nine did after drinking orange juice.

Since many seemingly healthy people who drink are not even aware that they have trouble breathing during sleep, and since even people who know they have apnea may succumb to occasional social pressure to drink, sleep experts are unanimous in urging moderation.

If you drink and then take a sleeping pill, the combined effects could endanger your life. Moreover, drinking might make you forget that you have taken a pill, and you might inadvertently take another.

If you now usually have several drinks during the evening, you may find it hard to stop all at once. Treat alcohol as the drug that it is and cut back gradually.

In heavy drinkers, sleep is vastly disrupted, with shortened REM periods and many awakenings. Chronic alcoholics who try to withdraw from alcohol take longer to fall asleep and experience a REM rebound that prompts frequent awakenings, jitteriness and sometimes nightmares or hallucinations. Some alcoholics resume drinking to protect themselves against this insomnia, thus perpetuating a vicious circle.

Abstinent alcoholics who get normal amounts of deep sleep may respond better to treatment for alcoholism than those who get low amounts of deep sleep, reports Richard Allen, Ph.D., co-director of the Baltimore Regional Sleep Disorders Center; the finding suggests they have not yet developed tolerance to alcohol's effects. Once alcoholics stop drinking, their sleep improves dramatically in as little as two weeks, but even recovered alcoholics may be troubled by long-lasting insomnia if their excessive use of alcohol has left them with permanent brain damage.

Children born to mothers who drank heavily during pregnancy were found to have abnormal sleep and sleep-wake patterns when they were recorded four days after birth.

L-TRYPTOPHAN

L-tryptophan is an essential amino acid, a building block of protein; it seems to play a role in triggering sleep. Since it is found in a variety of foods, including milk, meat, fish, poultry, eggs, beans, peanuts and leafy green vegetables, most of us normally consume one-half gram to two grams of it a day. There's about one gram, for example, in a typical American evening meal.

The well-known sleepiness that occurs after a large meal, particularly one containing meat, may be related to the L-tryptophan content of the meal. Insomniacs may have an inborn or acquired problem in making use of L-tryptophan.

While Grandma's insomnia remedy, warm milk at bedtime, contains L-tryptophan, a cup of milk contains only about one twenty-fifth of a gram of it. This amount is not likely to speed the time it takes to fall asleep, except perhaps in people who are exquisitely sensitive to it. For most of us, milk's soporific effect comes mainly from pleasant associations with childhood.

To look at the effects of L-tryptophan on sleep, Ernest Hartmann, M.D., director of the sleep laboratory at the Lemuel Shattuck Hospital, Boston, and his colleagues gave ten adult men who ordinarily took fifteen minutes or more to fall asleep at night doses of L-tryptophan ranging from one to fifteen grams, as well as a placebo (a chemically inert "look-alike"). On the placebo, the men averaged twenty-four minutes to fall asleep, but on all doses of L-tryptophan, they averaged only twelve minutes. In a later study of insomniacs, the researchers extended the dose downward to one-quarter gram. Doses of as little as one gram helped people fall asleep significantly faster at night; even the lower doses helped somewhat.

These studies and others tend to support the conclusion that people who ordinarily take a long time to fall asleep may be helped to fall asleep faster by a dose of one gram of L-tryptophan. Even smaller doses may help some people, and larger ones seem unnecessary, since they provide no added benefit and sometimes have undesirable effects, such as nausea or changes in the stages of sleep. L-tryptophan offers no advantage to people who do not have trouble falling sleep; it does not, for example, reduce awakenings during the night. Indeed, animal studies suggest that very high doses actually produce more wakefulness, rather than more sleep. Animal studies also show an association between L-tryptophan and bladder cancer; hence, further study is necessary before this treatment can be generally recommended.

Dr. Hartmann suggests, "Although L-tryptophan probably won't be powerful enough to calm someone who is highly anxious or agitated, my impression, based on clinical use of the substance with patients, is that it will be helpful to many insomniacs, especially on a short-run basis, and will replace many mild sleeping pills."

At this writing, L-tryptophan has not been approved by the Food and Drug Administration as a sleep aid in the United States. It is, however, sold in health food stores as a "dietary supplement."

OTHER SUBSTANCES

Aspirin: A basic item in the family medicine cabinet, aspirin relieves a variety of aches and pains. Now it appears that two aspirin may also help people who have trouble staying asleep.

At the Dartmouth Medical School, six of eight chronic insomniacs who participated in a study comparing aspirin with a placebo got more sleep the first three nights they took the aspirin. They woke less often, particularly in the latter half of the night. For three of the insomniacs, the benefits continued even longer. Aspirin did not help anyone get to sleep faster, nor did it change sleep stages. According to Peter Hauri, Ph.D., director of the Dartmouth Sleep Disorders Center, there was no evidence that aspirin in the evening led to hangovers or grogginess the next day.

"Considering the hazards often incurred with prescription hypnotics, it would seem prudent to use aspirin as a first line of defense against occasional insomnia," Dr. Hauri suggests. Of course, aspirin is not appropriate if you have ulcers or other intestinal disorders, and obviously it does not work for everyone. If you were to take it every night and then stop, you might experience a rebound effect leading to worsened sleep, just as you might with other sleeping pills.

Placebos: Although placebos, by definition, are inactive substances, the simple act of swallowing a pill seems to help some people feel better, particularly if they believe the pill will work. This fact may explain why some people who have taken sleeping pills for years insist that the pills still help them sleep better, although it can be shown by any laboratory measure that they do not.

The power of suggestion is demonstrated by this true story. A man on a business trip discovered at bedtime that he had forgotten the sleeping pills he took every night. He left his hotel but could not find an open drugstore. He stopped at a candy machine on the way back to his room and bought a package of chocolates with colored coatings. Noticing their resemblance to his pills, he took two with a glass of water. He then fell asleep promptly. He has now discarded his pills in favor of the candy, and after experimenting with all colors, insists, "The red ones work best."

The placebo effect may also account for personal testimonials to a wide variety of insomnia remedies, including specific foods or behaviors, such as checking the doors or arranging certain items on the dresser. (Bedtime routines may be helpful to you; for more information, see Chapters 15 and 16.)

How to Break the Sleeping-Pill Habit

Don't stop taking pills abruptly. Do it gradually, under your doctor's supervision, to minimize withdrawal symptoms.

About half of all sleeping-pill users develop withdrawal symptoms when they stop using the pills. Some people experience a "rebound insomnia" that manifests itself as frequent awakenings during the night. Less often, people have a "REM rebound," reflected by anxious dreams and possibly even nightmares. Sleep may be worse than it was before you started taking sleeping pills, and you may find that the disturbances last for several nights.

Although there is a wide range of individual differences, the higher the dose you have been taking and the longer you have been taking it, the more likely you are to have these problems. Drugs with a short half-life, because they are "washed out" of your body faster, are more likely to trigger withdrawal symptoms right away than those with a longer half-life. If you have been taking barbiturates, for example, you might have trouble sleeping the first night; with longer-acting benzodiazepines, your problems might begin only after five or six nights or longer.

It usually takes several nights, and sometimes a month or more, to readjust to the drug-free state. The problems you might have in the meantime are predictable and are not a re-emergence of your original symptoms. Don't let the apparent worsening of your ability to sleep trick you into starting medication again.

It's happy news that over half of all sleeping-pill users discover that they can sleep better without the pills. If it turns out that you still have trouble sleeping after you stop taking them, your doctor may want to refer you to a sleep disorders center to try to find out why.

The Bottom Line

In laboratories around the world, scientists actively seek the ideal sleeping pill, one that fosters good, sound sleep and helps people to feel and work better during the day, with complete safety. "One of the most promising areas of research is the study of sites on nerve cells in the brain where the commonly used benzodiazepine sleeping pills act," notes Solomon Snyder, M.D., chairman of the department of neuroscience at the Johns Hopkins School of Medicine. "The strategy is to find drugs that act at these same sites but in a different, nonaddicting way," he adds.

For now, the AMA's Council on Scientific Affairs has concluded that sleeping pills, despite their drawbacks, have certain specific uses. The council urges physicians to prescribe sleeping pills "judiciously and for brief periods of two to six weeks" and to explore nondrug treatment, such as better sleep hygiene, to help people who have long-standing insomnia but are otherwise healthy.

If you now use sleeping pills, or before you do, you owe it to yourself to weigh the benefits against the risks.

9

THE SNORING SICKNESS

Attempts to muzzle snorers have spawned a panoply of gadgets. Nose clips, chin straps and a collar that jolts the neck with a mild electric shock at every raspy snort are among the more than three hundred antisnoring devices registered at the United States Patent Office. Snoring inspires jokes. It's portrayed as a nuisance more to those whose ears are assaulted than to the snorer. But snoring is not trivial. Indeed, the implications of this nighttime cacophony may be quite ominous.

Snoring almost always indicates that something is wrong with breathing during sleep. It makes sleep less restful and may also subtly undermine the quality of waking life by inducing constant sleepiness, difficulty with concentration, headaches and even impotence. A particular pattern of raucously loud snoring heralds recurrent interruptions in breathing during sleep. If prolonged, these pauses may lead to high blood pressure, heart attacks and strokes.

The "snoring sickness" is not a new disease. What is new is the link between numerous seemingly disparate ailments and disordered breathing during sleep. Snoring does not cause all these troubles. It is simply an easy-to-recognize early warning signal.

Fortunately, once a breathing problem is recognized, it can often be treated successfully. In both adults and children, symptoms can frequently be dramatically reversed.

Why Do We Snore?

The sounds of snoring come from vibration of the soft palate and the uvula at the back of the throat. The vibration is prompted by narrowing of the passage through which air moves as it comes through the nose and throat, into the lungs and out again. Narrowing sufficient to trigger snoring may come from a cold or allergy that causes temporary swelling of nasal passages, enlarged tonsils or abnormal closure of muscles of the upper airway during sleep. The last problem is among the most worrisome, because there is no sign of it when a person is awake.

Millions of people of all ages snore—perhaps thirty million people in the United States alone. Fortunately, most of them snore lightly and intermittently. Their air flow remains adequate. They have no trouble obtaining the oxygen they need from incoming air to supply the body's organs and tissues or to get rid of the carbon dioxide that accumulates as a waste product of bodily activity.

But an estimated one person in ten—two and one-half million Americans—has seriously disturbed breathing during sleep. These people snore loudly enough to be heard in the next room and they often snore continuously. Their air flow is significantly reduced, so that less oxygen gets into their bloodstream and more carbon dioxide is retained. Their snoring may be punctuated by silence if the movement of air stops altogether.

At such times, their blood pressure may soar. It usually returns to normal when breathing restarts, but when interruptions in breathing occur in rapid succession, periods of high blood pressure may be sustained. After many years, and for reasons that still are not entirely clear, blood pressure may remain elevated even while these people are awake. Habitual snorers are twice as likely to have high blood pressure as nonsnorers.

When the flow of air into the lungs is reduced or interrupted, the heart, brain and other organs are deprived of oxygen. The heart does not pump efficiently. It slows down and may beat irregularly, prematurely or with extra beats. In severe cases, the heart pauses for several seconds. Sometimes, it stops completely.

Why does sleep cause all this trouble? First, we don't sleep standing up. The customary sleeping posture—lying flat—alters circulation, especially in the lungs, where oxygen and carbon dioxide are exchanged. If you are overweight, the fat on your abdomen compresses your lungs. Think how hard it would be to blow up a balloon if someone was squeezing it.

Furthermore, muscle tone falls during sleep. During REM periods, most muscles "turn off." If we are going to run into difficulty breathing during sleep, REM is our most vulnerable time. People most susceptible to this problem are those in whom the muscles involved in breathing have been weakened by disease or time (the elderly) or those whose the muscles are still immature (babies in their first months of life). This problem is a prime suspect in many cases of sudden and unexpected death during sleep, including those of the young victims of the Sudden Infant Death Syndrome (SIDS), sometimes referred to as crib death.

Anyone may have occasional brief pauses in breathing during the night, particularly just as sleep begins or along with bursts of rapid eye movements. However, in healthy people these pauses do not occur over and over again and they never last longer than thirty seconds.

People with breathing disorders may stop breathing during sleep more than one hundred times per hour all night long, in both REM and NREM sleep. These people may not breathe at all for three quarters of their time asleep. Some pauses have been recorded that lasted over three minutes, a striking length of time, since four minutes without oxygen often results in irreversible brain damage.

Cessations in breathing that last ten seconds or longer are termed "apneas," from the Greek word meaning "want of breath." When thirty or more apneas appear in seven hours of sleep, producing excessive sleepiness and other ill effects during the day, a person is said to have the sleep apnea syndrome.

This disorder can start at any age, although it becomes more common as we get older. Over half of the people who have it are forty or over when it is discovered. (For more information on the impact of sleep apnea and other problems that develop as we grow older, see Chapter 6, "The Later Years.")

Apnea Has Several Guises

Heavy snoring is the hallmark of the most common form of sleep apnea, upper-airway, or obstructive, apnea. In this disorder, a blockage at the upper end of the airway halts the movement of air. The muscles of the diaphragm and chest that help move air in and out of the lungs continue to work. Eventually, the rhythmic muscle contractions build up so much pressure that the airway is "uncorked." The person awakens briefly, gasping as air rushes in. Then he sinks back into sleep, an obstruction develops, breathing stops and the cycle repeats itself.

Sometimes the airway remains open but the diaphragm and chest muscles stop working. This form of apnea is known as central apnea. When it occurs, an alarm apparently sounds in the brain, awakening the sleeper. The act of awakening restarts breathing. Because the airway stays open, snoring may not occur.

In mixed apnea, a brief episode of central apnea typically is followed by a longer episode of obstructive upper-airway apnea, repeatedly throughout the night. People with mixed apnea sometimes snore. Waking makes it possible for breathing to begin again.

Although a person experiencing apneas might have all three forms in a single night, generally either obstructive apnea or central apnea predominates, and the former is more common. Partial blockages can occur, too; they're referred to as "hypopneas." Although less serious than complete interruptions in breathing, partial ones may cause trouble too.

Upper-Airway Apnea

In *The Pickwick Papers*, Charles Dickens gives us a classic description of the untoward effects of upper-airway apnea. Fat Joe, the red-faced serving boy, "goes on errands fast asleep, and snores as he waits at table." This combination of massive obesity, breathing difficulties during sleep, and daytime sleepiness came to be called the "Pickwickian syndrome."

Those with the Pickwickian syndrome, however, represent

only about 5 percent of all people who have upper-airway apnea. Obsesity can, indeed, make a bad situation worse. The most severely affected people tend to be extremely overweight; thin people, however, may develop apnea, too. Curiously, many people with this disorder have a short, thick neck, even if they are not fat. Before the age of fifty, far more men than women have it; in the older years, both sexes are afflicted nearly equally.

The twenty-seventh president of the United States, William Howard Taft, was notorious for dozing off in the midst of meetings. Weighing more than three hundred pounds, he may well have had sleep apnea.

Don is thirty-two years old and has snored loudly since he was four. Recently, the snoring has become much more persistent. Don's wife relates that at night he must make a supreme effort to breathe. He perspires so heavily that he drenches the sheets. In the morning, she often finds him sitting or kneeling on the side of the bed. Don falls asleep while visiting friends and even at work. His personality has changed, too. Previously, his wife notes, "he had a wide range of interests; he could converse intelligently on a myriad of topics and had a quick wit and a good sense of humor. Now his interests have greatly diminished; he no longer converses easily. He often simply does not think about anything and seems actually depressed much of the time."

Sid, fifty-one, complains, "I just don't seem able to manage sex anymore. I seem to have lost interest, but I think I'm too young to be running out of steam this way."

Sara, seventy-three, is considered senile by her children. She is constantly forgetful. Recently, a new and embarrassing situation has developed—she often wets the bed at night.

Howard, forty-two, finds it increasingly difficult to concentrate on the business forms he must process each day. He no longer trusts himself to return papers to the files, since he has become so absentminded that he frequently drops papers in the wrong folders. He's on the verge of being fired.

Dora, fourteen, has just been diagnosed as having sleep apnea, although hindsight suggests she's had it half her life. At the age of eight, she complained of morning headaches, and they have bothered her ever since. At nine, she started wetting the bed, a problem attributed to her parents' recent divorce. By ten, she had dropped to the bottom of her class at school and had been branded "borderline retarded." Her high blood pressure prompted a referral to the sleep clinic. Surgery to open her airway brought dramatic relief of her physical symptoms. Tragically, the oxygen starvation of her brain while it was developing makes it unlikely that she will regain her intellectual skills.

Upper-airway sleep apnea makes itself known in a variety of ways. The most common symptoms are raucous, nonstop snoring at night and sleepiness in the daytime.

The snoring is virtually universal. It occurs nightly and is often so loud that even neighbors complain. The characteristic pattern involves snores that are suddenly interrupted by silence, then followed by a loud, choking gasp as breathing restarts. In nine out of ten cases, the snoring becomes habitual before the person is twenty-one and often dates back to early childhood. Snoring may precede other symptoms by as much as twenty years.

It's a myth that snoring occurs only when you lie on your back. Ordinary snoring is more common then because gravity allows tissues in the mouth to fall backward and partially block the airway; but in people with upper-airway apnea, snoring occurs in all sleeping postures.

Although one fireman's snoring was said by his co-workers to rival the station alarm, and a businessman's snoring actually registered higher on a decibel meter than a chain saw, snorers greet reports of their nighttime "pillow squawk" with protestations of disbelief. After all, they're oblivious to it.

The excessive daytime sleepiness sometimes causes "sleep attacks." Some people say they merely feel more drowsy than usual while reading or watching television, but others say they can't keep themselves from falling asleep, even when behind the wheel of a car. One man fell asleep while he was taking his test for a pilot's license. Children sometimes try so hard to fight their persistent sleepiness that they are thought to be hyperactive.

Although extreme sleepiness also bothers people with another sleep disorder, narcolepsy (see Chapter 10, "Too Sleepy People"), those with sleep apnea are not refreshed by their naps, while those with narcolepsy typically are. Unlike people with narcolepsy, those with sleep apnea do not have attacks of muscular weakness triggered by strong emotions. Among people with narcolepsy, one in ten also has sleep apnea, a higher percentage than in the population at large.

The hundreds of awakenings that disturb the nights of individuals with upper-airway apnea are too brief to be remembered in the morning. People usually blame "unrefreshing sleep" for making them feel "tired all the time." The extreme loss of sleep does, of course, contribute to daytime sleepiness, but it's not the only reason for this common complaint. Sustained low levels of oxygen in the brain cause body-wide deterioration, interfering not only with thinking, but also with sexual functioning and other behaviors.

As the disorder worsens, usually over a period of years, additional symptoms are likely to appear. They may include one or more of those listed below:

Unusual body movements during sleep range from forceful thrusts of arms and legs to thrashing about like a beached whale. In the morning, some people acknowledge, "The bed looks like a battlefield." Bed partners complain of blows and kicks that cause bruises or force them out of bed; this, along with the noisy snoring, often leads them to sleep in separate beds or even separate bedrooms.

Sleepwalking may occur at least occasionally in people with upper-airway apnea. Sometimes the person merely stands up and then abruptly collapses back into bed. In the morning he may be found propped on an elbow or leaning against the head of the bed or an adjacent wall, or perhaps even asleep sitting on the floor next to the bed, having unconsciously sought an upright posture to make breathing easier.

Blackouts or episodes of automatic behavior occur several times daily during waking hours in the majority of people with severe sleep apnea. These episodes last from just a minute or two to several hours, during which a person might continue to perform familiar tasks, such as driving or assembly-line item-sorting. If involved in conversation, he probably will be incoherent and won't remember later what he said. This behavior occurs because the person is repeatedly falling asleep and waking up. The waking permits the activity to continue; the intermittent sleeping dulls the memory of it. Automatic behavior may cause traffic and industrial accidents. Because it's a result of extreme sleepiness, it plagues people with narcolepsy, too.

Intellectual fogginess in the daytime is sometimes linked with automatic behavior. Some people complain that they are unable to concentrate. Some complain of feeling disoriented, particularly right after awakening, a state described as sleep drunkenness. Confusion resulting from sleep apnea may cause some older people to be considered senile. Some children with this disorder have been labeled dull, lazy or retarded.

Hallucinations may occur when a person is fighting sleep. These bizarre illusions actually are bits of dreaming sleep that intrude into wakefulness. While a person is driving, he may brake abruptly to avoid a truck that turns out to be imaginary. Hallucinations are also characteristic of narcolepsy. They often make it hard for a person to separate real events from imagined ones and may lead him to question his sanity.

Personality changes are among the most disturbing symptoms of sleep apnea. Depression, anxiety, marked irritability and aggressiveness—all may be problems. Some people show sudden jealousy, suspicion and irrational behavior.

Loss of interest in sex affects both men and women with sleep apnea. Men may find it increasingly hard to have or to keep an erection; this symptom occurs in men in their thirties and forties, as well as in older men.

Morning headaches, in the front of the head or all through the head, may contribute to a general malaise upon awakening. They generally disappear by noon, but if a person with sleep apnea takes a long nap, headaches and general discomfort are likely to return.

Bed-wetting may start in children who have been dry for years, as well as in adults. Younger adults are likely to wake up during the night feeling the need to urinate; older people may have "accidents."

No one person is likely to have all of these symptoms, but most people will have several. The nighttime problems obviously are unknown to the sleeper; reports from a spouse or roommate are needed to document them. At first, daytime complaints usually don't seem severe enough to merit a trip to the doctor. Often the person makes no connection between his daytime complaints and his sleep.

What Goes Wrong?

No one knows *why* upper-airway apnea develops, but sleep specialists have a good idea of *how* it does.

Consider the mechanics of breathing: "The act of breathing itself requires a complex coordination of muscular activity within the entire respiratory tract," notes Christian Guilleminault, M.D., of Stanford University.

Ordinarily, as we breathe in, pressure within the upper portion of the airway, the part from the base of the tongue to just above the vocal cords, known as the oropharynx, is lower than the atmospheric pressure without. Since this area has no bones or cartilage to provide support, its muscles, as well as those of the diaphragm and chest, must work together to hold it open. If these muscles fail to work, the oropharynx collapses.

Since muscle tone drops during sleep, particularly during REM sleep, REM sleep is the time when problems involving muscle control are most likely to occur. Relaxed muscles sag. The narrower the airway, the more likely that sagging will lead to an obstruction. Obesity, enlarged tonsils, chronic nasal congestion and congenital physical abnormalities set the scene for the development of upper-airway apnea.

The muscle at the base of the tongue may also be involved in upper-airway apnea; this muscle's main job is to protrude the tongue to keep the airway open. If the tone in this muscle falls abnormally low, the tongue may fall backward and partially or completely plug the airway. Efforts of the diaphragm and chest muscles below will draw the tongue in tighter. Sleeping posture makes things worse; if a sleeper were sitting up, gravity would make the tongue fall forward.

The net effect of reduced muscle tone is that the upper airway acts like a floppy, soggy paper straw. Trying to draw air from one end while the other is narrowed makes the sides stick together.

This failure to coordinate muscles in order to safeguard the body during sleep is believed to stem from a defect not in the muscles but higher up, in the central nervous system. One theory is that there are feedback loops involved in central control. Frequent awakenings increase the need for sleep but also slow down muscle and nerve responses. The poorly working muscles and nerves make the frequent awakenings inevitable, but at the same time, they make it harder and harder for the person to wake up. It's a vicious circle.

Genetics may play a role. In one family, two sons and their father had apnea, while the child of a third son was a SIDS victim. In this family, muscle activity of the tongue during sleep was abnormal.

Central Apnea

When the diaphragm and chest muscles stop working, causing central apnea, it takes drastic action—partial or full awakening—to get breathing started again.

Harold, sixty-two, explains, "I just don't feel rested. I can't seem to sleep the whole night through. I wake up five, six, maybe ten times a night. Sometimes, I can't seem to catch my breath. I feel like I'm choking. Just when I start to relax, I feel my heart pounding. I get kind of edgy."

Frequent waking during the night prompts people with central sleep apnea to complain of trouble staying asleep—that is, insomnia. Some, newly diagnosed at sleep disorders centers, say they have had insomnia for more than twenty years.

Many such people had received an assortment of prescriptions for sleeping pills, without gaining relief. Some had tried tranquilizers or alcohol in the hope of reducing the anxiety they presumed was waking them up. However, since sleeping pills, tranquilizers and alcohol depress breathing, they not only can't help central apnea but may well make it worse.

While people with central apnea may snore, their snoring isn't usually as loud or as repetitious as that of people with upper-airway apnea. Like people with upper-airway apnea, those with central apnea may note loss of interest in sex, and men may have difficulty with erections.

People with central apnea tend to be older than those with upper-airway apnea. Central apnea is most frequent in people aged sixty and older. Unlike upper-airway apnea, which affects men primarily, central apnea affects both sexes nearly equally.

Central apnea also appears in people with diseases such as polio, or with spinal-cord injuries that have damaged or destroyed nerves.

Since people with central apnea often breathe quite normally during the day, establishing the reason for the frequent awakenings and other symptoms requries an evaluation during sleep.

If You Suspect Sleep Apnea

Ask your spouse or roommate to observe your sleep. Do you snore furiously, then seem to hold your breath before gasping for air? (Use a tape recorder to document your noises; take the tape with you to your doctor.) Do you thrash about in your sleep? Is it obvious that you're having trouble breathing while you sleep?

- If so, avoid sleeping pills, tranquilizers and alcohol. All of them depress breathing and, if you do have sleep apnea, may make the illness worse.
- Don't smoke; smoking irritates the passageways through which air travels to the lungs.
- If you have a cold, allergies or any other illness causing congestion in the nose and throat, use a vaporizer while you sleep to keep secretions from becoming stiff and further blocking the airway.
- Try using two pillows or elevating the head of your bed on six-inch to eight-inch blocks, because breathing is easier in a semiupright position than lying down.
- If you do have sleep apnea, home antisnoring remedies won't help. Because people with apnea snore in all sleeping postures, sewing a tennis ball, a sponge or metal jacks to the back of your pajamas to discourage sleeping on your back not only won't make any difference but, by making you uncomfortable, may further rob you of sleep. Devices that keep your mouth closed

may make it even harder for you to breathe, and hence may be dangerous.

• See your doctor if you feel sleepy all the time, frequently wake up gasping for breath, are extremely restless during the night or have other symptoms described in this chapter. If your spouse is the one with these problems, urge him or her to see the doctor.

The doctor needs a detailed description of your symptoms. In examining your nose and throat area, he or she will look for enlarged tonsils and adenoids, abnormalities of the soft palate, nasal polyps or other physical abnormalities that might interfere with your breathing while you sleep. Expect to have your blood pressure checked, too, because many people with apnea have elevated blood pressure. Your doctor may suggest that you go to a sleep disorders center for further evaluation.

What Will Sleep Specialists Do?

To identify people with apnea, sleep disorders centers may use a variety of daytime tests along with all-night sleep studies.

A comprehensive battery of lung tests provides information about daytime breathing. Tests that measure the flow of air when you breathe in and out while awake can often show whether or not you have an abnormal airway and hence are a likely candidate for surgery.

You may be asked to wear a portable heart monitor, known as a Holter monitor, for twenty-four hours. Electrodes applied to the chest will be connected to a device about the size of a standard tape recorder that you wear on a belt around your waist. In people with sleep apnea, the contrast between waking and sleeping is dramatic. During waking, heart rhythms are normal. During sleeping, when breathing stops, the heart rate may plunge from its normal 70 beats per minute to 30 beats per minute. A few seconds after breathing restarts, the heart rate may jump to 120 beats per minute. Sometimes the heart stops for three to six seconds. These patterns are so characteristic of sleep apnea that if twenty-four-hour monitoring shows you do not have them, you probably do not have this illness.

A promising new device for the evaluation of sleep apnea, developed at Stanford University, is a pocket-sized computer. It can simultaneously receive, analyze and store information on heart activity, breathing, body movements, the amount of oxygen in the blood and other functions for a week at a time, while the person wearing it pursues his normal daily life, simply pressing a button when unusual symptoms or events occur. When the device is brought back to the doctor, the information can be displayed on a video terminal or printed on paper. The device can be used to collect data before and after treatment and is therefore able to show how successful the treatment has been.

The monitoring of your sleep remains crucial in documenting sleep apnea. In the sleep laboratory you will wear several sensors that can help show what is going wrong. These are likely to include a light face mask or temperature-sensitive beads taped near your nose and mouth to measure the rate at which air enters and leaves your body; stretch bands with small gauges around your chest and abdomen to measure the effort you expend to breathe; and a device that clips on your earlobe, much like an earring, to show the changing level of oxygen in your blood, an indication of how efficiently you breathe.

If you are having apneas, that fact usually will be apparent on the first night. If your chest wall moves during sleep but no air enters or leaves your nose and mouth, your apnea is the upper-airway or obstructive type. If your chest wall fails to move, then no airflow is possible, and your apnea is the central type.

In the case of upper-airway apnea, several additional procedures are used to pinpoint the area where the narrowing occurs. Fluoroscopy involves placing a mobile X-ray image intensifier over the sleeper; when he stops breathing, a technician makes a videotape. The film might show, for example, just how the tongue falls back to block the airway. With tiny lights mounted on the end of thin wires—fiber optics—doctors can take a direct look at the airway.

Using the X-ray technique of computerized axial tomography (CAT), which yields pictures of cross-sectional "slices" of the body, doctors at the Baltimore Regional Sleep Disorders Center based at the Baltimore City Hospitals have found that people with severe obstructive apnea often have narrower than normal airways. The CAT scans show areas not visible during an ordinary physical exam.

Some sleep centers also monitor movements of the legs and arms, since people with sleep apnea not only are likely to thrash about during sleep but also are particularly prone to have periodic episodes of rapid leg jerks that further disturb their sleep. (For more information about how sleep studies are conducted, see Chapter 17, "Could a Sleep Center Help You?")

Treatment of the Sleep Apnea Syndrome

WHEN THE PROBLEM IS UPPER-AIRWAY APNEA

Weight reduction, medications, devices that assist breathing and surgery are the main approaches to treating upper-airway apnea.

Weight loss: People who are overweight are encouraged to shed excess pounds. Some studies suggest that people who lose as little as 10 percent of their body weight—thirty pounds in someone weighing three hundred pounds—have considerably fewer apneas during sleep.

Medications: A drug, medroxyprogesterone acetate, sometimes cuts daytime sleepiness and reduces the rate of apneas during sleep. The rationale for use of this drug came from studies at the University of Florida College of Medicine showing that men and older women were equally affected by breathing disorders during sleep, but younger women were spared. In younger women the hormone progesterone circulates; it is known to stimulate breathing. The hormone is absent in women after menopause, and in men.

Studies of other breathing stimulants, including theophylline, protriptyline, pemoline, thioridazine and clomipramine, are in progress. Some of these drugs also reduce REM sleep, the time when many, and often the worst, episodes of sleep apnea occur.

Devices: A mouthguard, worn during sleep, pulls the tongue forward by suction, thus opening the airway. It was developed by researchers at the Rush-Presbyterian-St. Luke's Medical Center, Chicago, who propose it as a reasonable alternative to surgery for people with moderate upper-airway apnea and note that it provides immediate relief, which can be helpful, for example, while a person is trying to lose weight.

A different approach involves the insertion of a rubber tube through the nose and into the windpipe at night. The tube permits airflow to continue during sleep, according to researchers at the University Hospital, Lund, Sweden, who found that the procedure did not cause chronic irritation.

Another device, developed at the University of Sydney (Australia), utilizes a nose mask and a blower unit; it keeps the airway open with continuous air pressure through the nose.

Surgery: For both children and adults with a physical abnormality such as enlarged tonsils or adenoids, nasal polyps or a deviated nasal septum, relatively simple corrective surgery is frequently recommended. One man comes to the Baylor College of Medicine, Houston, every six to twelve months for surgical removal of recurrent growths on his larynx that obstruct his airway.

Surgery on the interior of the throat enlarges the entrance to the airway. In a procedure similar to a face-lift, droopy tissues are tightened and excessive tissues that block the airway during sleep are trimmed away. If surgery—and, as a result, swelling—are extensive, an opening may be made in the neck to facilitate breathing; the hole is maintained for about a week and then permitted to close.

In this procedure, known as a tracheostomy, a T-shaped tube is inserted into the windpipe, or trachea, through a small hole just above the notch of the breastbone. The protruding end of the tube is closed when the person is awake, allowing him to speak and breathe normally. At night, the tube is opened, so that air flows through it directly to the lungs.

At present, a permanent tracheostomy is likely to be advised only for someone who is having one hundred or more interruptions in breathing in six hours of sleep, whose apnea is causing obvious heart problems and whose daytime symptoms, such as sleepiness and grogginess, are harming work and social life. Some people monitored in a sleep laboratory have had such severe apnea —more than eight hundred episodes during the night—that they have gone directly from the laboratory to the operating room.

A tracheostomy is not a cure for sleep apnea; it merely bypasses the obstruction in the upper airway. To sample its benefits, doctors sometimes encourage their patients to sleep one night with a tube threaded through the nose into the windpipe.

The typical response to a tracheostomy is rapid and dramatic. The person feels better after the first night's sleep. A frequent comment is "I haven't felt so well rested in years." One man dropped from an average of 142 apneas per hour to two. Sleepiness and other daytime symptoms vanish immediately, and nighttime heart irregularities are greatly reduced. Sleep studies show sleep patterns become more normal, showing less light sleep and more deep sleep. Most people can go back to work a few days after leaving the hospital.

A tracheostomy is not free from complications. Some people develop growths around the opening, irritations, infections or other physical problems. The opening requires daily care and hence serves as an unsettling reminder that one has a chronic illness. A person with a tracheostomy should not smoke and needs to use a humidifier at night. Some spouses, and even some patients themselves, are bothered by its appearance. However, women can conceal the opening during the day with a high collar, scarf or jewelry and men can hide it with a shirt collar and tie.

WHEN THE PROBLEM IS CENTRAL APNEA
Drugs that stimulate breathing, such as medroxyprogesterone, help some patients with central apnea.

Since this problem is one in which the diaphragm muscle stops working, a pacemaker device, modeled after the heart pacemaker, also may be used. It stimulates the nerves in the diaphragm, causing it to descend and pull air into the lungs.

Sleep and Other Breathing Disorders

In addition to the different types of apnea, there are other disorders of breathing that show up in sleep. Many have colorfully descriptive names.

"*Ondine's curse*" takes its name from the fable concerning the revenge taken by the water nymph Ondine on the mortal man who jilted her. According to the legend, her curse was that he had to remember to breathe. When he fell asleep, he died.

Some people with this disorder have difficulty breathing both while awake and while asleep; others breathe normally while awake and have difficulty only during sleep. People suffering from Ondine's curse may breathe only a few times a minute during sleep, far less than is normal. They may become chronic nighttime invalids, their life sustained only by such breathing aids as iron lungs, rocking beds and tank respirators.

The Quasimodo Syndrome is the problem thought to have afflicted the Hunchback of Notre Dame. A deformity of the chest makes the heart and lungs work harder than is normal during waking, and even more so during sleep, when sleep posture and the loss of muscle tone are added stresses. This combination of factors makes sustained low oxygen in the blood likely, with personality problems a possible result.

Certain people with chronic obstructive lung diseases, such as chronic bronchitis or emphysema, may be classified as "blue bloaters" or "pink puffers." The former are "blue"—that is, look dusky —particularly around the mouth and fingernails, because they have lower rates of oxygen and higher rates of carbon dioxide in the blood than is normal, and "bloated" because they suffer failure of the right side of the heart, which results in water retention; additionally, they are usually overweight. The latter are "pink"— that is, of normal coloration—because they get enough oxygen, but they "puff" or breathe rapidly because their lungs aren't working properly. During sleep, both may have even more difficulty breathing than they have during the day; blue bloaters are more susceptible than pink puffers to sleep apnea. In order to get sufficient oxygen during the night, some people with these disorders need to sleep wearing a masklike device or nasal tubes.

For information on asthma, see Chapter 13, "In Sickness and Health."

Summing Up

Sleep apnea, of which the most common form is upper-airway apnea, is a potentially life-threatening illness. Yet its most familiar early symptom, snoring, sparks wisecracks. The other most frequent symptom, excessive daytime sleepiness, is often overlooked until it becomes extreme, and when it does, the cause of the sleepiness is sometimes not recognized, for sleep apnea is not yet a well-known disorder, even among physicians. It was only in 1980 that the standard reference guide to topics in medical publications, the *Index Medicus*, adopted "sleep apnea syndromes" as a new subject heading. Nonetheless, one out of every four people seeking help at sleep disorders centers proves to have sleep apnea. Sleep researchers believe the problem is far more common than has been thought, particularly among older people.

If you suspect that you may have sleep apnea, see your doctor. Make the appointment SOON! Ask if a referral to a sleep disorders center is appropriate.

10

TOO SLEEPY PEOPLE

Driving down the highway at fifty-five miles an hour, William Baird was horrified to see a man standing on a huge wooden beam directly in his path. He slammed on the brakes but still smashed into the beam, throwing the man up and over his car. Trembling, his heart racing, he struggled out and looked around. There was no man, no beam and no damage to his car. The road was entirely clear.

The scene had been an illusion.

Such apparitions—nightmares in the daytime—are part of a constellation of symptoms that characterize narcolepsy, a lifelong illness that is among the most disabling of sleep disorders. In this chapter we'll examine the nature of narcolepsy and its impact on the lives of those who have it and on their families.

The most common symptom of narcolepsy is uncontrollable sleepiness. Like many people, those with narcolepsy doze off easily in lectures, at the symphony or lying on the couch watching television. Unlike most people, they may also be seized by sleep while spooning soup at the dinner table, being interviewed for a job, pedaling a bicycle or even while making love. Someone with narcolepsy may, in fact, fall asleep behind the wheel of his car in the time it takes a stoplight to turn from red to green.

Falling asleep at inappropriate times is distressing in itself, but these attacks of sleepiness do not merely interrupt otherwise normal alertness. People with narcolepsy are almost always sleepy, relentlessly sleepy. Indeed, many are hobbled by sleepiness for their entire lives.

Nor is their sleepiness restricted to the drowsiness or lethargy that anyone might have after lunch or after a night without much sleep. A splash of cold water on the face or a change of activity revives most people, but attempts at stimulation do little for those with narcolepsy. Their sleepiness is closer to the eye-burning, head-nodding feeling that most people would experience if they tried to add columns of numbers at three in the morning after three days and two nights with no sleep.

We all experience several surges of sleepiness and alertness during the day. Precisely because the major debilitating symptom of narcolepsy is a feeling that occurs naturally in everyone, the recognition of a disorder of sleepiness is often delayed. People with narcolepsy typically have had their symptoms for fifteen years and have seen five doctors before the diagnosis is made, says William Baird, president of the American Narcolepsy Association, the national organization for patients and their families, with headquarters in Stanford, California.

Yet narcolepsy is not a rare disease. In the United States alone, by a conservative estimate, at least 250,000 people have it, as many as have multiple sclerosis and more than have muscular dystrophy or Parkinson's disease, all of which are far better known. Men and women are affected in equal numbers.

Narcolepsy accounts for more than one quarter of all cases of excessive daytime sleepiness diagnosed at sleep disorders centers. Yet the condition has not yet been diagnosed in perhaps half of all people who suffer from it. Some are erroneously thought to have disorders such as hypothyroidism or hypoglycemia that also cause sleepiness. Many simply plod through life, their sleepiness a barrier to full participation and enjoyment.

Although someone whose condition is diagnosed today as narcolepsy may be the first in his family in whom the disease is recognized, narcolepsy can be inherited. Relatives of people with narcolepsy are sixty times more likely to have it themselves than are members of the population at large.

The Marionette Syndrome

The symptom that makes the diagnosis of narcolepsy virtually certain is sudden muscle weakness, known as cataplexy, which makes a person feel like a marionette whose strings have been cut.

Most of us have at one time or another been so convulsed by laughter that we couldn't talk and had to lean on someone else for support. Cataplexy has a similar effect. This condition is usually triggered by a strong emotion, such as exhilaration, anger or surprise, and ranges from complete collapse to weakness of only certain muscle groups. A father raises his arm to chastise his son and suddenly swoons. A policeman clasps handcuffs on a suspect, then finds himself weak in the knees. A businessman laughs at a joke, only to have his face contorted by grimaces and twitches of the eyelids.

Excessive sleepiness may trouble a person for five, fifteen or even thirty years before cataplexy appears.

People with narcolepsy may have additional symptoms, such as seeing things that aren't there, like the man on the road. Sometimes they also hear unreal noises. Such experiences are called hypnagogic hallucinations.

Sometimes the hallucinations are coupled with a temporary inability to move, which occurs just as the person is falling asleep or waking up. Frequently the theme is impending attack. This story is typical: "I was lying in bed when I heard footsteps approaching my room. A prowler kicked open the door and strode to the bed, knife in hand. I wanted to leap out of the way, but I couldn't move even a finger. I tried to scream but the sound was locked in my throat." Such episodes of sleep paralysis are sometimes accompanied by the feeling that something is pressing on the chest. This experience is believed to be the basis for Henry Fuseli's famous painting "The Nightmare," in which a demon is hunkering on the chest of a terror-stricken woman, who appears unable to move. Sleep paralysis usually lasts just a few seconds, but it may continue for as long as twenty minutes.

As an isolated incident, this paralysis is no cause for concern—it occurs occasionally in people who do not have narcolepsy and usually ends by itself. It can also be terminated by touching the person or calling his name. Hence, a spouse or parent who is alert to the problem can often abort it.

Sometimes people with narcolepsy experience blackouts. At such times, they may drive fifty miles past their destination and come back to their senses with no memory of what has transpired and no concept of how much time has passed.

What Causes These Bizarre Symptoms?

Sleepiness, muscle weakness, frightening visions, an inability to move just before or after sleep and episodes of forgetfulness have no connection that is immediately apparent to the person who suffers them. He might not think to mention all of them to the doctor, or might even refrain from doing so for fear of being thought "crazy."

But all of these symptoms are indeed tied together, for narcolepsy is a disorder of the basic brain mechanisms that regulate sleep. In narcolepsy, sleep persistently intrudes into wakefulness, engulfing the person with a constant feeling of sleepiness and triggering during wakefulness events that are usually confined to sleep.

While we sleep, two distinct states alternate. In nonrapid-eye-movement (NREM) sleep, muscles are ready for action and thoughts are vague. By contrast, in rapid-eye-movement (REM) sleep, muscles twitch but large movements are suppressed, while the mind is filled with the vivid images we call dreams. A normal night's sleep begins with NREM. After about ninety minutes, the sleeper enters a brief REM period. Four or five cycles continue throughout the sleep period, at approximately ninety-minute intervals, with REM periods growing progressively longer as the night moves on. In persons with narcolepsy, the usual order is reversed. The person goes from wakefulness to REM sleep, immediately or within fifteen minutes. Early REM periods are longer than usual.

REM sleep episodes that sneak in during the day produce many of the symptoms of narcolepsy. The same "off-switch" that keeps the body from moving in normal REM sleep triggers the muscle weakness of cataplexy, as well as the momentary sense of paralysis at the times of falling asleep and of awakening. During such episodes, as in REM sleep, eyes move even though the body does not. While experiencing cataplexy, a person can usually see what's going on around him and follow instructions to move his eyes in a specific direction or track an object.

The vivid sights, sounds and feelings characteristic of hypnagogic hallucinations are thought to be dreams occurring while the person is awake, both during the day and just at the edges of nighttime sleep. Some of these illusions, like nightmares, are terrifying. The episodes of automatic behavior resemble sleepwalking and sleeptalking.

Not only are people with narcolepsy more sleepy during the daytime than people without the disorder, but they also seem to be "more awake" during the night. Many find sleep is marked by more frequent awakenings, brief or lasting for hours, and more than the usual number of nightmares, with murder or persecution a common theme. Many talk or cry out during the night and thrash about. Even their deep sleep is punctuated by bursts of REM sleep. Hence, despite their sleepiness, people with narcolepsy average about the same amount of sleep at night—seven to eight hours—as do people without the disorder. They may hold the misconception, however, that their excessive daytime sleepiness is caused by insufficient nighttime sleep, and as a result, they may spend inordinately long hours in bed. But people suffering from narcolepsy are sleepy during the day, regardless of how much sleep they get at night.

One in ten people with narcolepsy has an added complication. These people, mostly men, suffer from sleep apnea, recurrent interruptions in breathing during sleep. They are particularly sleepy during the daytime, and, in contrast to most people with narcolepsy, they awake from naps feeling as sleepy as before. (Sleep apnea is the subject of Chapter 9, "The Snoring Sickness.")

Once viewed as "all in the mind," narcolepsy is now recognized as a disorder of the nervous system. The cause remains unknown. Narcolepsy is not contagious. While at present it remains incurable, treatment with medication can help people with this illness to live more normal lives.

Growing Up Sleepy

Sleepy children don't bother their teachers or parents; as a result, their sleepiness is easily overlooked. At the other extreme, some children who show hyperactive behavior actually have narcolepsy; they are working frenetically to keep themselves awake.

Although narcolepsy has been diagnosed in a five-year-old, its symptoms most frequently appear for the first time during adolescence. Mary Carskadon, Ph.D., of Stanford University found that the increase in sleepiness that accompanies normal maturation was intensified in the teenage daughter of a mother with narcolepsy. Dr. Carskadon hypothesizes that the extra sleepiness characteristic of adolescence may make it a particularly vulnerable stage in the development of narcolepsy.

A teenager who sleeps in class may be dismissed as lazy, lying about not getting enough sleep at night or merely inept, when in fact the child is suffering from narcolepsy. William Baird recalls that, beginning in junior high school, he wasn't much of a student. He often slept during class. After school, rather than participating in sports or clubs, he came home to nap. Not only are people with narcolepsy often too tired to get involved in social activities, they frequently avoid them because of the chance that they might fall asleep or be overtaken by cataplexy.

While growing up, Sue had to contend with the nickname Lazy Susan. Recently, sharing with a friend her interest in a public television series, she was startled to learn that it was based on a novel that had long been standard fare in high school English classes. "I now realize that I never was awake long enough to read the classics," Sue relates.

When a child has narcolepsy, parents must resign themselves to patiently explaining the situation to each new teacher.

The Sleepy Employee

In work situations, people with narcolepsy have to struggle to keep up. "You don't go up the corporate ladder with narcolepsy," says one man. "You slide down, or, if you're lucky, you manage to hold on." People who fall asleep at work often are viewed as "goofing off."

George arranged his office furniture so that a file cabinet blocked the view of his desk from the door, enabling him to put his head down frequently for a minute or two. To take a longer nap, he retreated, like many people with narcolepsy, to a bathroom stall. "I took off my belt and strapped myself to the toilet paper roll to avoid falling over," he recalls.

A graphic artist, George might devote hours of exacting work to a complex electrical plan, only to fall asleep, splattering ink all over the paper. Although his employer encouraged him to take projects home, he found he rarely could complete them successfully. By his forty-second birthday, he had left work, certified as completely disabled. Indeed, of all people with narcolepsy seen at the Stanford Sleep Disorders Center, more than half have been completely disabled with respect to employment by the age of forty.

Baird comments: "Many people with narcolepsy who are taking medicine can hold a nine-to-five job and do it well, but their work comes at the expense of the rest of their lives. Almost no one with narcolepsy is capable of the same level of performance as he would be if he didn't have it." Baird himself, a stockbroker, experienced such severe cataplexy when making sales that he had to abandon his career in his mid-thirties.

He adds, "There are a few hours each day, perhaps five or six, when I can be as productive as anyone. During the rest of the time, I'm far from alert. I have no social life, no hobbies, no recreation."

The Sleepy Spouse

Husbands and wives have a tough time accepting narcolepsy. Patti, George's wife, says, "It's hard not to be peeved when he claims he lacks the energy even to take out the garbage." (Baird says he has never married because of his illness.)

Vicki describes how narcolepsy can interfere with marital relations. "My husband and I would go to bed and I'd fall asleep instantly. If he woke me, I'd be irritable. Later I'd wonder, Did we have sex or didn't we?" Her husband found a way to resolve the problem; he started coming home at lunch time.

Women married to men with narcolepsy sometimes find it hard to accept the necessity of being the family's only wage earner. A Stanford study found that when one partner has narcolepsy, a marriage has a 50 percent chance of ending in divorce. Hence, marriage counseling and family counseling now are often offered at the time of diagnosis.

Of continuing concern are the hereditary aspects of the illness. A parent with narcolepsy may feel guilty if a child develops it. Some couples abandon plans to have children.

The Insidious Effects of Sleepiness

Sleepiness has far-ranging consequences. It affects one's ability to perform, to think and to concentrate. "People who are sleepy have to make an extra effort just to keep up with others," comments Arthur Spielman, Ph.D., co-director of the Sleep/Wake Disorders Center at Montefiore Hospital, New York. "Sleepiness begets feelings of inferiority. This central core of inadequacy has a radiating effect on the quality of life," he says.

Charlotte, a former director of a social service agency who was forced by narcolepsy to leave work, reflects, "If I could choose, I'd rather be in a wheelchair for the rest of my life than have narcolepsy. I'd find it easier to cope with a physical impairment. My mind would be alert; I could think, read or type. I'm barely able to do any of those things now. Mostly, I just sit around."

Sleepiness also erodes motivation and judgment. "It can paralyze a person's will to resist falling asleep even when there could be disastrous consequences," comments Stanford sleep researcher William Dement, M.D.

In our society, sleepiness is scorned. We say a sleepy person is lazy or stupid. No one wants to be "caught napping." We encourage people to deny fatigue. We are offended when someone falls asleep while we are talking with him. People with narcolepsy are sometimes assumed to be drug abusers or closet drinkers. Sleepiness is "acceptable" only when it's clearly associated with illness (although being ill carries stigmas, too).

Because sleepiness is part of everyone's frequent experience, and because the symptoms of narcolepsy usually are mild when they first appear, the person with this illness typically spends years wondering, Am I sick? Or do I merely lack initiative? These are nagging questions that can undermine self-esteem. Baird notes, "You find lots of things in your life to explain symptoms: You stayed up too late. You worked too hard. In your heart, you have nagging doubts about your ability and motivation."

Vicki describes life before she learned she had narcolepsy and began treatment: "On weekdays, I barely finished work, went home and went to sleep. On weekends, I got up, did a few chores and went back to sleep. I could explain all this to myself: After all, I had two active children, a full-time job and I was getting older." Vicki's job was just a block from the grocery store, but she was unable to shop after work for even a single item for dinner without first going five miles to her home for a nap.

Most people find it hard to accept the notion that sleepiness can't be controlled. Because occasionally excitement, even in a person with narcolepsy, overrides sleepiness, family members, friends or employers may insist that the person could be more alert if he worked at it. Unfortunately, in people with narcolepsy the usual link between interest and wakefulness is almost always flimsy. Rather than being spurred into wakefulness by excitement, the enthusiastic football fan with narcolepsy is more likely to fall asleep in the midst of a cheering crowd when the ball is on the ten-yard line.

If he is aware of extreme drowsiness, someone with narcolepsy may try to fight it by opening a window, blinking rapidly, flexing his hands, pinching himself, biting his cheeks—behaviors that an observer may well view as odd. Baird puts ice on his neck, since he finds that cold acts as a stimulant. When assigned to jury duty, Vicki resorted to digging her fingernails into her hand to force herself to stay awake. Many people with narcolepsy chain-smoke, using the activity involved in handling a cigarette as an impetus to stay awake. Drinking copious amounts of coffee and other caffeine-containing beverages is a common practice.

Someone who knows he has narcolepsy often can forestall periods of overwhelming sleepiness by taking regular naps. Usually, he can recognize the warning signs of an impending sleep attack long enough in advance to seek out a spot to sleep. It is excruciatingly difficult, and frequently impossible, to ignore the urge to sleep, no matter how inconvenient or inappropriate. Occasionally, a person will be overcome by sleep with no warning at all. Some people say that after a brief period of sleep, sometimes just a few minutes, they feel relatively alert, but others report that they are merely not as sleepy.

Wiped Out by Blackouts

A person with narcolepsy frequently wobbles back and forth between sleep and wakefulness in a state that's been likened to sleepwalking. This automatic behavior is one of the most distressing consequences of extreme sleepiness.

In this state, a teacher wrote algebraic equations on the blackboard during an English class. A woman headed home from the supermarket with her groceries, but left her baby behind in the shopping cart. Another woman was repeatedly arrested for shoplifting, behavior she denied being able to remember. A businessman habitually misplaced everyday objects; he might find his watch in the refrigerator or his toothbrush in the mailbox. Because he often lost track of the flow of conversation during meetings, he began using a tape recorder. Even that proved inadequate; he sometimes failed to note that the tape had stopped and needed to be turned over. A receptionist, expected to cover all office phones at lunchtime, could not get messages straight. A man put a kitchen sponge between two slices of bread—and then ate the sandwich.

The consequences of such episodes may be severe: One woman last remembered walking into the kitchen to do the dishes. "When I 'woke up' about thirty minutes later, the kitchen was a complete mess," she recalls. "I had put all the plates in the clothes dryer and turned it on." A computer programmer reports, "My last mistake was to run a completely inappropriate program for three hours. During that period of time I had to do a certain number of tape rewindings, which I did. It seems that I even talked appropriately to one of my assistants. Had I not awakened before it was too late, my error would have cost the company twenty-five thousand dollars. However, I don't remember anything at all."

People in this altered state of consciousness may even jeopardize their lives. A driver crashed into a gate at a railroad crossing. A woman plunged her hand into boiling soup. A housepainter walked off a roof. One man sounds a universal cry of anxiety, saying, "The most frightening thing is not being able to remember what I have done in the minutes, usually hours, that have just passed."

Sometimes the episodes are so brief that the person himself is unaware of them. Reading a newspaper, he may doze off and return to a story numerous times. People in the company of someone like this may not notice such behavior either, unless he replies inappropriately or with meaningless phrases when asked a complex question. Often, after such an incident, the person recalls just one or two scenes, as in a broken movie. The episode may be forgotten if no evidence is at hand that something has happened.

People with narcolepsy have such experiences frequently, often daily, usually at times when sleepiness is most common, such as in the afternoon or early evening, but almost never in the early morning. Most of those with the disorder have had such episodes while driving, and many also have them while doing a monotonous task alone in a warm room. Some find that these events are triggered by eating sweets.

In one study at Stanford, people with and without narcolepsy wore sleep-monitoring devices for an hour while they added columns of figures and performed other tasks requiring concentration. The narcolepsy patients complained that the experimenters had reduced the testing time. They skipped over problems and made far more mistakes than the others. They wrote unintelligible sentences that they couldn't interpret afterward or even remember writing. Periodically, they sat motionless. Their eyes remained open but had a glassy look. The sleep records showed that they slept for periods ranging from two to ten minutes. Overall, they performed only half as well as people without narcolepsy.

Living with Cataplexy

Unlike the physical paralysis of nighttime REM sleep, the loss of muscle control that occurs during cataplexy is usually not accompanied by a loss of consciousness, although it may be. More typically, someone with cataplexy is able to think clearly and to hear and see activities around him; sometimes his vision is blurred. He may feel that he has difficulty breathing, although breathing is not in fact altered.

Because cataplexy is most frequently triggered by emotional arousal, some people choose to constrict their emotional lives by dampening their feelings. "That means removing yourself from life's pleasures," sighs Baird. "It also may mean seeming not to care. A person with narcolepsy often avoids confrontation by giving in before demands are pressed."

Sometimes the precipitating event for cataplexy is startlingly idiosyncratic. People have reported that they get weak only in such specific situations as hooking a fish or slicing rare roast beef.

After many years, some people with narcolepsy find that less emotional stimulus is required to induce cataplexy and that increasingly more muscles are involved. Other people find the symptom diminishes; possibly, they simply have become more adept at anticipating and avoiding situations that would trigger attacks.

Most attacks of cataplexy last less than a minute; occasionally, they go on for ten to twenty minutes. Typically, they last as long as the precipitating experience continues and perhaps a minute more. During longer attacks, hallucinations—those nightmares in the daytime—are more likely to occur. Brain-wave records taken during an attack of cataplexy often show a mixture of both wakefulness and REM sleep, a fact that explains why people frequently report, "I knew where I was, but I saw things I later realized weren't there." Some people feel they are leaning sideways or floating. Some people have attacks of cataplexy as infrequently as once a month; others have them dozens of times a day.

Cataplexy is not an easy symptom to explain to other people. Baird comments, "After you once have an attack in the cafeteria and find your face in your spaghetti, you begin to eat lunch somewhere else alone."

How Is Narcolepsy Diagnosed?

Excessive sleepiness in the daytime is not sufficient evidence of narcolepsy, although some people with only this symptom worry that they have the disease, with all of its lifelong disabling implications. Sleepiness is a prominent characteristic of a number of other disorders, including sleep apnea. An all-night sleep study may be necessary to identify the specific cause of the sleepiness.

The appearance of attacks of muscular weakness triggered by strong emotions makes the diagnosis of narcolepsy almost certain. Someone who experiences sleepiness, hypnagogic hallucinations, sleep paralysis and disturbed nighttime sleep may have narcolepsy but needs further evaluation. Only one of every four people with narcolepsy has all symptoms of the disorder. If you have any of these symptoms, see your doctor; an evaluation at a sleep disorders center may be indicated.

The major diagnostic test used at most sleep centers is the multiple sleep latency test (MSLT). Patients are given five or six opportunities to sleep at two-hour intervals during the day. Falling asleep in less than five minutes is considered abnormal. People with narcolepsy often fall asleep within a minute. At Stanford, a large group of people with narcolepsy fell asleep on the MSLT in an average of four minutes. Moreover, they frequently fell immediately into REM sleep, while people without narcolepsy almost never do.

There is some evidence that narcolepsy can be diagnosed, even before the classical clinical symptoms appear, by the abnormal rapidity with which a person enters REM sleep during the MSLT. The test would be most useful for screening the child of a parent with narcolepsy; early detection and treatment as soon as warranted might avert some of the negative psychological fallout.

How Is Narcolepsy Treated?

Treatment aims at controlling the two major symptoms of narcolepsy, excessive sleepiness and cataplexy. Although both arise from the same disorder of basic sleep mechanisms, they require separate treatment.

FIGHTING SLEEPINESS *naps*

To relieve sleepiness, the first step is to *schedule naps* at the times of the day the person is most sleepy. Because it's easy to underestimate sleepiness, someone may not realize how much more alert he could be with regular naps. Hence, keeping a "nap diary" and rating one's own alertness at regular intervals throughout the day can help provide needed insight.

A person with narcolepsy can nap by putting his head on a desk or leaning back in a chair. A nap of just a few minutes may ward off sleep attacks, but doctors often advise people with severe sleepiness to try to sleep for at least fifteen or twenty minutes several times a day.

In siesta cultures no one apologizes for napping. Indeed, the existence of the midday nap may explain why fewer people with narcolepsy come for treatment to sleep clinics in Italy that otherwise have a mix of patients comparable to those seen at sleep clinics in the United States. In the United States, people who take naps—particularly those who nap more than once a day or in public—arouse suspicion. Some people manage to conceal the illness from co-workers by saying they are "meditating" or "just thinking."

Naps are particularly valuable in treating children, because the consequences of a lifetime of medications on their development or on the course of the illness are unknown.

As an adjunct to napping, people with narcolepsy are advised to *keep regular sleep habits*, with particular emphasis on getting enough sleep so that, as often as possible, they awaken spontaneously.

For people with mild sleepiness, regular naps may provide adequate relief. But for more severe problems, *stimulant drugs* generally are used. The most commonly prescribed drugs are pemoline, methylphenidate, dextroamphetamine or related compounds. These drugs may be able to reduce sleep attacks from two or three a day to as few as one or two a month.

The aim of treatment is to reduce sleepiness without resorting to excessive doses of the drugs. Unfortunately, many people quickly develop tolerance to the drugs and require increasingly larger doses to maintain alertness. At the same time, they become dependent upon the drugs. Doctors try to monitor patients carefully to determine the lowest effective dose and the best time for taking the medication. However, even on low doses, some people become aggressive, nervous and irritable. Occasionally, a patient develops a drug-related psychosis. To avoid adverse reactions, people with narcolepsy often have to stay away from certain foods and medications. Because the specific drug and the dosage schedule may have to be altered frequently, patients may repeatedly have to face drug withdrawal symptoms such as intensified sleepiness and disturbing dreams.

Success of treatment with a particular drug can be evaluated at many sleep clinics. The patient is asked to lie down in a quiet, darkened room and to try to stay awake. His ability to stay awake during five separate twenty-minute sessions two hours apart is tested on days he takes medication and on days he doesn't; a comparison of the results tells how well the drug is working.

How a patient feels when using medication is not the only criterion for assessing the medication's effectiveness. Indeed, for some patients, the result of performance tests given as part of the drug evaluation are troubling: While they feel much better, their ability to add numbers, sort cards and manage other tasks is actually worse. Outside the lab, the discrepancy between how a patient feels and how he performs might have a disastrous outcome, if, for example, he or she is tempted to try a lengthy drive. Moreover, the primary benefit of stimulant drugs—improving alertness—may permit marital and social problems previously submerged by the sleepiness to emerge. A patient on medication may be more aware of his limitations and more frustrated by being passed over for a promotion at work, for example. Hence, individualized counseling about driving, employment and other activities of daily living is a part of continuing care.

Finally, use of stimulant drugs, or "uppers," even for illness, may be stigmatizing or viewed as morally wrong. In a day when drug abuse is common, someone with narcolepsy must often put up with extra scrutiny at the prescription counter.

TREATING CATAPLEXY

The symptoms of cataplexy can often be reduced or eliminated by protryptiline, imipramine and monoamine oxidase inhibitors, drugs commonly used in the treatment of depression. The effect of these drugs on cataplexy can be observed within an hour; by contrast, when the same drugs are given to relieve depression, their effects take a week or more to become apparent.

Treatment of cataplexy can reduce its occurrence from three times a day to three times a month. The aim is not to block cataplexy completely, because excessive doses would be required; instead, treatment aims to reduce the symptom's frequency and duration. Because these drugs may also aggravate sleepiness, determining the best timing and dose is critical. Again, the development of tolerance to the drugs is common.

Effective treatment for cataplexy usually also relieves two of the other symptoms of narcolepsy, sleep paralysis and hypnagogic hallucinations.

However, side effects may occur. One of the most frequent is impaired sexual functioning in men. Some men must choose between cataplexy or impotence, a situation certain to put stress upon a marriage. Some men discontinue the drugs every few days for one or two days in order to sustain sexual relations.

None of the drugs used for narcolepsy is known to be safe for use during pregnancy.

Much like diabetes or arthritis, narcolepsy is a lifelong disorder that is best managed when patient and doctor form a comfortable partnership that permits frequent tailoring of treatment. People with narcolepsy need to see the doctor approximately every three to six months.

Counseling Can Help

Because employment, social and family life all are acutely affected by narcolepsy, supportive counseling is a strong component of treatment.

With regard to employment, people with narcolepsy have difficulty in jobs that require vigilance and prolonged attention; the disorder limits both the type and amount of work a person can do, as well as his motivation to do it.

However, "when the broadest possible definition of 'employment' is applied to encompass part-time, homebound and self-employment, it appears likely that most persons with narcolepsy can benefit from rehabilitation services," according to Brian McMahon, Ph.D., a rehabilitation counselor at the Illinois Institute of Technology, Chicago, and James Walsh, Ph.D., director of the Sleep Disorders Center at Deaconess Hospital, St. Louis.

The illness imposes many restrictions: Because of the potential danger to themselves or others, most people with narcolepsy are advised not to work with moving objects, flames, hot surfaces, explosive materials, mechanical or electrical hazards, at heights or on moving surfaces. Many should not operate vehicles. They may need to avoid emotional excitation, stress or strenuous physical effort. Someone suffering memory deficits won't be able to handle jobs requiring frequent learning of new material or instructions. If a person has visual problems involving eye fatigue, focusing, maintaining a single image and involuntary eye movements, he would not do well at jobs that require extensive reading or close attention to detail, such as inspecting. Jobs that are boring or involve extensive driving may bring on sleep attacks, while exciting jobs may increase cataplexy. Long hours, infrequent rest periods or irregular schedules that interfere with normal sleeping hours are likely to increase a person's sleepiness and hence are poor choices.

"There are, however, many jobs a person with narcolepsy can do well, particularly in an enlightened office where it's possible to take three or four nap breaks a day," asserts Merrill Mitler, Ph.D., senior staff scientist at the Scripps Clinic and Research Foundation, La Jolla, California. The key criterion is that the tasks can be divided into parts that can be performed in relatively short periods.

Driving is a touchy issue for anyone with narcolepsy. Some states require a physician to report a patient who experiences lapses in consciousness to the state's licensing bureau. To avoid having a restriction placed on their driver's license, some people, regrettably, avoid seeking medical care.

However, a person with narcolepsy who is *properly* trained and medicated can drive safely. Patients learn to take a stimulant before a drive and to get off the road before the medication wears off. Use of medication also gives them time to respond to irresistible sleepiness, so that they can pull over before a sleep attack overwhelms them.

Physicians and sleep clinics may ask patients to sign an agreement that they will respond affirmatively on any application asking about their illness and will drive only when their symptoms are under control.

The accident rate of drivers who are known to have narcolepsy is actually lower than that of drivers without the disorder; once people understand and respect the limitations of the illness, they deal with driving responsibly. Baird asserts, however, that in 20 percent of automobile fatalities that occur in the United States the cause is a mystery. Falling asleep at the wheel is often suspected.

Self-help groups, such as those sponsored by the American Narcolepsy Association (ANA), aid people with narcolepsy and their families to cope with the illness. This organization, started in 1975 by Baird and eight other patients who met at Stanford, has over two thousand members and groups in many cities around the country. For more information on narcolepsy and the address of a group in your area, write the ANA, P.O. Box 5846, Stanford, California 94305.

Research Advances

Many important pieces of the narcolepsy puzzle are beginning to fall into place as the result of studies of narcolepsy in animals. Such studies can provide information that it would be impractical or unethical to seek using human subjects. The effects of narcolepsy on behavior, the way the disorder is inherited and the benefits and risks of specific drugs are being evaluated by studies of dogs with the disorder. Narcolepsy occurs naturally in animals (unlike, for example, diabetes, which must be induced with diet or surgery) and has been identified in seventeen different breeds of dogs, and in ponies as well.

Monique, a French poodle sent to the Stanford Sleep Disorders

Center by a veterinarian who recognized that she had narcolepsy after reading about the disease in humans, provided the impetus for a dog colony there; a breeding colony was begun in 1977 with two Doberman pinschers who had narcolepsy. Now, at any one time, it houses two to four dozen animals.

In the dogs, as in humans, novelty triggers symptoms of narcolepsy. The appearance of a visitor causes one dog's hind legs to crumple under him. After a few seconds, the dog jumps up; on noticing the visitor again, he topples down. When a litter of puppies is let out of the pen into a yard to play, they get so excited that four or five flop to the ground at once. When tossed a food pellet, a dog collapses with excitement, struggles awake and forward a few inches, collapses again, then wakes again. When it finally gets the food, it falls asleep before it can take a bite. Like people with sleep paralysis, the dogs can be aroused by a handclap or by petting.

Dogs with narcolepsy have considerable difficulty breeding. Because sex is emotionally arousing, they keel over while attempting intercourse. Often, artificial insemination is necessary.

In humans, narcolepsy is known to run in families, but the pattern of inheritance is not clear. Few families are known in which both parents have narcolepsy. Dog studies show that if both parents have narcolepsy, all puppies born to purebred Doberman pinschers and Labrador retrievers have the disease themselves. However, that's not the case with poodles, a fact that suggests that both genetic and nongenetic factors are involved in the disorder's development. As is the pattern in humans, the mating of a dog with narcolepsy to a dog without it will yield puppies who may not show symptoms of narcolepsy themselves but may pass it on to their progeny.

In familiar settings and as they get older, dogs, like people, have fewer attacks of cataplexy. The finding that in both dogs and humans there is no obvious relationship between the age at which cataplexy first appears and the severity of the disorder eases the anxiety of people whose narcolepsy is diagnosed relatively early in life. Cataplexy in dogs with narcolepsy can be elicited in the first few weeks of life if the dogs are given a drug, physostigmine salicylate. Normal dogs have no response to it, but dogs that will later show evidence of narcolepsy drop to the ground, a fact that may lead to the development of a screening test for the families of people with narcolepsy.

Sleepiness can be studied in animals by keeping them awake for certain periods and then allowing them to sleep as long as they wish. Sleep attacks, cataplexy and the appearance of REM sleep earlier than is normal can also be assessed. A new system of EEG telemetry, in which a self-contained, self-powered signaling device is implanted under the skin of the dog's neck, allows researchers to observe the dog while it is moving freely.

The dog colony further benefits humans by providing a way to evaluate medicines that inhibit cataplexy. A dog with narcolepsy who is going through a maze to get food will ordinarily have an episode of cataplexy in the middle. A drug that permits the dog to make it through the maze will get a more intensive look for possible use in people.

The discovery that dogs with narcolepsy have unusually high concentrations of the brain chemical dopamine suggests that narcolepsy may involve a defect in the way the body uses or processes dopamine, or both. Since amphetamine drugs, which often benefit people with narcolepsy by making them more alert, are known to stimulate the release of dopamine, this finding may lead to the development of even more effective drugs for humans.

The surge of recent knowledge about narcolepsy gives rise to the hope that better treatments will soon be available. These, along with more widespread recognition of the problem, are long overdue and will surely make it easier for persons with narcolepsy to cope with their invisible disability.

11

THE TIME
OF OUR LIVES

Our lives are governed by a set of clocks located in the brain. These clocks regulate the timing of sleeping and waking, feelings of hunger, ups and downs in body temperature, release of hormones, response to pain, daydreaming, and even our moods. All of these functions of body and mind show cyclic fluctuations, most following a schedule that is roughly twenty-four hours long, the direct result of our living on a twenty-four-hour planet. Hence, they are termed "circadian" from the Latin *circa*, approximately, and *dies*, meaning "day."

But most humans would prefer to live on a twenty-five-hour day, as has been demonstrated by experiments in which people live in a cave or laboratory apartment with no windows, clocks or other indicators of time, going to sleep and getting up whenever they wish. (Such studies have also shown that most of us can easily adjust to a day length that is one to two hours more or less than twenty-five hours.) As a result, while most of us are able to manage quite well in a twenty-four-hour world, we are more prone to stay up later than to go to bed earlier.

Living in the real world, we must reset our inner clocks each day by about an hour. Various clues in the outside world—wristwatches and alarm clocks, for example—help us to do this. Events that occur periodically in our lives, called zeitgebers, are time setters that also aid us to adhere to a twenty-four-hour day. For most animals, light and dark are paramount in synchronizing such functions as waking and sleeping, body temperature and hormone secretion; the changing amounts of light and dark during the course of a year even regulate annual rhythms such as breeding, migration and hibernation. But for people, social factors are more important. "The ringing of the morning alarm clock probably is the most powerful zeitgeber for humans," asserts Elliot Weitzman, M.D., director of the Institute of Chronobiology at the New York Hospital-Cornell Medical Center. "It makes a statement that you have to get up to get to work or school or take care of your family," he adds. "Alarm clocks make us aware of the consequences of not following society's rules."

The scheduling of sleep helps set your internal clocks. The "awake at day, asleep at night" routine most of us pursue is merely a convention. Prior to the invention of electricity, this schedule was eminently practical. But there is no innate reason why we must sleep when it is dark. For most of us, there's a time when it's easy to fall asleep and stay asleep and a time when, even if we're utterly frazzled and are resting comfortably in a darkened room, sleep eludes us. People who set their own schedules in time-free environments instinctively choose to go to sleep and get up in step with the daily ups and downs of their body temperature, a range that goes from about 97°F to 99°F.

The biological rhythms discussed here have nothing to do with the notion popularly referred to as "biorhythms," which purports to predict "critical days" in your life solely on the basis of the day of your birth. Biorhythm theory, first developed by Wilhelm Fliess, a Berlin nose-and-throat specialist and a friend of Sigmund Freud, posits a twenty-three-day cycle of physical stamina and endurance, a twenty-eight-day cycle of emotional sensitivity and a thirty-three-day cycle of intellectual performance. According to the theory, these cycles are fixed and unchangeable throughout a lifetime; days of transition between the highs and lows of each cycle supposedly are more stressful, "critical days," on which people are more accident-prone.

"Biorhythm theory is a hoax," asserts chronobiologist Charles Ehret, Ph.D., senior scientist at the Argonne (Illinois) National Laboratory. "The only relationship this so-called biorhythm theory has to genuine knowledge of biological rhythms is like that of astrology to astronomy. Our internal rhythms do change; that's why we develop problems when we travel through many time zones or work different shifts. Illness, the times when we take medications or eat our meals, light and social interactions—all can change the timing of our inner clocks," he adds.

"Imagine a master clock in your house to which all other clocks are attached, even though all can also run independently," suggests Dr. Weitzman. "If the wires between the master clock and the other clocks were cut, the other clocks would still run. After a while, however, they would not all run on exactly the same frequency. They would tend to drift away from each other, some running faster, others slower."

Similarly, our internal clocks normally are tied together. If you upset their relationship, your body will try hard to adapt. But this process takes time; the separate and distinct clocks reset themselves at different rates. Some people have lived for many years with their inner clocks continually out of sync with the world at large; fortunately, the findings from chronobiological research are already being translated into practical ways to help them.

This chapter looks at how inner clocks govern our daily lives.

Jet Lag: Coping with Time Travel

It's six-thirty in the evening. Ordinarily at this time, Helene and Dick would be at the dinner table, but tonight they're at Kennedy Airport boarding a flight that leaves at seven for Paris. Shortly after takeoff they sip cocktails and then have a large dinner with two cups of coffee. They flip through magazines, watch a movie and listen to music. At midnight, the stewardess arrives with breakfast and more coffee. At two, long past their usual bedtime, they step off the plane and into the noisy traffic-jammed streets of a Paris morning, where it's now eight o'clock. They arrive at their hotel, only to find their room isn't yet ready; so, with eyes blinking in the bright sunlight, at a time when they normally would be fast asleep, they set off for the Eiffel Tower.

For the next few days they fight sleep—not always successfully —during their tour guide's talks. But at bedtime, they're ready to go. They stay up later than they desire and sleep fitfully; when it's time to get up, at an hour when they would ordinarily be asleep, they must fight inertia. Despite their enjoyment of the trip, they feel a bit peevish and short-tempered. They eat when their watches and the local crowd tell them it's mealtime, although they're not always hungry. Occasionally they feel chills and queasiness, which they blame on the change in food and water.

In fact, along with the millions of other people who travel quickly across several time zones, Helene and Dick have jet lag. Trying to sleep and stay awake at unaccustomed times, in addition to changing the times for eating and other activities, causes the synchronized beat of a host of inner clocks to go awry. The body acts like an orchestra without a conductor; over here the tempo is too fast and over there it is too slow. Many different systems of the body are in disharmony.

After about two days in a time zone six hours different from your home time—the difference between New York and Paris—you'll find it easier to sleep on the new schedule. But your sleep may remain fitful for several more days; you're likely to awaken more frequently during the night to urinate, for example, because this process also takes time to adjust to your new waking hours. Body temperature, which normally goes up and down during the day in a pattern that is tied to the times you are awake and asleep, stays out of sync with your new sleeping time longer, often for over a week and sometimes for two weeks.

Since body temperature is correlated with your alertness during the day, you may find yourself feeling out of sorts when you least expect to be or are least able to tolerate it. All of us, for example, have a time during the day when we are at our worst. For people who are normally asleep between midnight and six, this low point usually occurs between three and five in the morning. When you travel from New York to Paris, your low point is at the same "body time," but that's nine to eleven in the morning by Paris time. In general, you can expect to have the most trouble with lethargy in the morning if you travel eastward, and in the afternoon if you fly west.

Tourists can give in to this sluggishness by sitting down in the nearest sidewalk café or taking a nap back at the hotel, but business travelers and diplomats are at a decided disadvantage. This fact helps account for the popularity of the Concorde jets, which whisk travelers from the United States to Europe in about three hours;

although they don't, of course, eliminate jet lag, they permit business to be conducted on the same day. At international conferences, high officials have been known to insist that talks be conducted on their time rather than that of the meeting place. Some firms require that no contracts be signed within twenty-four hours of arrival by their representatives who have traveled from the United States to Europe, and within seventy-two hours, by those who have traveled to Asia.

Rapid travel across several time zones upsets the patterns of secretion of hormones. Some, like growth hormone, whose release occurs mainly during sleep, shift quickly. Others, like cortisol, which is crucial to the normal functioning of every cell in the body, take eight days or longer to adjust. Digestion and elimination may take a week or more to return to normal.

The array of disturbances that you may experience tends to last longer going east, when the contrast between your usual bedtime and activities in the new time zone are greater. Going west, you literally race the sun across the sky. Going east, you're likely to miss a lot more sleep, and sleep deprivation seems to further aggravate the symptoms of jet lag.

The maxim that it takes one day to adapt for each time zone crossed is just an approximation. It doesn't seem to take as long to readapt once you return home, whether home is east or west of where you've been, since familiar surroundings and schedules accelerate your adjustment. However, it probably will be at least a week before you're completely "back to yourself" again. Of course, there's a wide range of individual differences. About one person in four is hit hard by jet lag and one in four seems able to shrug it off. Larks, or morning people, whose body temperatures normally rise and peak earlier in the day, seem to suffer more than owls or evening people, whose temperatures rise and peak later on. The older you are, the more likely you are to feel the symptoms of jet lag. If you're already an insomniac, grit your teeth. You'll probably feel jet lag acutely.

It's a mistake to think that jet lag is "all in the mind." It's a physical response that reflects the temporary disparity between internal rhythms and the rhythms of the external world; that's why the scientific name for it is "circadian desynchronism." Jet lag, incidentally, isn't the result of travel per se, but rather of the rapid crossing of time zones. If you travel across time zones by ship or train, you'll adapt more easily to the slowly changing local time. If you fly between north and south but don't cross time zones, even if your trip takes many hours, all you're likely to feel is the fatigue of traveling.

You don't even have to leave home to develop "jet lag." If you go to bed late on weekends and then try to return to an earlier bedtime for the rest of the week, you may suffer the symptoms of jet lag. If you sleep late on Saturday and Sunday mornings, you're likely to have trouble falling asleep Sunday night. Our "travels" into and out of weekends produce the well-known Monday morning blahs, the bane of students and teachers, employees and employers. If you usually have trouble falling asleep, irregular schedules are likely to give you even more grief.

The change to or from daylight saving time may trigger jet lag symptoms, no small concern because more than two dozen countries around the world now spend several months a year on daylight saving time. In the United States, most states "spring forward" by an hour in April and "fall back" in October. Even so small a change may alter our biological rhythms enough to produce measurable effects. It takes a week or longer to adjust after both spring and fall time changes, according to work by Drs. Timothy Monk and Simon Folkard of the Perceptual and Cognitive Performance Unit at the University of Sussex, England. They found that, in the spring, people spontaneously awakened about fifteen minutes later than usual; in the fall, they awakened that much earlier. In the spring, people woke up feeling more tense and more drowsy than usual and felt they had slept poorly; in the fall, the opposite was true. Daylight traffic accidents were higher the week after the spring change than the week before.

In the spring, you lose an hour of sleep; in the fall, you gain one. Losing an hour of sleep disrupts your waking life more than adding an hour on. "But the disadvantages presented by the change to daylight saving time don't outweigh the benefits of having long summer evenings," notes Dr. Monk, now at the Institute of Chronobiology at the New York Hospital-Cornell Medical Center. You can make the changeover easier on yourself by acknowledging that you may have problems, particularly in the spring. "Don't schedule important appointments early in the day the first week after the change and don't start off with a sleep debt," he suggests.

HOW TO PREVENT JET LAG

If you could gradually alter in advance the time you go to bed and the time you get up by as many hours as the number of time zones you will cross, you'd be all set. But this goal is not feasible for most of us. Right up to the time we leave, we must go to work or school. We would find it inconvenient to eat at times different from our usual mealtimes. In fact, since many of us are gripped by a last-minute frenzy, trying to accomplish certain tasks before we go and at the same time to complete our packing and other trip preparations, we often sleep less than usual. Few of us manage to set off on a big trip relaxed.

If you're planning a trip, however, there are steps you can take before you leave home to move your inner clocks in the proper direction. Dr. Ehret has developed a program that takes account of the multiple cues for time-keeping in our daily lives. His plan is based on the following concepts:

- Food taken on an empty stomach acts as a starting gun for the new cycle. Meals taken at regular times help to synchronize our other body clocks. Further, eating is usually a social event, and social factors play an important role in setting human clocks.
- Protein foods seem to promote wakefulness, while carbohydrates appear to foster sleep.
- Coffee and tea contain chemicals known as methyl xanthines, one of which is caffeine. They seem to have an effect on the body's time-keeping system entirely separate from their effect as a stimulant, in that they seem to be able to speed up or slow down inner clocks, depending on the time of day at which they are consumed. Taken in the morning, they seem to be able to move the clock ahead (as in flying from west to east) and, in the evening, backward (as in flying from east to west).
- Exercising, working, watching television and engaging in

social activities help set body clocks. So can light and dark, which you can control to some extent by wearing an eye mask or turning lights on or off, for example.

Going from west to east: Here are Dr. Ehret's suggestions on how to prevent jet lag if you fly from west to east and leave in the evening, as you would on most flights from the United States to Europe:

Four days before takeoff, start the "World Travelers' Diet."

- Day 1: "Feast" with three full meals. Eat a high-protein breakfast and lunch, with high protein cereals, eggs, meat, chicken or fish. Eat a high-carbohydrate supper, such as pasta.
- Day 2: "Fast" by eating three small, low-calorie, low-carbohydrate meals consisting of salads, light soups, fruits and juices.
- Day 3: Repeat the menu for Day 1.
- Day 4 (day of departure): Repeat the menu for Day 2.

On the first three days, drink coffee or tea, if you wish, but only between three and five in the afternoon. On Day 4, follow the plan described below.

The feast/fast plan burns up the liver's store of glycogen, a storage form of glucose, the body's most important energy source, setting a scene that makes it easier for inner clocks to realign themselves, Dr. Ehret says. Those of us who normally sleep at night ordinarily have our peak supply of glycogen in the body after our largest meal, generally dinner; we burn it through the night and start off in the morning like a car with an empty gas tank. The aim of these dietary manipulations is to allow us to arrive in Europe with a "gas tank" at the same level as that of a European.

You can further shift yourself to European time by your behavior on the plane. Once aboard, turn your watch to the time of your destination. Skip the cocktails and cola drinks. Instead, drink one to three cups of coffee or tea, but don't use cream or sugar, because the sugar will build up glycogen, when your aim is to burn it.

Pass up the typical heavy supper; ask the stewardess to give it to you at breakfast time. Don't watch the movie or read; turn out

the light. Even though you've just consumed caffeine, try to ignore its stimulant effect, overlook the noise and get some sleep. If
you can't sleep, at least stay quietly in your seat. Just before
breakfast service begins, get up, walk down the aisles, stretch and
talk to other people. When they're having breakfast, enjoy your
supper, but forgo the coffee or tea. Once in Europe, do as the local
folks do. Eat meals on their time. Have a high-protein lunch and
a high-carbohydrate supper. Restrict consumption of caffeinated
beverages to three to five in the afternoon. Don't nap during the
day; go to bed early and get up the next morning at your usual
hour, but by local time.

Going from east to west: Going west, follow the same feast/fast
routine, with one difference. Drink caffeinated beverages early in
the day you depart but not after noon.

IT REALLY WORKS!

The United States Army's 82nd Airborne Division, based at Fort
Bragg, North Carolina, has successfully adapted this approach for
training exercises that involve transatlantic flights. "Our troops
usually parachute into an area to begin their day's mission," explains the division surgeon, Major Harold Timboe, M.D. "They
have to work a full day, so it's important that they are fresh when
they jump out."

"Operation Brightstar" brought 1,200 troops to Egypt in 1981.
They went to a "lock-in" area twenty-four hours before departure; there, they set their watches on destination time. The planes
left North Carolina in the afternoon. As Major Timboe reports,
"Once on board, we gave the troops a high-carbohydrate meal but
no caffeine. After supper, we turned out the lights, turned up the
heat, and said, 'No talking. Go to sleep.'

"The planes had been turned into flying bedrooms; instead of
seats, there were litters, so people could sleep comfortably. About
three hours before the jump, we turned on the lights, turned down
the heat, got everyone up and moving around and gave them a
high-protein meal with caffeine, if they wanted it.

"There's a seven hour time-zone difference, but they had breakfast and were ready to jump into Egypt at nine in the morning
Egyptian time and to stay on that time."

In 1982, "Operation Reforger" brought 1,800 troops from the United States to Germany to participate in annual North Atlantic Treaty Organization exercises; similar procedures were followed. The jet lag countermeasures were judged useful, and they are now under consideration for more wide-scale military adoption.

HOW TO COPE WITH TRAVEL FATIGUE

If you don't care to fiddle with your diet and you hate to pass up the movie on the plane, here are a few simple measures that may at least minimize jet lag and the travel fatigue that aggravates it. Most will also be helpful if you follow the travelers' diet.

- Drink plenty of water or fruit juices; airline cabins are low in humidity, a condition that may make the mucous membranes of your nose and throat dry and suppress urination. Carbonated drinks may make your abdomen uncomfortably distended, as may gas-forming foods, such as peas and beans.
- A drink of alcohol at a high altitude packs a more potent wallop than the same drink on the ground. Further, when you drink on an empty stomach, as is the usual routine on a plane, alcohol is absorbed faster and you'll feel its effects sooner.
- Shed your shoes, loosen your belt. Put a pillow in the small of your back.
- Don't spend the entire trip in your seat. Walk up and down the aisles. Bend and stretch. Jog in place. Roll your shoulders, rock your head; you'll find these practices relax your muscles and ease your joints.
- When you arrive after a trip east at night, don't go right to your hotel and drop into bed. Push through the day without sleeping. Spend as much time as possible out-of-doors with other people; exposure to daylight and social contacts seems to help inner clocks shift faster. Have meals on local time. Go to bed at nine or ten o'clock in the new time zone.
- When you fly west, go to bed as close to your usual bedtime as you can. If you go from the East Coast to the West Coast, the local time is three hours earlier; if your usual bedtime is midnight, turn off your lights at nine o'clock.
- For trips of only a few days, do as pilots who crisscross the

world do. Don't reset your watch. It will be easier to bow to the demands of your body time if you easily can tell what time it is.

When Work Hours Shift but You Don't

The effects of time changes may be merely a minor inconvenience to vacationing travelers who are bound by few obligations, but they often present a serious hardship to shift workers.

If you were to live for more than three weeks in a different time zone, your body clocks would re-establish their synchronous performance. In the new time zone, waking, sleeping and social activities would most likely have the same time relationship to each other as they do at home. But shift workers seldom have as long as three weeks on a single rotation. They must reset their clocks over and over again. Their time of work frequently changes by eight hours, a difference comparable to flying from Washington, D.C., to Moscow. Further, shift workers generally don't live completely in each new time zone; they may follow one schedule on workdays but a different one on weekends and days off, to be with their families and friends and to enjoy leisure activities.

The industrial revolution, followed by the invention of the electric light—just a century ago—made possible the twenty-four-hour workday. Steel furnaces roar constantly, giant computers hum, cake batter churns, letters careen through mail sorters, disc jockeys chatter, newspaper presses roll. People in many occupations may work at all hours of the day; these include doctors, nurses, airline pilots, air-traffic controllers, police, fire and rescue workers, military personnel, long-distance truck drivers, train engineers and diplomats.

To satisfy society's needs and whims, one in four American workers now puts in some or all of his hours during the evening or night. Eight-hour shifts are most common, but many people work longer or shorter shifts. Hospital interns may be on duty for thirty-six hours straight. United States Navy nuclear submarine crews may work for six hours and then have twelve hours of rest, which gives them an eighteen-hour "day."

While some employers offer "flextime," to allow workers to tailor their schedules to their personal preferences, shift workers often are out-of-sync with their families.

Consider this all-too-typical example: The father is a police officer. This month he's stuck on the night shift from midnight to eight in the morning, and there are times when he must work outside of his shift to make arrests or appear in court. The mother is a nurse. For two weeks, she'll be working evenings from three to eleven; then she'll rotate for two weeks to days, from seven to three, before switching back to evenings again. She races to get home before her husband leaves for work. Their nine-year-old son goes to elementary school from eight-thirty to three. His thirteen-year-old sister goes to an overcrowded junior high school that operates on split shifts; she attends classes from eleven to four.

It's rare for the entire family to sit down together to share a meal. The mother has weekends off, but her husband works for six days and is off two. The nine-year-old leaves for school before his father gets home. When he returns from school, Dad's asleep and gets angry if he makes too much noise. Mom isn't home after school to supervise the kids. The thirteen-year-old daughter assumes some household jobs; she makes dinner, for example. Family members seldom have a long conversation; their talk focuses for the most part on immediate and practical concerns, such as who needs money. In this family, shift work impinges dramatically on the quality of every family member's life.

But in other families where both parents work outside the home, particularly those with preschool children, shift work may permit parents to be more available to their children. In a study of households in the United States with children and with both parents employed full time, sociologists Harriet Presser, Ph.D., and Virginia Cain, of the University of Maryland, found that in one third of the households at least one spouse worked a shift other than a regular day shift. In one tenth of the households, both spouses worked completely different shifts and had no overlap in hours. A schedule of this kind reduces the time in the evening or night that both parents can be with their children but maximizes the time that at least one parent can be present in the home. Nonetheless, such a schedule may strain the marital relationship, since the couple has less time to be with each other.

HEALTH PROBLEMS ARE COMMON

Many shift workers say they seldom sleep as long as they wish. Shift workers average six to seven hours of sleep per twenty-four hours, compared with an average of seven to eight hours for other adults. They have more trouble falling asleep and staying asleep, too. This loss of sleep may, of course, make it harder to stay awake and to work effectively. Sleep loss reduces skill, increases reaction time, upsets judgment and interferes with complex decision-making.

Digestive complaints, such as diarrhea and irregularity, prompt the most frequent worker complaints. The problem is not psychosomatic; moving sleep and mealtimes around alters release of digestive enzymes and habits of elimination. "Pilots ending a long day want a light meal right before they go to sleep," notes veteran Delta Airlines pilot Captain Richard Stone. "When they get up, even if it's four in the afternoon, they still want breakfast," he says. "As a result, more than half of a pilot's meals may consist of breakfast foods. But breakfast isn't easy to find at all times of the day. We eat a lot of our meals in waffle houses," he adds.

Other common problems for shift workers include marital difficulties, emotional troubles, colds, ulcers, leg and foot cramps and other aches and pains. Stewardesses have a higher-than-usual rate of chronic menstrual-cycle disorders. Shift workers tend to use more sleeping pills and drink more alcohol, to combat trouble falling asleep. However, these substances often add to their problems, because they not only may be addictive but also may worsen work performance and disrupt normal patterns of sleep. Shift workers also tend to consume more caffeine and use more stimulants to help compensate for fatigue while they are awake. Older workers seem to have more problems than younger ones. Some studies suggest as many as one in five people who try shift work cannot tolerate it, but whether shift work has long-term effects on health and length of life is not yet known.

While some people prefer to work at night, few choose to have shifts that frequently change. Nights and weekends are viewed as the worst shifts. The weekend is particularly bothersome because someone working then often misses out on social activities; he feels doubly isolated. The most demanding shift schedule is a random one, where work time and time off have no relation to the schedule of the day before or the day after.

Labor wage agreements generally provide a financial premium for working shifts, and in fact, the extra pay is often the primary reason why a person is willing to take on shift work. In nursing, a field in which shift work is standard, the dropout rate today exceeds the entry rate; how shift work is arranged is a key factor in job satisfaction.

SHIFT WORK AFFECTS PUBLIC HEALTH

Many health and safety problems are felt keenly by the individual worker; shift work may pose dangers to the general public, too. The issue is the circadian rhythm concept of "subjective night," that is, the time during each twenty-four hours when a person is least able to work and most susceptible to fatigue and sleepiness. Remember that for people who customarily sleep at night, this time usually is from three to five in the morning. Even for people who generally sleep at other times but, like most shift workers, often follow a conventional schedule on days off, the night is the time of poorest performance. Meter readers jumble numbers on dials; train engineers are more likely to miss warning signals; truck drivers are more prone to accidents.

The series of mistakes that led to the breakdown of the reactor at the Three-Mile Island nuclear power plant in Pennsylvania in 1979 was made at four in the morning by men who had been rotating from days to nights to evenings every week. "The time course of this accident strongly suggests that poor circadian chronohygiene was a contributing factor," notes Dr. Ehret. According to the *Report of the President's Commission on the Accident at Three-Mile Island*, "Except for human failures, the major accident at Three-Mile Island would have been a minor incident."

Pilots frequently work on schedules that play havoc with their internal clocks. "A typical rotation lasts from three to five days," explains Captain Stone. "A person who sleeps at night while he's off duty might find himself flying nights. Even worse, a pilot might end up with very short or very long 'days.' With a twenty-three-hour layover, for example, a pilot wants to sleep after coming off duty and he ought to sleep again before going back on duty; that, however, is hard to do."

The National Aeronautics and Space Administration (NASA) is exploring the potential hazard of allowing a pilot to take the controls of a plane at the time he ordinarily would be sleeping. Curtis Graeber, Ph.D., of the NASA Ames Research Center, Moffett Field, California, observes that senior pilots, who get first choice of schedules, frequently pick those that are the most attractive because of premiums, such as better vacation allowances, but also are the most disruptive. "The older pilots experience the most sleep loss and, at the same time, are most susceptible to its effects," he notes.

The Air Lines Pilots Association has raised the question of whether flying at the "wrong" time of the pilot's biological day may have have contributed to several tragedies, among them the 5:30 A.M. crash of a Western Airlines plane in Mexico City in 1980, in which the pilot landed on runway 23-left instead of 23-right, for which he had been cleared. That crash killed seventy-nine people. The pilot of an Eastern Airlines plane that went down in North Carolina in 1974 had had more than a twelve-hour reversal in his sleep/wake schedule during the days preceding the crash.

The National Transportation Safety Board, in investigating aircraft accidents, has always evaluated the prior schedules of work and rest of the crew and the air-traffic controllers; but recently, it has also begun to look more systematically at circadian factors, such as the amount and timing of sleep of the people involved, the time of day that the accident occurred, the trip direction and time zone changes.

Pilot flight-time limitations and minimum rest requirements in the United States are regulated by the Federal Aviation Administration. Current rules, in effect for more than thirty years, do not take circadian rhythms into account. They compute rest time solely on the basis of accumulated flight time, a practice that results in a random shift of hours of work and hours off from one day to the next.

The Air Line Pilots Association, along with The Center for the Design of Industrial Schedules, a nonprofit organization in Boston, Massachusetts, whose members include the world's experts on sleep/wake schedules and biological rhythms, feels that the pilot's "subjective night" also should be taken into account. Britain, Germany and the Scandinavian countries, unlike the United States, have regulations that do take biological clocks into consideration in drawing up flight schedules.

BETTER CONDITIONS FOR SHIFT WORK

Research is under way to identify people who can best handle shift work, an important task since increasing numbers of us are rotating the hours we work. Night people, or owls, seem to be better at shift work than morning people, or larks. People who can sleep at unusual times, then wake up easily and "snap to" fully, seem better at it than those who cannot. Outgoing people seem to have less difficulty than introverts. People whose normal daily temperature has a narrow range between up and down seem to have the fewest problems. However, "the primary factor for successful adjustment to work at odd times of day," asserts Paul Naitoh, M.D., of the Naval Health Research Center, San Diego, is "the individual's commitment to live and work in the world of night work and shift work."

In the future, some workers, along with their entire families, may choose to work and live permanently in communities that run on time schedules different from those of the outside world. Their children might think it is natural to go to school at midnight and be tucked into bed at four in the afternoon. Stores would be open, prime-time shows would be on television and guests would come to dinner just as they do now, but at times different from those in other areas.

Until this new world comes about, scientists are trying to devise schedules for shift work that would place the least burden on workers. "Permanent" shifts would still be most desirable. But few employers offer them, and most workers don't want them, since they would keep the worker perpetually out-of-sync with the rest of the world. Moreover, shift workers would still have to contend with different schedules on weekends or days off.

Fortunately, the application of circadian principles to the design of shift-work schedules is beginning to have a major impact in the workplace. Workers at the Great Salt Lake Minerals and Chemicals Corporation, Odgen, Utah, recently compared different directions and lengths of rotation. They found that rotations that go from days to evenings to nights—similar to a westward flight—were easier than the reverse. Charles Czeisler, M.D., Ph.D., of the Center for Design of Industrial Schedules, Boston, and his colleagues, found that when rotations followed this direction and changed every three weeks, as compared with every week, personnel turnover dropped and productivity not only increased immediately, but also was higher months later. The workers' preference for rotations in a clockwise direction reflects the inborn tendency to function on a day that is longer than twenty-four hours.

While consensus grows on the desirability of the clockwise direction for work rotations, the optimal speed of rotation is still under debate. Some researchers believe that rapidly rotating shifts, changing every one to four days, are better, because temperature rhythms don't shift that fast; hence, workers remain anchored to the schedule of people who work only during the day. Such schedules are more popular in Europe than in the United States. Other scientists think that if people spend more than seven days on a fixed shift, they have time to adapt to a new sleep/wake schedule. Additional studies, such as the one at the Utah chemical plant, may provide the answer within the next few years.

WAYS TO COPE WITH SHIFT WORK

If you are a shift worker, try these suggestions:

- Sleep at the same time each day. It's not necessary to sleep at night, although you may find it's quieter then. Most people seem to follow a routine in which the "day" moves from work to leisure to sleep. Most of us, in fact, would find it hard to fall asleep immediately after work, unless our work is less demanding than our leisure pursuits. Someone who works as a waiter in order to concentrate on writing plays, for example, might well reverse the traditional pattern.
- If you take naps, the time you take them makes a difference. See Chapter 3, "How Much Sleep Do We Need?"

- When you sleep, see that your bedroom is as dark and sound-proof as possible. A fan or air conditioner can help mask outside noises.
- Eat the same type of meal at the same time each day. Don't snack constantly at work.
- Use the "World Travelers' Diet" (discussed earlier in this chapter) in anticipation of a rotation to make your adjustment easier.
- Limit the amount of coffee, tea and cola you drink. Caffeine can make it harder to fall asleep and stay asleep.
- Don't use alcohol to make it easier to fall asleep. It's likely to make you wake up more often during the night.
- Before you turn to sleeping pills, read Chapter 8, "Sleeping Pills and Other Drugs for Insomnia," and Chapter 15, "How to Get a Better Night's Sleep."
- If you have digestive-tract disorders or metabolic problems such as diabetes, recognize that shift work may have an adverse effect on your health. If you can, choose a job with regular hours.

Faulty Clocks and a Complaint of Insomnia

Many of us have trouble falling asleep at night. But some of us who don't fall asleep until the middle of the night could slumber peacefully for as long as we would like and wake up feeling fine if we were not dragged out of bed by the demands of our children or the need to get to work or school. We complain of "insomnia." But it's not really our sleep that's disturbed; it's the *timing* of our sleep.

If we force ourselves to get up after only three or four hours of sleep, of course we're likely to be sleepy during the day. Many people "catch up" on lost sleep on weekends or days off, thus making it even harder to get to sleep the following night. Some try sleeping pills or alcohol, both of which can disrupt sleep. If you have trouble falling asleep, you need to reset your inner clock to get it back in line with the rest of the world.

Elaine, a thirty-four-year-old psychotherapist, sought help at a sleep disorders center. She said she had stayed up late since child-hood and remembers that her mother had to force her to get up in the morning. She reported that now she usually went to bed around three in the morning but often couldn't fall asleep for an hour or more. Since she was sluggish if she got up before noon, and sometimes even fell asleep during morning therapy sessions, she started scheduling patients between four and nine, so that she could sleep until one in the afternoon.

A single night in the sleep laboratory showed that she slept normally for 7.5 hours but did not start to sleep until just before dawn. Like other people with this complaint, Elaine was asked to keep a careful record of her sleep/wake schedule for four weeks and to refrain from using sleeping medications and alco-hol. The diary confirmed her pattern, which the doctors refer to as delayed sleep phase syndrome. They prescribed chronoth-erapy (literally, "time therapy") to help Elaine fall asleep at an earlier hour.

Chronotherapy is based on the fact that our inner clocks have a natural period of twenty-five hours. While the natural tendency to drift later and later around the clock by about an hour a day seems to be more pronounced in people with the delayed sleep phase syndrome, these people do not ordinarily keep moving completely around the clock. They could not do so and still live in society. For people who are not shift workers, a bedtime of, say, ten in the morning, is usually not compatible with holding a job and having a family life. By dint of forcing themselves to get up at a "normal" time, people with this problem maintain their tena-cious hold on a middle-of-the-night bedtime. During treatment, however, their bedtime is progressively delayed around the clock until a more suitable bedtime is reached.

During chronotherapy, they are usually asked to live on a twenty-seven-hour day, the upper end of the range of day lengths that most people can manage. If you had been falling asleep at 3 A.M., for example, bedtime the first day would be at 6 A.M. You would get your usual amount of sleep and would be instructed to remain in bed for seven to eight hours. The next day, bedtime would be at 9 A.M.; the third day, at noon; until, after six days, you would reach midnight, which would now become your regular bedtime.

Maintaining the new schedule requires self-discipline, with careful attention to keeping regular bedtimes. It has been done successfully in dozens of cases, and most patients find it as easy (or as difficult) to stay on the new schedule as on their old one.

Treatment often is carried out in a sleep laboratory. Some centers use a special time-isolation suite. Since it's hard to follow the rigid schedule in a world with ringing telephones and family members watching television, most people need a "helper" to protect their sleep time, see that they get the appropriate meals at the proper times and provide encouragement. Elaine, however, lived alone, and she brought it off by herself, checking in with the sleep center staff each day.

If you think you may have the delayed sleep phase syndrome, see a sleep specialist before you attempt chronotherapy on yourself.

Too Early to Bed, Too Early to Rise

Some people have the opposite problem. If you're among them, you probably can't stay awake past nine at night and awaken well before dawn. Your sleepiness at parties is legendary and it is probably a major inconvenience to you. In the early morning, it's frustrating to lie in bed while everyone else is sleeping. Doctors call this problem advanced sleep phase syndrome. It's not as common a complaint as the syndrome of delay, but we do seem more susceptible to it as we grow older. "Early to bed, early to rise" tends to be viewed as a virtue, not something to see the doctor about, but if you feel it is interfering with your activities, you can try to alter it.

What's the best remedy? Trying to go backward around the clock is difficult; humans have a built-in tendency to have longer, not shorter days. Most of us simply can't fall asleep early. You may, however, be able to force yourself to stay up later. Postpone bedtime for just fifteen minutes, and hold to the later schedule for a week at a time. Even if at first you don't sleep later in the morning, with luck, you eventually will. Again, once you achieve your desired bedtime, it's important to keep regular hours.

Living on Twenty-five-Hour Days

Every day, most of us disobey our natural proclivity for a longer day and reset our inner clocks to conform to the twenty-four-hour real world. Not all of us make this adjustment smoothly. Some of us end up with unusual bedtimes, as in the delayed sleep phase syndrome. But some of us, it seems, can't maintain regular bedtimes at all.

Jim Stevenson, now in his mid-thirties, has been blind from birth. His days are precisely 24.9 hours long. If he were living in a cave, his "free-running" schedule would be viewed as perfectly normal. But since he lives in the real world, in Palo Alto, California, there are only a few days out of every month when he goes to bed comfortably and gets up in step with most other people. The rest of the time he either has a hard time sleeping at night or is sleepy during the day.

"My natural desire would be to go to bed fifty minutes later every day," he explains. "I would wake up eight or nine hours later without an alarm. Of course, I couldn't do that and still hold a job. I try to go to sleep at the same time every night, and I rely heavily on my alarm clock."

After Stevenson's lifelong problem was documented during a lengthy hospital stay by Laughton Miles, M.D., and his colleagues at Stanford University, the researchers tried to lock him into a normal schedule. He went to bed at eleven and was awakened at seven. He observed strict times for meals and other activities and did not nap. Nonetheless, his nighttime sleep became progressively more disrupted and his days were increasingly invaded by sleepiness.

A biostatistician and experimental psychologist who holds a Ph.D. from Stanford University, Stevenson has tried numerous measures to stabilize his life. These include cold showers, loud music and exercise in the morning, dietary manipulations with proteins, carbohydrates and caffeine, and an "electrosleep" machine that allegedly stimulated the sleep centers in the brain. All such efforts have been unsuccessful.

Stevenson manages his weekday activities with the aid of medication. "If I have trouble falling asleep, I take a short-acting sleeping pill; if the trouble is in the middle of the night, I take a longer-acting one," he explains. "Sometimes I need stimulants to keep awake during the day, although I find it easier to fight sleepiness if I've gotten at least a little sleep the night before. On weekends and vacations, I do nap and I try not to use drugs." Once a month he plots the coming month's schedule. That allows him, for example, to arrange in advance an important meeting at work or make a dinner date without worrying that he'll fall asleep at an inopportune moment. His employer, fortunately, is tolerant of his problem.

"Since one of the major manifestations of a circadian rhythm abnormality is a complaint about sleeping and waking, you'd expect to hear this complaint more often from blind people, and indeed we do," Dr. Miles comments. Although it's generally held that social cues are the most powerful synchronizer for humans, it has not been documented that social cues are sufficient in the absence of light/dark cues.

When Dr. Miles and his Stanford colleagues surveyed more than two hundred people with varying degrees of blindness, they found, to their astonishment, that nine out of ten reported sleep/ wake disturbances. The majority said they were excessively sleepy during the day and had trouble falling asleep or staying asleep at night. Of course, not every blind person has trouble maintaining a twenty-four-hour rhythm and the problem is not limited to the blind. Indeed, several fully sighted people who suffer from it have now been identified. Older people who spend most of the time indoors or people of any age who live isolated lives seem particularly susceptible. Notes Dr. Miles, "It's not generally appreciated that insomnia or excessive fatigue that comes and goes a couple of weeks a month may be symptomatic of a rhythm disorder. Such problems may be far more common than has previously been thought."

If you have such periodic problems, try to document your pattern by keeping a sleep/wake diary. (You'll find instructions and a sample diary at the back of this book.) Most people with such problems feel better if they have regular hours to go to bed, get up, eat, exercise and pursue other activities.

Body Time in Health and Disease

The realization that temperature, blood pressure, heart rate, breathing and other aspects of bodily functioning follow predictable and often interrelated circadian cycles is helping to refine the diagnosis and improve the treatment of illnesses as diverse as arthritis, asthma and cancer. By monitoring cycles of cell division, for example, cancer specialists can time the use of anticancer drugs in order to cause the most harm to cancer cells and the least harm to normal cells.

Studies of jet lag have direct application to the treatment of depression. Having observed that the changes in the organization of sleep stages in people who skip rapidly through time zones are similar to those of people with manic-depressive illness, scientists have tried treating their depressed patients by advancing their sleep time—that is, by inducing a state like the jet lag after an eastward flight. Although most people would find this experience discomforting, it switches some people out of their depression, if only temporarily, suggesting that depression represents, at least in part, a disorder of the body's internal clocks. (For more on inner clocks in depression, see Chapter 14, "Troubled Minds/Troubled Sleep.")

Better treatments for depression are also emerging from studies of the effects of the light/dark cycle in humans. A sixty-three-year-old scientist had documented his seasonal mood changes for over thirty years. He regularly suffered depression in the fall and winter but improved dramatically beginning in January. Researchers at the National Institute of Mental Health began lengthening his day in the fall, just when days were shortening, with six hours of exposure to bright lights. The procedure made spring come early for him, and in four days, he switched out of his depression. He went home, did not have a relapse, and reported that for the first time in many years he had a pleasant Christmas.

For all of us, recognition of the inexorable ticking of the inner clocks offers guidelines for structuring our everyday lives and prompts new respect for the consequences of bending time out of joint.

12

THINGS THAT GO BUMP IN THE NIGHT

From ghoulies and ghosties
and long-leggety beasties
And things that go bump in the night,
Good Lord, deliver us!

—Scottish prayer

On the dark continent of the night, some sleepers babble. Others wail and moan. Some rise from their beds and wander about their homes. One tumbles down steps; another walks through a plate-glass door. A father whacks with a flashlight a "burglar" who turns out to be his own four-year-old daughter. Such events violate our notion of sleep as a peaceful and quiet state.

Once, such behavior was thought to be the acting-out of dreams. Now, it is recognized that during REM (rapid eye movement) sleep, when most vivid dreams occur, our bodies are paralyzed. Sleepwalking and attacks of sleep terrors, experiences that endlessly capture popular imagination, most often occur during the deepest stages of nondreaming (NREM) sleep. At such times, the sleeper starts to awaken but, for some unknown reason, goes only part of the way. No one knows what misfiring in the brain triggers waking at the wrong time or why the sleeper rouses imperfectly. Rather than simply entering a lighter stage of sleep, the person's brain straddles sleep and wakefulness, making his body awkward and his mind befogged. Indeed, brain-wave recordings made at such times show a mix of the alpha waves characteristic of relaxed wakefulness and the delta waves of deep sleep. It's left to witnesses to record the events of the night, for the sleeper rarely wakes long enough to set memory in motion.

Sleeptalking, bed-wetting and tooth-grinding also occur during partial arousal from sleep. In the transition to and from light sleep and wakefulness, some of us occasionally find ourselves unable to move, a sensation described as sleep paralysis. In the process of falling asleep, children sometimes bang their heads repetitively against headboard or wall; some adults drift off while rhythmically rocking their bodies.

These curious behaviors occur more often in children than in adults. A still-immature central nervous system may favor their appearance in people who are genetically predisposed to them. Such behavior frequently runs in families, affecting boys more often than girls, adult men more often than women. Several of these problems seem to share a common genetic background. Sleepwalkers are more likely than others to have sleep terror attacks and trouble staying dry at night, for example.

If your child has these problems, you may be relieved to know that "tincture of time" usually is the only treatment needed. Most of these behaviors gradually diminish and disappear by adolescence. Of course, there are ways to make it easier for your child to cope and to avoid embarrassment, as well as ways to help the rest of the family sleep more easily. We offer some guidelines in this chapter, as well as in Chapter 5, "The Growing Years."

When sleepwalking, terror attacks, bed-wetting or other nighttime behaviors that are perceived as problems continue into adulthood or start then, medical evaluation is definitely indicated. While "cures" aren't always possible, ways to minimize the disruptive effects on both the person involved and the rest of the family are discussed here.

Sleepwalking

The sleeper sits up abruptly. His facial expression is blank. He opens his eyes, which appear glassy, but his gaze is undirected. After fifteen to thirty seconds, he sinks back down on the bed. Such behavior disturbs no one and is usually observed by someone else only by chance. This is "sleepwalking," even though the typical episode doesn't actually involve walking.

Sometimes, however, the child or adult gets out of bed. Although the sleepwalker is usually clumsy and poorly coordinated, he may dress, open doors, use the bathroom, eat and perform other simple, often repetitive acts, such as opening and closing a drawer or picking at a blanket. His eyes may be open but his vision is unfocused. He sees well enough to avoid many objects in his path, including the often-tried pan of water in the doorway, but it's only a myth that sleepwalkers can make their way up ladders, across rooftops and through traffic-filled streets unscathed.

Violence toward other people, though we may hear of sensational incidents, actually is rare. Far more frequent are the injuries sleepwalkers themselves suffer: shins bruised on coffee tables, heads bumped on doors, fingers smashed in drawers and bones broken by falls.

The sleepwalker may moan or grunt. If asked a question, he may murmur a brief, usually garbled reply. Occasionally, he speaks a word or two spontaneously.

When people live in close proximity to one another—in college dormitories or at summer camps, for example—the odds are higher that sleepwalking will be witnessed. Judy recalls a camp experience: "When the shouting woke me, I saw Mary Ann, our counselor, sitting up in bed. She kept saying, 'I'm going to do it.' Finally, she got up, walked across the cabin and ripped down the window screen. She said, 'There, I did it.' Then she went back to bed. In the morning she claimed she didn't remember a thing."

Sleepwalking typically occurs during the first three hours of sleep; the person arouses from stage 3-4. Most sleepwalking episodes last just a few minutes but some continue for over thirty minutes. Sleepwalking more than once a night is rare. However, some people walk in their sleep nearly every night, a practice that is understandably disruptive to the rest of the family.

Children who are prone to walk in their sleep, as well as those who are not, can on occasion be provoked to do so if they are made to stand up during deep sleep. Parents sometimes put this phenomenon to good use by walking a still-sleeping child to the bathroom or getting a child who's fallen asleep on a car trip into his own bed without fuss.

Children who are extremely tired or who have recently had less sleep than usual are more likely to walk in their sleep. Sleepwalking sometimes starts after a high fever.

Adults who sleepwalk often report that the episodes began just after some major life stress, such as being fired or getting divorced. Shakespeare gave us the classic portrait of extreme provocation in Lady Macbeth. When under stress, adults who sleepwalk seem to do so more often. Such people commonly feel frustrated and get angry when things don't work out, according to Anthony Kales, M.D., and his colleagues at the Pennsylvania State University College of Medicine. Their anger is outwardly directed, rather than self-directed, as in people who become depressed. While awake, and if awakened while sleepwalking, they may become overly talkative, disoriented and panicky. They act in their sleep as they act while awake.

If you find someone sleepwalking, the best approach is to gently steer him back to bed, without trying to wake him. Indeed, a sleepwalker usually resists efforts to awaken him and, if aroused, will be confused and disoriented. If you must awaken him, say his name over and over; don't slap or shake him or throw cold water on his face. If left alone, a sleepwalker may fall back asleep on a couch or on the floor, mystified the next morning about how he got there. Often, even without help, he makes his way back to his own bed.

You need to protect a sleepwalker from injury. To make your home safer, install protective gates on stairways and across the doorway to a sleepwalker's bedroom. (These will discourage sleepwalking but not pose a hazard if a fire starts and a fast exit is necessary.) Hide knives and put away the car keys. Don't leave windows wide open at night. Lock doors to balconies. If you are a sleepwalker, ask someone else to watch out for you, and agree in advance on what should be done.

Sleepwalking that starts before the age of ten is usually outgrown by the age of fifteen; children who sleepwalk generally aren't given medical treatment. An estimated 15 percent of all children sleepwalk at least once. One to 6 percent of all adults are sleepwalkers.

Because fatigue seems to increase attacks, both children and adults are encouraged to keep regular hours. Afternoon naps are often advised; they may decrease the amount of stage 3-4 sleep at night and, hence, may further reduce the likelihood of sleepwalking. Psychotherapy may help adults who sleepwalk to manage their waking lives better. In some cases, sleepwalkers benefit from hypnosis, where they learn that placing their feet on the floor is the cue to wake up.

The use of drugs such as imipramine, diazepam or flurazepam is usually reserved for people who are frequent sleepwalkers and who suffer injuries despite precautions: someone who smashed his hand through a glass door and another person who walked into the embers of the family fireplace. The drugs seem to reduce the number of times a person shifts from one stage of sleep to another, making arousals less likely.

Some elderly people wander about the house at night in a dazed state often believed to be sleepwalking. They are not truly sleepwalking. They are awake, but disoriented and most often suffer from organic brain deterioration. But whatever the cause of nighttime activity, the sleepwalker needs to be protected from harm.

Sleep Terrors

An hour or so after four-year-old Timmy goes to sleep, his hysterical screams pierce the air. His mother relates, "My husband or I, or sometimes both of us, run to his room. I'll never get used to it; those shrieks still make my heart pound. We usually find Timmy, sitting up in bed, obviously frightened and agitated. His eyes will be wide open, although he doesn't seem to see us, and he'll be sweating and breathing hard.

"He sometimes looks as if he's in pain but he pushes us away if we try to comfort or wake him. It usually takes five or ten minutes before he calms down. Then, suddenly, he sinks back into sleep. In the morning, he never remembers any part of what went on."

These attacks are known as sleep terrors. While just what causes them remains unknown, scientists have learned that sleep terrors occur during a partial awakening from deep sleep. In this respect they are different from nightmares, which occur during REM sleep, the period in which most vivid dreams take place. When a child or adult awakens from a sleep terror attack, he usually can recall only a nameless feeling of dread. Bob reports, "Sometimes, I have the sense I am being smothered but can't fight back. Other times I feel as if I am choking to death." By contrast, someone who awakens from a nightmare, even though distraught, usually can recount a vivid and frightening story, often involving catastrophes and violence. In both terror attacks and nightmares, the sudden awakening causes the heart to race, a phenomenon that triggers feelings of intense anxiety. (For more on nightmares, turn to Chapter 4, "The Stuff of Dreams.")

Sleep terrors are more common in children than in adults. Because children have lengthy periods of stage 3-4 sleep in the first third of the night, they may be particularly vulnerable to terror attacks. Indeed, such attacks usually ebb by adolescence, paralleling the normal decline in stage 3-4 sleep. Sometimes sleep terrors reappear or show up for the first time in people in their twenties and thirties, although seldom in anyone older.

Children with sleep terrors do not as a rule have a personality disturbance, although sometimes terror attacks in children can be related to stress. One sleep researcher reports, "My own son had sleep terror attacks nearly every night for about six months when he was three. I could think of lots of possible reasons: His grandfather had just died; his brother had just been born, and as a result, he'd been moved to a different room. Nonetheless, it certainly was frustrating to stand there as a supposed expert in these things, unable to do anything but wring my hands."

Unlike children, adults with sleep terrors are more likely to have psychological problems than are adults who simply sleepwalk. Frequently, they have severe chronic anxiety. Unlike sleepwalkers, who seem to respond to stress with outwardly directed action —both awake and asleep—people who suffer sleep terrors characteristically react with fear and apprehension, Dr. Kales and his colleagues at Pennsylvania State University found.

Terror attacks that occur several times a week put considerable stress on other members of the family. Children may be too embarrassed to sleep at a friend's house or go to summer camp. In a college dormitory or in the military service, a person with sleep terrors is likely to be the butt of jokes.

Sleep terrors, like sleepwalking, can sometimes be reduced if a child or adult keeps regular hours to avoid fatigue and takes a late-afternoon nap to decrease the amount of stage 3-4 sleep he gets at night. In severe cases, the doctor may prescribe drugs such as diazepam, imipramine or flurazepam, which seem to reduce the number of shifts from one stage of sleep to another, making arousals less likely.

Don't try to awaken someone gripped by a sleep terror. Do stay nearby to keep him from hurting himself. As the attack subsides, a comforting hug may help ease him back to sleep. If you interrupt the attack, you may find the person becomes even more terrified and confused. If you get him out of bed and stand him up, you even may trigger sleepwalking. In such cases, the sleepwalking is likely to be more vigorous and frantic than ordinary sleepwalking; during a sleep terror attack a person may bolt out of bed and dash around frightened and confused. One boy even jumped out of a second-story window.

Sleepwalking and sleep terrors may be inherited together, Dr. Kale and his colleagues say. They suggest that sleepwalking, with its mild confusion, represents a more moderate state than the intense, anxiety-filled sleep terror. Someone may develop both disorders at the same time or at different times; however, sleepwalking is more common. Close relatives of people who both sleepwalk and have terror attacks are more likely to have these problems than the rest of the population.

Some people first have terror attacks after a head injury or high fever. A child who seems to be having sleep terrors may, in fact, be suffering from ear pain or stomach upsets. In rare cases, seizures that occur during sleep may mimic sleepwalking or terror attacks. That's why frequent attacks call for a visit to the doctor.

Sleeptalking

Contrary to myth, sleeptalkers rarely blurt out corporate secrets or confessions of love affairs. "I've never heard anyone say anything in his sleep that he would be embarrassed to say while awake," reports Allan Rechtschaffen, Ph.D., director of the Sleep Research Laboratory of the University of Chicago.

Sleeptalking often is slurred or garbled. Even when articulate, it usually is brief and has little meaning to the listener; much sleeptalking sounds like fragments of ordinary conversation or words a person might say to himself when alone. Samples of sleeptalking collected in the laboratory include "OK," "Wow!," "That was that" and "Something's wrong." Occasionally, sleep-talking resembles one side of a telephone conversation, as the sleeper speaks, pauses and speaks again.

Hypnotic suggestion, flashing lights and other measures have stimulated some people to speak up more often during sleep, but researchers have not yet been able to elicit live "on-the-spot" reports of dreams as they progress. When asked a question, most people who are truly asleep, not merely in the transition between wakefulness and sleep, do not reply.

People may be in any stage of sleep when they start talking. Sleepers awakened after talking in REM sleep, the state when most vivid dreams occur, are more likely to report dreams related to what they said than people awakened after talking in NREM sleep.

When someone having a sleep terror shrieks, "It's after me," the assertion may actually come on waking. You might feel that way, too, if you were to wake up with your heart racing, your breathing rapid and your body dripping with sweat.

Sleepwalkers sometimes respond to queries, although not always coherently. They may also talk spontaneously, usually just a word or two, but they rarely carry on a true conversation. Lady Macbeth's soliloquy is marvelous theater but not accurate science.

Sleeptalking is more common in children than adults, but most of us probably engage in this harmless behavior now and then. It is not regarded as a problem that requires treatment.

Tooth-Grinding (Bruxism)

Millions of sleepers, an estimated one in seven people, chomp and gnash their way through the night, a habit known as bruxism. Few of us realize that we are grinding our teeth during sleep, for we seldom awaken because of it. Complaints of disturbed sleep are more likely to come from members of our families, who report that the usual high-pitched grating and clicking noises can be heard several rooms away. A tendency to have this problem seems to be inherited.

If you are an extreme bruxist, as is the case for about one or two out of every one hundred people, you probably awaken in the morning with aching jaws. Some people have pains that radiate up into the face and even headaches, usually just on one side of the head. Occasionally, people who seek help because they are sleeping poorly or are sleepy in the daytime are discovered to be bruxists. In such people, grinding is so furious it rouses them repeatedly during the night, yet they remain unaware of the trigger for these awakenings.

Bruxism usually occurs during the lighter stages of sleep and during transitions from one stage to another, but when it occurs during REM sleep, it may have more serious consequences; in REM sleep, bite reflexes that ordinarily keep upper and lower teeth from touching each other, and, hence, help protect teeth, are suppressed.

A dentist can easily spot signs of bruxism. The biting surfaces of the teeth show excessive wear and teeth are often chipped. After many years, teeth actually may be ground down to the gum line. They may become loose, and there may be damage to the bone and soft-tissue supporting structures.

Some people who grind their teeth at night are jaw-clenchers during the day. Others grind their teeth even while awake, although seldom noisily. When under stress, some people grind their teeth, just as others develop ulcers, headaches or insomnia. Some people, predictably, grind more on Sunday nights, anticipating the work week. Many grind less on vacations.

The specific life-events that trigger tooth-grinding in particular individuals can be identified with the aid of a portable monitor worn around the clock. The device, developed at the University of Texas Health Science Center by behavioral psychologist John Rugh, Ph.D., and his colleagues, uses a recorder about the size of a deck of cards and three electrodes taped over the jaw muscle to tell whether a person has excessive muscle tension and under what circumstances it occurs.

The Texas researchers demonstrated that stress can increase tooth-grinding. The night after watching a scary movie (one of which was *Jaws*), people who habitually ground their teeth while asleep did it more often.

If you grind your teeth, you may benefit from learning stress-management aids such as relaxation skills. Some people are helped by short-term biofeedback, which involves wearing to bed a device that emits a tone loud enough to wake you when grinding starts; after a while, you may be able to anticipate the tone by not grinding your teeth as often.

For a few bruxists, stress is not a factor. Instead, a central nervous system abnormality seems to be involved. These people grind their teeth during deep sleep and do not benefit from stress-management techniques. Debate continues on the role of allergies that trigger inner-ear swelling, possibly prompting a person to "chew" during sleep in order to open the eustachian tube, much as chewing gum while on a descending airplane relieves pressure.

Dental problems sometimes worsen tooth-grinding. An overbite, in which upper teeth overhang lower teeth, may trigger frequent side-to-side movements of the lower jaw; here, orthodontic adjustment may lead to relief.

Although tooth-grinding seldom can be eliminated entirely, its damage can often be minimized by wearing a custom-fitted acrylic bite plate over upper or lower teeth during sleep. This appliance keeps the biting surfaces of the teeth from coming together and often forestalls jaw clenching. The device may seem annoying at first, but children as well as adults generally learn to adapt to it within just a few nights.

Head-Banging and Body-Rocking

Parents may notice rhythmic to-and-fro head-rocking or body-rocking in infants and toddlers just as they are falling asleep. Young children sometimes bang against the side of the crib or a headboard or wall, but they almost never bang hard enough to hurt themselves.

A child who is vigorously banging his head or who is injuring himself should, of course, be taken to the doctor. Head-banging sometimes occurs as a result of emotional stress or in association with epileptic seizures. It's also more common in children of below-normal intelligence. For these youngsters, helmets may be necessary and sedative drugs sometimes provide relief.

In most children, the rocking is simply a habit, not a disorder. It diminishes with age. However, some adults continue to rock their feet or head as they drift off to sleep.

Sleep Paralysis

Perhaps you've experienced the sensation—while awakening or falling asleep—of not being able to move. You discover that your body is paralyzed. Although you may try to call out, the sound remains locked in your throat. Meanwhile, your mind is clamoring to know what's going on.

Seconds, or possibly one or two minutes, pass; perhaps someone calls your name or touches you. Suddenly, the spell of this sleep paralysis is broken. You feel like the Sleeping Beauty, roused from her hundred years' sleep by the kiss of a prince.

About one in twenty of us is occasionally lassoed by sleep paralysis. For most of us, it is nothing to worry about. The sensation may have been the basis for Jonathan Swift's description of Gulliver in the land of the Lilliputians, awakening to find himself secured by so many bonds that he could not move.

During sleep paralysis your body is asleep, although your mind is not. The paralysis is the same loss of muscle tone that occurs during normal REM sleep. Ordinarily, you're not aware of it because you have been asleep for some time before it starts. Sometimes, particularly if you have been getting too little sleep, you fall into REM sleep sooner than usual, early enough in sleep so that you become aware of your inability to move.

Most often, however, sleep paralysis occurs in the morning if you happen to awaken abruptly from REM sleep. If the paralysis is accompanied by fragments of a dream, particularly images of being chased or attacked, you may, understandably, be terrified. Some people feel, rarely correctly, that they are struggling to breathe.

Even when you are otherwise immobilized by sleep paralysis, you can move your eyes, just as in REM sleep. Looking up and down and side to side rapidly is a Houdini-like trick for loosening the straitjacket ties. If you have frequent episodes of sleep paralysis, enlist the cooperation of your bed partner or another member of the family who can be especially attentive to rousing you in the morning.

People—most often teenage boys—whose bouts of paralysis after sleep are triggered by high-carbohydrate meals and alcohol may have an inherited disorder called periodic paralysis, which involves the way the body handles potassium, a chemical essential for muscle function. In rare cases, thyroid disease may produce a similar disorder. These morning muscle-weakness attacks are not over suddenly; rather, it may be an hour or two before strength has returned to normal. If you have such symptoms, see your doctor.

If you also suffer sudden episodes of muscle weakness during the day, you need to see the doctor; muscle weakness and sleep paralysis are both associated with a specific sleep disorder, narcolepsy. (For more information on narcolepsy, see Chapter 10, "Too Sleepy People.")

Summing Up

Illuminating these shadow states makes them both less and more mysterious. As disorders of incomplete arousal, they tell us that the paths connecting sleep and wakefulness are labyrinthine. At the same time, their appearance underscores a miracle most of us take for granted: No matter what difficulties we may have falling asleep, we clamber back up to wakefulness with relative ease, day after day, year after year.

13

IN SICKNESS AND HEALTH

Some illnesses become worse during sleep and a few appear only at this time, facts that challenge the popular belief that "sleep restores." From a cold to a sunburn to the chest pain of angina, "any illness or discomfort that bothers you while you are awake probably will disturb your sleep as well," notes Robert L. Williams, M.D., chairman of psychiatry at the Baylor College of Medicine, Houston, Texas, and co-director of its Sleep Disorders and Research Center.

Pregnancy, menstruation and puberty may affect sleep. Better ways to evaluate certain waking disorders have come from sleep studies. Clues to the cause of impotence, for example, may be derived by monitoring penile erections, which normally occur in males of all ages during REM (rapid eye movement) sleep. Similarly, the appearance of hot flashes during sleep in menopausal women confirms that this sensation is not, as once was thought, "all in the mind."

In this chapter, we will look at common illnesses and show you some of the ways in which your health affects your sleep and your sleep affects your health.

Headaches

The ten to twenty million Americans who have migraine headaches know that the excruciating pain can chip a large hole out of the day. Often, one can't do anything but "wait it out."

Similar headaches may disrupt sleep, but unlike the typical migraine, they often occur in clusters—sometimes one to four headaches during the day for several weeks or even months. *Cluster headaches* typically start about three hours after sleep begins— that is, in the latter half of the night, when REM periods are longer. During REM sleep, blood pressure rises and the rate of blood flowing through the brain increases; such changes, in people susceptible to cluster headaches, may be related to the development of pain.

The pain, often likened to that of a burning poker, may be so severe it rouses the person during the night, although sometimes the victim simply awakens in the morning with a headache. Even so, the pain may give him the impression that he has spent a restless night. In a person with a regular bedtime, attacks may recur at the same hour, night after night. Shifting the sleep schedule has shown, however, that the attacks are tied to sleep itself, rather than to the time of day.

Cluster headaches seem to occur exclusively on one side of the head or the other, often causing reddening and tearing of the eye and a stuffed nostril on the side where the pain occurs. Usually the headaches last thirty to ninety minutes, and the steady, penetrating pain is so intense that a person cannot lie still. Pacing around the room and even performing vigorous calisthenics may give some relief.

People with cluster headaches can sometimes be recognized by their "lionlike" face; they tend to develop deep creases between the eyes, furrows on the forehead and folds beside the nose.

The headaches usually recur in periodic sieges, with pain-free intervals often lasting months or years. For an unfortunate 10 to 15 percent of people who have these headaches, pain-free intervals are few and brief. Medication that suppresses REM sleep sometimes brings relief.

Another type of headache, *chronic paroxysmal hemicrania*, causes similar pain for shorter periods, usually five to fifteen minutes, but as often as twenty-four times in twenty-four hours. Headache-free days are rare. When this type of headache occurs during sleep, it occurs only in REM periods. Again, drugs that suppress REM sleep are sometimes helpful.

One type of sleep-related headache, usually noticed on awakening, has an easily remedied cause. The aptly named *turtle headache* may plague you if you bury your head under the blanket for long periods. The headache stems from a lack of oxygen and a buildup of carbon dioxide in your blood.

Another type of headache is also noticed on awakening from sleep or soon after. Some people call it the *weekend headache*, or the *Sunday morning headache*, because they get it when they sleep late. Oversleeping, although often blamed, is usually not the culprit. (See also the "blah syndrome," discussed in Chapter 3, "How Much Sleep Do We Need?") If you drink several cups of coffee, tea or cola drinks during the day, your headache is probably a *caffeine withdrawal headache*. It may occur during the daytime, too. The time elapsed from the last "dose" of caffeine is the determining factor. The remedy is straightforward: Cut back on caffeine. Because everyone reacts differently to caffeine, you may need to experiment to find the amount you can consume without problems. Withdrawal symptoms may take a week, or even longer, to disappear.

Asthma

Asthma gets its name from the Greek word meaning "panting." The disease's most obvious symptom is wheezing, a rough, raspy, whistling sound that accompanies each breath as air is forced through constricted bronchial tubes and other airways in the chest. Coughing is another common symptom; it represents the body's attempt to expel the excess mucus clogging the air passages and lungs.

Asthma attacks are more frequent during the evening and during sleep than during the day. Coughing may occur only at night or may be worse then, as a result of the sleeper's position rather than of sleep itself, since lying down further narrows the airways.

Asthma attacks seldom occur in the early half of the sleep period, the hours of deep NREM sleep, perhaps because the person is too deeply asleep to respond to the asthma attack trigger. However, people with asthma have less deep sleep than those without this disorder; the attack signals may disturb their sleep without fully arousing them. Even though breathing is more irregular during REM sleep, attacks occur randomly in the latter half of the night, in both REM and NREM sleep. Hence, the notion that disturbing dreams trigger asthma attacks may be true in only some cases.

Some people with asthma also have sleep apnea; the combination of relaxed muscles and already narrowed airways produces greatly worsened breathing at night. In severe cases, patients may breathe better with both medication for the asthma and a tracheostomy to provide a permanent opening in the windpipe.

Other Lung Diseases

Breathing is likely to be more difficult at night for people who already have trouble with it during the day, not only because we lie down while we sleep, but also because muscles, including those involved in breathing, relax during sleep.

In people with chronic obstructive lung diseases, the most common being chronic bronchitis and emphysema, oxygen in the blood is lowered by such minimal daytime activities as eating, urinating, sitting up and coughing. During sleep, particularly during REM sleep, oxygen levels go even lower. The shortage of oxygen puts an added burden on the heart and may be life-threatening. People with these disorders may need to sleep wearing a masklike device or nasal tubes to supply them with oxygen.

Diseases of the Heart and Blood Vessels

Cardiovascular diseases cause more than half of all deaths in the United States. Despite recent advances in treatment, some 400,000

Americans die every year within hours of a heart attack. Most are middle-aged men and one in four has never shown symptoms of heart trouble.

A sleep recording of a healthy fifty-year-old man showed that he had 500 to 1,100 heart blocks and heart rhythm interruptions during a single night. Such abnormalities, which may cause the heart to cease its normal beat and twitch irregularly, are believed to be a key cause of sudden death. This man was fortunate; more typically, the abnormalities come to light only after the person's death, when an autopsy is performed. French Army physicians found that the irregularities of this man's heartbeat occurred mainly during REM sleep and never during waking, not even after exercise. When heart irregularities are recognized, a pacemaker often is used to correct them.

Whether we are healthy or ill, blood pressure, heart rate and breathing all are more variable during REM sleep. If a person has chronically elevated blood pressure, the REM surges may further strain his heart and damage arteries. If someone has a disease of heart and blood vessels, the added stress of REM theoretically may make a heart attack or stroke more likely at this time; whether it does, in fact, do so, has yet to be shown. Contrary to popular lore, it has not been proven that the most common time of death during sleep from heart attacks and strokes is the REM-rich period at the end of the night. (For more on this subject, also see Chapter 2, "What Is Normal Sleep?")

It is still customary to treat heart disease with bed rest, which usually makes a person sleep more. In a hospital coronary care unit, sleep is likely to be highly disturbed. The physical aspects of the illness and the attendant worries, as well as the presence of monitoring equipment and the necessary activities of the staff, all interfere with sleep. Some drugs used to treat heart disease are known to disrupt normal sleep patterns. The impact of sleep on the heart and the need to provide the best possible environment for sleep, even in an intensive care unit, have only recently begun to be appreciated. Studies are in progress to determine whether drugs that suppress REM sleep can prevent worsening of heart problems.

Interruptions in breathing, or sleep apnea, may lead to or worsen high blood pressure, trigger irregular heart rhythms and possibly cause the heart to stop beating altogether. (For more information on sleep apnea, see Chapter 9, "The Snoring Sickness.")

People with narcolepsy and certain other disorders of excessive sleepiness also have a higher incidence of heart abnormalities than people without these disorders; the reason for this association is not clear. One heart problem common to these conditions is mitral valve prolapse, a deformity of the valve that controls the amount of blood flowing into the left ventricle.

Chest Pain (Angina)

Angina is brought on by exertion. Hence, it is far more common during wakefulness than during sleep. But even before modern sleep-laboratory studies began, physicians speculated about the link between chest pain during sleep and anxious dreams. Many episodes of sleep-related angina do appear to occur during REM periods. If it is determined that a person experiences angina mostly during REM, he may be treated with REM-suppressing drugs.

Heart Failure

When the heart is unable to pump the amount of blood necessary to maintain normal circulation, fluid collects in the abdomen, legs and/or lungs. Merely lying down in bed, not necessarily sleeping, may produce uncomfortable shortness of breath. Some patients suffer "air hunger" so extreme that they can sleep only in a sitting-up position.

Heartburn and Choking (Gastric Reflux)

A feeling of pain or tightness in the chest, with or without a sour taste in the mouth, sometimes wakes a person several times during the night. Coughing, choking and difficulty breathing may also be complaints.

The symptoms occur when food and gastric acid backs up from the stomach into the esophagus; even acid alone in the esophagus may wake you up. If you frequently belch or suffer "heartburn" while awake, you're more likely to have such symptoms while asleep as well.

Of course, when you are awake, a few swallows will clear the acid material; it does not maintain prolonged contact with your esophagus. Further, saliva is a natural antacid. But sleeping posture, combined with the fact that people swallow ten times less often while asleep than awake, causes irritating substances to stay around in the esophagus longer, reports William Orr, Ph.D., director of the Sleep Disorders Center at Presbyterian Hospital, Oklahoma City, Oklahoma. Coughing and choking are the body's way of speeding up the "clearance" process.

Because the disorder can have such serious complications as inflammation of the esophagus or inhalation of contents into the lungs, it requires treatment. A doctor can diagnose the disorder during the daytime by assessing an individual's ability to "clear" certain test solutions placed in the esophagus. To document the existence and frequency of gastric reflux, a twenty-four-hour portable monitoring system has been devised by Thomas Hendrix, M.D., and his colleagues at the Johns Hopkins Swallowing Center, Baltimore.

At night, elevating the head of the bed on six-inch to eight-inch blocks may help prevent the problem. If you have this disorder, you may feel better if you do not recline immediately after eating, if you don't wear clothing that fits tightly around the chest and if you lose weight. You may want to avoid foods and substances that produce heartburn by local irritation (such as citrus juices, vinegar or tomatoes), that increase acid output (such as caffeine and alcohol) or that hamper the ability of the sphincter muscles to contract (such as chocolates, fats, alcohol and cigarettes). Your doctor may suggest antacids or drugs that increase the pressure of the sphincter muscle in the lower esophagus. In serious cases, surgery to tighten the muscles may be necessary.

Abnormal Swallowing Syndrome

Some people wake briefly but frequently during the night with the sensation of choking and blocked breathing. Although they have no trouble falling back to sleep, they understandably complain of restless nights.

These short-lived episodes of coughing and gagging occur when saliva drips into the windpipe just below the larynx or voice box, instead of being swallowed in the normal way and sent through the esophagus to the stomach. Gurgling sounds that precede the gagging as the saliva pools in a pouched area in the throat can alert a bed partner to the cause of the distress. Some people complain the pillow is drenched in the morning as a result of their nighttime drooling. Occasionally the problem is so severe that a person could choke to death.

The disorder may stem from several factors, including the excessive production of saliva during the night, difficulty swallowing or failure of the muscles of the lower esophagus to relax and allow saliva down. Sleep posture complicates matters; it's harder to swallow when lying down.

Because of loss of sensation associated with aging or strokes, elderly people are more likely than younger ones to inhale droplets of saliva into the lungs and, as a result, to develop lung infections.

Raising the head of the bed on six-inch to eight-inch blocks may provide relief.

Ulcers

Pain from an ulcer may awaken a person during the night. The gnawing or burning sensation is usually limited to a small area in the abdomen between the naval and the lower end of the breastbone. The ulcer pain is a response to both an empty stomach and the increase in secretion of gastric acid that occurs at certain times of the day and night. There's no relationship between acid secretion and specific stages of sleep.

While acid secretion drops during sleep in nearly everyone, it falls less in people with ulcers of the upper intestine, or duodenum. Because of a faulty control mechanism for acid secretion, they may secrete three to twenty times as much gastric acid during sleep as people without ulcers.

If you have an ulcer, you may be able to get a better night's sleep by having a bedtime snack that contains protein, such as a glass of milk. The protein neutralizes gastric acid. Unfortunately, protein also stimulates the production of more acid, a key reason why diet treatment of ulcers usually isn't sufficient. (Ulcer patients usually are advised to avoid substances that stimulate acid, including coffee, tea, cola drinks and alcohol.)

A recent boon for ulcer patients was the introduction of the drug cimetidine, which cuts down on acid secretion.

Waking to Urinate

If you awaken frequently during the night and urinate, you need to find out whether you are waking because of a need to urinate or waking for some other reason and then heading for the bathroom. A urinary tract infection might trigger frequent waking. Less obvious causes include enlargement of the prostate gland in men or, in persons of either sex, an obstruction that prevents complete emptying of the bladder.

Someone with mild congestive heart failure may accumulate excessive fluid in soft tissues at night; waking might be one symptom of this illness. People taking diuretics for high blood pressure or other illnesses also may awaken because they have to urinate.

If you have this problem, a first step is to restrict fluids from dinnertime onward. If that doesn't help, see your doctor.

Bed-Wetting

Bed-wetting is by no means a problem for children only, although it is indeed the most common childhood sleep disorder. It also occurs in the elderly. For some people, it is a lifelong problem. However, the incidence of the disorder is not known; people have an understandable reluctance to admit having it.

While bed-wetting may happen in any stage of sleep, it occurs most often in the deep sleep stage 3-4 and in periods of transition to lighter stages. After urinating, the person usually does not awaken spontaneously. Others find him hard to awaken; he is likely to remain disoriented for several minutes.

When bed-wetting begins in adulthood, urinary tract disease is not the only possible cause; diabetes, epilepsy or sleep apnea may also lead to bed-wetting. The symptom demands a visit to the doctor. Often the cause is correctable. (For more information on bed-wetting in children, see Chapter 5, "The Growing Years.")

Dark Urine in the Morning

Brownish-red urine in the morning may be the first sign of one form of anemia. In this disorder, called *paroxysmal nocturnal hemoglobinuria,* red blood cell destruction increases during sleep, and excessive pigments spill out into the urine. A person may also develop weakness and pallor. If large numbers of red blood cells are destroyed, transfusions may be necessary. The disorder can appear at any age but usually occurs between the ages of twenty and forty. If your urine appears dark in the morning, see your doctor.

Kidney Failure

When the kidneys stop working, the body retains progressively larger quantities of water, salt and other substances. Body tissues swell and toxic waste products accumulate, eventually threatening life.

Two methods of treatment are available today to maintain the lives of people with kidney failure: artificial kidney machines that take over the damaged kidneys' blood-purifying function, and kidney transplants.

People using artificial kidney machines show characteristic sleep disturbances; on days they receive treatment, as well as between treatments, they sleep less and get less deep, stage 3-4 sleep than healthy persons.

People who receive transplants show similar disturbances, even a year after the surgery. Kidney failure appears to be accompanied by an irreversible change in the mechanisms responsible for sleep, say researchers at the Baylor College of Medicine.

Arthritis

Arthritic pain normally diminishes during the night, but it may well disrupt sleep, particularly when you change positions. If you have arthritis, you probably will be most comfortable if you use a moderately firm mattress. Some people with arthritis prefer water beds; your doctor can advise you about the most appropriate sleeping surface for you.

Place pillows strategically to limit your turning during the night. If your knees or hips are affected by arthritis, don't put a pillow under your knees; you might develop a stiff contracture of the muscles or tendons. Your doctor may advise that you wear splints at night to ease pain and rest the more severely affected joints. A warm bath and mild exercises at bedtime may help relax you and make it easier to fall asleep.

Epilepsy

In one of four people with epilepsy, seizures are nearly always confined to sleep. In "sleep epilepsy," seizures occur most frequently in the first two hours after sleep begins or in a second two-hour peak, an hour or so before awakening. In some people, seizures are associated with awakening and generally occur in the first hour after arising. About 40 percent of people with epilepsy have seizures both while awake and while asleep.

Sleep-related seizures occur at all ages but are most common in children. Indeed, parents may mistake the thirty to one hundred brief seizures that may occur in a night for simple body movements. Or they may focus on other behaviors triggered by seizures, including bed-wetting, bowel incontinence, sleepwalking, head-banging or leg jerks. These disorders, it is important to note, also occur in the absence of epilepsy. (For more information on such disorders, see Chapter 12, "Things That Go Bump in the Night.")

Seizures that occur during sleep cannot be said to be either more or less serious than those during the day. No particular waking activities seem to make seizures at night more likely.

Sometimes seizures are caused by brain tumors, periodic low blood sugar or other problems; these, of course, require specific treatment. When no underlying cause is apparent, anticonvulsant drugs may reduce the frequency or severity of seizures. In children, the drugs are used to reduce the likelihood of seizures and can often be stopped when the brain matures, say researchers at the Johns Hopkins Epilepsy Center. Happily, evidence is accumulating that most youngsters with epilepsy outgrow it.

If it can be determined that an individual's seizures occur most often during a specific sleep stage, treatment with drugs that suppress that sleep stage may be helpful.

In Men Only

IMPOTENCE

Although "to sleep with" is an often-used colloquialism for sexual intercourse, "there is more to the relationship between sleep and sexual functioning than the bed in which both often take place," notes Ismet Karacan, M.D., a pioneer in the use of the sleep laboratory to diagnose sexual disorders, and co-director of the Sleep Disorders and Research Center at the Baylor College of Medicine.

Healthy normal males of all ages, from newborn babies to centenarians, have long-lasting erections of the penis during sleep, mainly during REM sleep. Recognition of this fact prompted studies of sexual functioning during sleep in men who complained of difficulty obtaining or keeping erections while awake.

Before these studies, this difficulty—often referred to as impotence—was believed to be almost always "all in the mind." Now it is known that in two out of every three cases, physical illnesses or abnormalities are to blame. Many can be corrected, restoring a man to normal sexual functioning and sparing him years of frustration as well as inappropriate, often expensive, treatment.

When a man fails to have erections during sleep or has only partial erections, he probably has some physical disorder. Impotence in a man who has normal erections during sleep probably has a psychological rather than a physical basis.

Erections occur when blood enters the penis faster than it leaves, engorging the organ and increasing its size. Blood flow is controlled by two sets of muscles surrounding the blood vessels that lead to and from the penis; these muscles respond to commands from nerves. The male hormone testosterone, produced by the testicles, also is needed for this normal sexual functioning. Hence, any problem involving the critical blood vessels, nerves or hormone supply may lead to impotence.

More than one hundred different physical causes of impotence have been identified. Diabetes is the most common of these; high blood pressure, obesity, prostate disorders, kidney disease, multiple sclerosis and Hodgkin's disease are among the many others. A wide variety of drugs, including those used to treat high blood pressure and heart disease, as well as sleeping pills and alcohol, may affect a man's erectile ability.

Some illnesses, particularly those caused by blood vessel blockage, may cause transient inability to sustain erections. Anxiety, depression, hostility and other psychological states have been linked to impotence. Such problems by themselves may cause impotence; however, they may also accompany or aggravate impotence that has a physical cause, particularly if the physical cause goes unrecognized.

Most men occasionally experience impotence. Exhaustion or worries about business, for example, can interfere with sexual arousal. Even social drinking can do it. As Shakespeare noted, alcohol "provokes the desire, but it takes away the performance." Potency declines with age but does not, as was once thought, invariably vanish. Older men generally require more vigorous stimulation and more time between orgasms but may retain the ability to climax throughout life.

Healthy men in their twenties average four full erections a night, lasting in all about 191 minutes, or one third of their total time asleep. Healthy men in their seventies have three erections a night, totaling an average of ninety-six minutes or about one fifth of sleep.

Erections during sleep (also referred to as nocturnal penile tumescence) usually occur during REM periods. However, men deprived of REM sleep continue to have erections during the night. Erections occur regardless of recent sexual activity or dream content.

REM periods typically last thirty minutes to an hour or longer in the last half of the sleep period. The fact that awakening in the morning usually occurs from REM sleep or soon after accounts for the familiar morning erection. Waking with a full bladder, contrary to a popular misconception, has nothing to do with this phenomenon. In Baylor studies, men were awakened about an hour early and permitted to empty their bladders. They then returned to sleep; if they experienced REM sleep just prior to awakening, they awoke with erections.

The reason why erections occur during REM sleep, a time of otherwise mostly lower muscle activity, is uncertain. One possibility is that during REM, the brain acts like a computer on "self-test," making sure that important bodily functions still work properly.

Whatever your age, you'd be wise to see your doctor if you have difficulty achieving erections and keeping them long enough for intercourse, or if you experience any drastic change in your usual functioning or levels of sexual desire.

When a man complains of impotence, diagnosis requires a comprehensive exam. Any diseases he has and specific medications he uses will be documented carefully. Laboratory studies of blood and urine are often performed; many sensitive measures of hormone imbalance have been developed only recently. Psychological questions are generally asked. Usually, the doctor will want to know if the impotence started suddenly, if it occurs only with certain partners and if an erection can be produced by masturbation. A man's wife or other sexual partner may be interviewed.

No matter how thorough, an exam performed only during waking can't address all possibilities. Not all cases of impotence in men with diabetes, for example, are caused by that disease. Impotence in a man who has had a heart attack may stem from side effects of certain blood-pressure-lowering drugs, or it may originate in fear that sexual excitement will trigger another attack. The first cause might be corrected by a change of drugs and the second by counseling; it's possible that both may compound the impotence.

"An evaluation involving both waking and sleep studies prevents anxiety by giving quick answers to a man with erectile problems," notes Merrill Mitler, Ph.D., senior staff scientist at the Scripps Clinic and Research Foundation.

Three consecutive nights are standard in many sleep disorders centers. During sleep, brain waves, eye movements and muscle activity, as well as erections, are monitored to see if sleep-stage or other abnormalities exist. A man who is to undergo such a series of tests usually arrives at the sleep center an hour or so before bedtime, has the necessary monitoring devices applied to him and then retires to a private bedroom, where he stays in bed until his usual time for arising the next morning. During the days of the study, he is asked to skip naps and nonessential medications and to restrict use of caffeine and alcohol, all of which may alter nighttime sleep. The first night a man sleeps undisturbed; since many people require a night to get used to the strange environment, patterns of sleep and erections are apt to be different from the usual ones. The second night provides a basic profile. The third night the man is awakened during at least one of his monitored erections. (He knows in advance that he will be awakened.)

"This procedure often is therapeutic," Baylor scientist Dr. Karacan explains. When a man learns that he is capable of normal erections, he frequently regains his self-confidence. On the other hand, a man with abnormal erections may be relieved to know that the cause is physical, because specific treatment may be possible.

Occasionally, a man with normal erections is disappointed that there is no physical problem he can blame for his daytime difficulties. "For men in this last group, we have to decide if sex therapy, individual therapy, couple therapy or family therapy will help most. The impotence may be merely a weapon in a couple's war," Dr. Karacan says.

The evaluation of impotence at sexual disorders centers at first may seem time-consuming and costly, but in the long run it provides a relatively inexpensive and quick answer to a longstanding problem. Efforts to develop simpler methods of diagnosis are in progress. A do-it-yourself approach that has garnered considerable publicity calls for circling the penis before sleep with postage stamps. An erection supposedly would snap the stamps apart. Experts in the field point out that a simple body movement during sleep could have the same effect; they deem the method worthless. It may even be dangerous, warns Dr. Karacan. The stamps can't be counted on to break; the tightening during an erection could produce pain and bruising.

When impotence stems from a blockage in a blood vessel, it often can be remedied with microsurgery. When the problem results from nerve blockage, a man may be helped to have erections with an implantable device that is inflated and deflated when desired with a pump also inserted under the skin. Hormone deficiencies can also be corrected; Harvard researchers found that thirty-three of thirty-seven impotent men with previously unsuspected hormonal disorders could be restored to normal sexual functioning with drug treatment.

PAINFUL ERECTIONS DURING SLEEP

Some men awaken from sleep with painful erections. As a rule, during waking they have no difficulty achieving erections and no pain. This disturbing problem can sometimes be traced to a transitory blockage in the blood vessels leading to or from the penis or, in uncircumcised men, a too-tight foreskin. Both of these problems may be corrected with surgery.

In Women Only

MENSTRUAL SLEEPINESS

Many women complain that they are excessively sleepy in the week or so preceding menstruation. This feeling is only one of a variety of unpleasant physical and emotional symptoms, collectively called the premenstrual syndrome (PMS).

Other symptoms of PMS include swelling and tenderness of the breasts, bloating of the abdomen, swelling in the ankles, feet and hands, fatigue or depression, anxiety, constipation, skin eruptions, headache and cravings for sweet or salty foods. All appear to stem from a common biochemical abnormality in the body's handling of the premenstrual cascade of hormone changes, say Robert Reid, M.D., and S.S.C. Yen, M.D., of the University of California, San Diego.

The few women with excessive sleepiness before their menstrual periods whose sleep has been monitored in a sleep laboratory have turned out to have lower than normal amounts of the deep sleep stage 3-4, as well as of REM sleep. Studies of people selectively deprived of deep sleep or REM sleep show that most feel sleepier than usual the next day. Women who do not experience excessive sleepiness get their highest amounts of stage 3-4 in the premenstrual period when hormone levels are at their peak.

Although there is no specific treatment to relieve the sleepiness, some women report that merely recognizing that it is periodic relieves their anxieties. If you are troubled severely by sleepiness or other PMS symptoms, you may want to plan your work and home activities accordingly. Unfortunately, pain relievers taken for other PMS symptoms may make you even sleepier.

PREGNANCY

For some women, extra sleepiness during the daytime precedes morning sickness as an early sign of pregnancy. One possible explanation is that the hormone progesterone is elevated in pregnancy; this hormone is known to have a sedative effect. Indeed, the sleepiness may be nature's way of telling a mother-to-be to take life a bit easier.

About midway through pregnancy, many women begin to have trouble sleeping through the night. No sleeping posture is comfortable for long. Sleeping on the stomach is no longer feasible, sleeping on the back becomes painful because the weight of the baby presses down and sleeping on the side is awkward. As time for delivery nears, the baby's head pushes on the mother's bladder and prompts frequent trips to the bathroom, night and day. Toward the end of pregnancy, women generally get much less of the deep sleep of stage 3-4.

Despite this discomfort, sleeping medications are not advised. It's an erroneous notion that drugs that can be bought without a prescription are harmless. Moreover, alcohol, which makes some people fall asleep faster, is taboo during pregnancy because of its possible harmful effects on the baby. If you are pregnant, check with your doctor before taking any drugs.

Even with the easy birth of a healthy child, many women suffer "new baby blues." That a joyous event should trigger crying, unpredictable mood changes and irritability seems paradoxical; biological events, including a precipitous fall in certain hormones following delivery, are implicated. Most women feel essentially back to themselves again by the end of the second menstrual cycle following childbirth. It is true, however, that a new mother's sleep will be disrupted for many months by her baby's demands and that lack of sleep may engender an achy, washed-out feeling associated with feelings of depression. Should you have such problems, you probably will find that sharing your feelings with other new mothers makes it easier to cope. Talk to your doctor, too; you may have developed an unrelated problem that requires treatment.

DISORDERS OF SEXUAL AROUSAL

Women of all ages, like men, undergo physiological changes in sexual organs during REM sleep. The clitoris becomes engorged with blood and vaginal pulse and lubrication both increase. As in men, these changes occur regardless of recent sexual activity or dream content.

Researchers are trying to devise ways, comparable to nocturnal penile tumescence monitoring in men, to measure female sexual arousal objectively. The hope is that studies made during sleep will eventually be able to help determine whether disorders of sexual arousal in women have a psychological or physiological basis.

HOT FLASHES

Sudden flooding with warmth, accompanied by sweating and dizziness, constitutes one of the most disconcerting symptoms of menopause. These hot flashes trouble eight out of ten women for a year or longer; some women have them many times a day and so severely that they are dragged from sleep repeatedly during the night.

Hot flashes may be a key component of the insomnia often experienced by women of menopausal age. The insomnia, in turn, may help provoke the feelings of irritability and not being up to par that many women associate with menopause. Since some women turn to sedative drugs and alcohol to relieve their insomnia, hot flashes may instigate some cases of dependency on these substances.

Documentation of flashes during sleep demonstrates that they have a physical origin and are not, as once thought, a psychosomatic complaint. "We have unequivocal evidence that hot flashes are not just a figment of the imagination," asserts Howard Judd, M.D., of the University of California School of Medicine, Los Angeles. The flashes appear to be triggered by biochemical events in the brain. Alterations in hormone release associated with menopause may cause a sudden downward setting of the body's central thermostat. In response, the body's furnace flips on. It sometimes overcompensates, creating excess warmth and other sensations.

Observing nine women with severe hot flashes one night in the sleep laboratory, Dr. Judd and his colleagues found that forty-five of forty-seven episodes involving changes in skin temperature and other signs of hot flashes were associated with waking five minutes before or after the flash occurred. When women suffering hot flashes were given estrogen drugs, they had fewer flashes and fewer awakenings during the night.

At the Royal Edinburgh (Scotland) Hospital, Joan Thomson and Ian Oswald, M.D., compared two groups of menopausal women. Members of one group took a placebo, or inactive substance, for six weeks and then took estrogen for eight weeks. The others took only the placebo. Estrogen made a big difference. While taking the drug, the women woke fewer times during sleep and went back to sleep more quickly.

Estrogen therapy is not without risks: Long-term use of estrogen has been associated with a higher rate of cancer of the lining of the uterus. However, when hot flashes are unremitting, the benefit of improved sleep may outweigh the risk, brightening a woman's whole outlook on life.

14

TROUBLED MINDS/ TROUBLED SLEEP

Clothes rumpled, hair unkempt, Naomi rarely spoke; when she did, she mumbled. She spent most of her hospital day slumped in a chair, oblivious to the activity going on around her. At meals, she picked at her salad but ignored the rest. Most people would guess her age as "over sixty," although Naomi was only thirty-six-years old. Diagnosed as having manic-depressive illness, Naomi (not her real name) agreed to have her sleep recorded throughout her stay in a psychiatric research unit at the Clinical Center of the National Institutes of Health.

On four of the fifty-eight nights on which she was monitored, Naomi went to bed in her usual depressed state, but awakened during the night and appeared at the nurses' station minutes later, thoroughly transformed. Her manner was vivacious, her face animated and her hands expressive. Chattering rapidly, she flirted with a male attendant, promised to bake him a cake and outlined elaborate plans for a party. At other times, during waking hours, she switched suddenly, with equal drama, from the crushing lows of depression to the energetic highs of mania and back again, also within the space of minutes.

Few other real-life events are as theatrical as these polar switches in mood. The fact that the change from depression to mania may occur while a person is asleep as well as when he or she is awake suggests that the trigger for the switch is inside the person, not in events in the outside world. Indeed, it supports the idea that this illness itself is an endogenous disorder, that is, one generated from within, independent of outside influences.

Studies of sleep in people with a variety of mental illnesses are helping to enlarge our understanding of these disorders. Sleep problems occur not only in people with the highs and lows of manic-depressive illness (sometimes called bipolar disorder), but also in those in whom depressive symptoms alternate with more normal moods (sometimes called unipolar disorder), and in those with acute schizophrenia, anxiety, obsessive-compulsive disorders and other disorders of the mind. Indeed, sleep problems often serve as a "ticket of admission" to the doctor's office, for most of us seem to find it easier to talk about trouble with sleep than to focus on underlying mental difficulties that we may be having.

"The sleep laboratory has helped bring the notion of using lablike tests and objective measures in the diagnosis and treatment of major psychiatric problems closer to reality," asserts David Kupfer, M.D., chairman of the department of psychiatry and director of the Sleep Research Center at the University of Pittsburgh Western Psychiatric Institute and Clinic.

Sleep in Depression

Depression that causes loss of interest or pleasure in all or almost all of a person's usual activities and pastimes for at least two weeks develops in about one in five women and one in ten men (so many of us that it has been described as the "common cold" of mental illness). As with colds, many people suffer recurrent bouts of depression throughout their lives.

"Depression seems to be a distinct illness," says Christian Gillin, M.D., professor of psychiatry at the University of California, San Diego. He observes, "It is not merely an extension of the normal feelings of sadness or discouragement we all experience in the course of daily living." We can't truly "understand" depression by relating it to ordinary "blues," any more than some one who indulges in a second dessert at the buffet table can "understand" massive obesity or someone who gets giddy on champagne can "understand" alcoholism. Depression may occur without an obvious instigator such as getting divorced or losing one's job. It may even be irrational, yet the person who has it usually can't be talked out of it.

Fluctuating between the lows of depression and more normal mood states, or unipolar disorder, is more common than bouncing between the lows and highs of manic-depressive illness. People like Naomi who ricochet between extremes may have intervening periods of normal mental health that last for weeks or years.

Depression may affect many different systems of the body. In addition to causing trouble with sleep, it may manifest itself as difficulty in thinking, working and eating, as feelings of helplessness and hopelessness and as lack of energy. Physicians diagnose depression on the basis of a person's current symptoms and physical condition, along with his individual and family history. However, they continue to search for more specific aids to diagnosis. The assumption that the brain and body function abnormally in certain types of depression has prompted the recent development of several laboratory tests.

Some of these tests focus on substances that appear in blood, urine or spinal fluid. Many people who are depressed, for example, secrete an excess of the hormone cortisol. The dexamethasone-suppression test identifies people who continue to secrete cortisol after receiving a steroid that ordinarily suppresses its secretion for at least twenty-four hours. Cortisol secretion is particularly interesting to sleep researchers because the area of the brain that is thought to regulate it may also control certain aspects of sleep.

The search for biological markers for depression also focuses on abnormalities of brain waves; sleep studies can further this research. Certain sleep disturbances have long been known to be more prominent in depression than in other mental illnesses or to occur only in this disorder. Some 2,400 years ago, Hippocrates described a woman with melancholia as someone who "became affected with loss of sleep." About 500 years later, Aretaeus observed that depressed people were "sad, dismayed, and sleepless." He wrote, "They became thin with their agitation and loss of refreshing sleep."

The following combination of sleep problems is most common in depression.

SLEEP IS SHORT

Compared with normal sleepers, and even with people who have insomnia but are not depressed, those with depression take longer to fall asleep and get less sleep during the night. They also are more likely to wake up before the alarm goes off. Waking "too early" once was viewed as the hallmark of all depressive illness. Now it is recognized that early awakenings are prominent only during the depressive phase, but not the manic phase, of the illness.

Insomnia may become a problem before the depressed mood becomes obvious. It also shows up in "masked" depression, that is, in people who deny feelings of sadness, try to cope despite such feelings or blame flu, stomach trouble, overwork or other stress for their emotional discomfort.

Although four in five people who are depressed have insomnia, one in five tends to oversleep. Among the depressed as well as the population at large, some of us respond to stress by sleeping less than usual and others sleep more than usual. Similarly, when under stress, some of us eat less than usual, and others overeat. Those who oversleep are likely to be the same ones who overeat; those who sleep less seem to be those whose appetite disappears. Age influences these patterns; when depressed, younger adults tend to oversleep or overeat, while older ones are more likely to forgo sleep and food.

Changing patterns of long and short sleep also appear to be common in people with a type of depression that occurs regularly in the winter. Such people have high energy levels in spring and summer but are so sluggish in fall and winter that they cannot work. In winter they may sleep nine or ten hours a night whereas in summer they sleep only four or five hours. Discovery of this pattern by researchers at the National Institute of Mental Health has led to the development of an effective treatment. Two weeks of daily exposure to bright artificial lights in winter months, in effect, makes spring come early.

SLEEP IS SHALLOW

People with depression have less deep sleep (stage 3–4) and more light sleep (stage 1) than normal sleepers do. They also are easier to awaken. These findings suggest that depressed people are over-aroused.

SLEEP IS FRAGMENTED AND INEFFICIENT

Depressed people wake up frequently in the middle of the night and spend more time in bed, although they get less sleep, than nondepressed people do. While a normal sleeper may shift from one stage of sleep to another about two dozen times during the night, a depressed person may shift four dozen times; the higher the number of these shifts, the more likely a person is to view the night as "restless."

REM (RAPID EYE MOVEMENT) SLEEP OCCURS "TOO EARLY" IN THE NIGHT

In normal, healthy adults, the first REM period of the night starts about ninety minutes after the beginning of sleep. Adults with insomnia tend to enter REM sleep earlier, but rarely sooner than an hour after the start of sleep. But adults with depression tend to have their first REM period thirty to fifty minutes after sleep starts. REM periods beginning twenty minutes or less after the start of sleep are common in severely depressed people. The earlier in the night the REM period occurs, the more severe the illness, notes Dr. Kupfer. The early REM period is a biological marker of depression, that is, a physiological indicator of the illness, he says.

As we get older, the first REM period of the night tends to occur earlier. But at all ages, depressed people have substantially earlier REM periods. Hence, accelerated, or premature "aging" of sleep seems to be another characteristic of depression. Depressed people generally have higher amounts of REM sleep in the first third of the night and lower amounts of REM sleep in the last third of the night, a pattern exactly opposite that of healthy nonde-pressed sleepers.

EARLY NIGHT REM SLEEP IS MORE "INTENSE" THAN IT IS IN NORMAL SLEEPERS

Depressed people often have storms of rapid eye movements,

especially in the first REM period. During the night they have more rapid eye movements than healthy sleepers.

Sleep in Manic-Depressive Illness

In contrast with the depressed person, who lacks interest or pleasure in life, someone who is manic may be ebullient or irritable. Often he or she is hyperactive and easily distracted, talks rapidly and has grandiose ideas. Depression typically drags on for six to twelve months, whereas mania usually lasts only three to four months. About one person in one hundred experiences manic episodes, far fewer than those who suffer only from depression.

Sleep during a manic episode differs from that experienced during depression. These are its key characteristics:

SLEEP IS SHORT

Unlike sleep in depression, sleep in a manic episode is not fragmented or shorter than desired. Instead, during mania, a person may awaken after only two to four hours of sleep and claim to be fully refreshed.

The switch from depression to mania is often preceded by a night or two with significantly less sleep, perhaps only half as much as usual. The sleep disturbance comes before obvious changes in mood and behavior, suggesting that the switch process has already begun.

Although the switch may occur during REM sleep, the time of most vivid dreams, its relation to dream content is unclear. People with mania often are too distracted and incoherent to relate dreams. Nonetheless, they may attribute their condition to bizarre dreams. Naomi, for example, once reported, "My brain is whirring at a high rate because of that insane dream." On another occasion, she said she had had "fourth-degree dreams," which were "dreams about dreams about dreams."

Rapid switches most often take place between seven in the morning and three in the afternoon; during these hours, they are associated with a less intense, less explosive mania than shifts that take place later in the day. Once mania begins, a person is likely to go a whole night without sleep. Indeed, people with mania often follow a pattern of alternating a night of no sleep with a night of sleep. They often have trouble falling asleep. Gradually, they begin to sleep longer at night and their mania diminishes.

People who sleep for short periods when manic often sleep for long periods when depressed, instead of suffering the more typical depression insomnia. While depressed, some take naps during the day but still complain of being more sleepy than usual.

SLEEP IS SHALLOW

People experiencing mania continue to get little of the deep sleep stage 3–4.

REM SLEEP STILL OCCURS "TOO EARLY" IN THE NIGHT

As in depression, the first REM period of the night in someone with mania may occur just a few minutes after the start of sleep.

New Treatment for Depression

Although scientists still don't know what particular purpose any specific state or stage of sleep serves, they have focused their attention on the prominent disruptions of REM sleep in depression.

All medications known to be effective in relieving the symptoms of unipolar disorder also suppress REM sleep. Drugs useful in the treatment of other mental illnesses do not share this property. Moreover, drugs that increase REM sleep produce depressionlike symptoms in some people who take them.

Armed with these facts, Gerald Vogel, M.D., director of the sleep laboratory at the Georgia Mental Health Institute, Atlanta, postulated that it might be beneficial to deprive people who are depressed of REM sleep. He monitored the sleep of fourteen patients in his laboratory and awakened them every time the polygraph tracings showed they were in REM sleep, as many as thirty times a night. About half of the patients who were deprived of REM sleep for two to three weeks did as well as people treated with a commonly used drug, and the benefits lasted as long as the drug treatment would have. Patients who did not get better after REM sleep deprivation also failed to improve when given the standard drugs. These people needed more rigorous treatment, such as electroshock therapy.

Depriving people of REM sleep requires a sleep laboratory with technicians who monitor sleep stages and wake the patients at the appropriate times. Because this procedure is too costly to be practical for everyday treatment, researchers have explored other ways to gain the same effect.

One approach is to deprive people of sleep entirely. Astonishingly, roughly 40 to 60 percent of depressed people deprived of sleep for thirty-six to forty-eight hours get better. They usually improve between three and eight in the morning if the deprivation starts at midnight; that is, they start to get better after only three to eight hours without sleep. This treatment hasn't become part of patient care because the benefits last only until the next time the person goes to sleep. Even a nap as short as ten minutes can drop a person back into depression.

Another tack involves depriving patients of part of the night's sleep. When depressed people go to bed at their usual time, say, eleven at night, but are awakened at three in the morning, they also get better.

Although it seems contrary to common sense to treat people who complain that they can't get enough sleep by keeping them awake, this approach works, as these experiments show. "The fact that it does highlights our general ignorance about the functions of sleep," Dr. Gillin comments. These studies raise an interesting question: Is sleep, or a certain amount or type of sleep, somehow bad for people who are depressed? Or is it the timing of sleep that has gone awry in depression? The success—even though temporary—of these various manipulations of sleep gives credence to the notion that depression involves at least in part a fault in the body's internal clocks. The benefits of manipulating sleep may be transient because internal rhythms eventually return to their natural state, which in depressed people is abnormal.

One way of testing this theory is to advance the time of sleep, that is, to induce a kind of therapeutic jet lag. In an experiment at the National Institute of Mental Health, a fifty-seven-year-old depressed woman agreed to go to sleep and get up six hours earlier than usual. She rapidly got better, Thomas Wehr, M.D., and his colleagues found. Two days after her first six-hour shift, which moved her sleep time from the conventional 11:00 P.M. to 7:00 A.M. forward to 5:00 P.M. to 1:00 A.M., her depression evaporated. Her mood ranged from normal to slightly manic. Two weeks later, while still on the shifted schedule, she relapsed into depression. Again, her sleep time was moved forward six hours and again, she improved. Unfortunately, when she relapsed again, the same therapy failed to work.

In trying to determine if a flaw in internal clocks occurs in depression, researchers have looked at the internal REM clock, the twenty-four-hour body-temperature curve and the release of the hormone cortisol. These processes were selected because previous studies suggest that all may be controlled by the same area of the brain.

Studies of REM periods show that people who do not have depression are more likely to have REM periods at certain times of the day than others. If we regularly sleep at night, we are more likely to have REM periods during sleep at seven in the morning (close to the end of the night's sleep) than during an after-dinner nap at seven o'clock (close to the beginning of the night's sleep), for example. But someone with depression may have high amounts of REM sleep at midnight. Waking him up at three means that his night ends much like that of a healthy person, just after lengthy REM periods. Sending him to bed earlier means that his REM periods will occur later in his sleep period. Waking someone up during REM periods early in the night causes later REM periods to be longer.

Similarly, in people without depression, body temperature peaks in the early evening and is at its low several hours after the start of sleep. In depressed people, body temperature seems to be at its low earlier. Delays or advances in sleep time temporarily change this temperature curve.

Moreover, in healthy people who live in environments free of time cues, going to sleep and arising when they wish, the hormone cortisol is secreted in advance of the sleep period. This hormone appears to be secreted even earlier in depressed people.

In summary, then, the various studies suggest that the internal REM clock, the body temperature clock and the clock for the release of cortisol may be set too early, relative to bedtime, in people who are depressed. This finding opens the door for the development of ways to treat and prevent depression by changing bedtimes, using drugs, lights or other techniques to manipulate these rhythms, says Dr. Wehr.

The activity of chemicals in the brain may also be ill-timed in depression. In the brain, nerve cells communicate with each other by sending chemical messengers with instructions to either "turn on" or "turn off" a particular activity or function. A key chemical messenger is acetylcholine; initiating REM sleep is believed to be among its jobs. Scientists can study how acetylcholine functions by giving drugs that either increase it or block it. For example, when a drug that enhances acetylcholine is given during NREM sleep, by way of a tube previously inserted into a vein, scientists can measure how long it takes before the REM period begins. People with depressive illnesses enter REM sleep much faster than normal people, not only when they're obviously ill but even when they seem much improved. This finding suggests that certain chemical systems in the body may be overactive in people with depression and provides the rationale for treatment, now under investigation, that would involve changes in these chemical systems.

Better Ways to Assess Drugs

When medications are given to treat depression, it typically takes three or four weeks before improvement, if any, becomes apparent. But changes in sleep are obvious in the first two nights the drug is used, Dr. Kupfer and his colleagues have found. People who will improve on the drug under study take longer than they previously did to enter REM sleep and fall asleep faster, and the closer these times get to normal, the more likely a person is to respond well to the drug in other ways. Those who are going to respond also show a more normal number of rapid eye movements. Since antidepressant drugs help only about two thirds of nonhospitalized depressed people and only about half of those so ill they require hospitalization, early identification of those who won't be helped by the drugs can spare them ineffective treatment and enable them to get other treatment sooner.

Naps, which can be studied far more efficiently than whole nights in the sleep lab, also can provide evidence as to whether drugs are going to work. Drs. Kupfer and Gillin and their associates asked fifteen people with depression who were not using medications to try to nap at ten in the morning and four in the afternoon. Most had difficulty going to sleep, even though they complained of insomnia and of feeling achy and washed out. Those who had the most trouble napping—that is, were the most overaroused—later proved to respond best to antidepressant drugs.

Sleep in Schizophrenia

Schizophrenia is the mental illness most of us have in mind when we use the terms "insanity" or "madness." Schizophrenia, which literally means "splitting of the mind," is probably not a single disorder but rather a group of disorders with certain symptoms in common. A person with schizophrenia is, on occasion, out of touch with reality, seeing things no one else sees, and having thoughts so jumbled and so rapid that he finds it difficult to "catch" them. Communication with others becomes difficult, if not impossible, and as a result, the person with schizophrenia retreats still further into a lonely, frightening world. His emotions are blunted, and those that are expressed are often inappropriate. He may suspect other people are out to get him, feel invisible fingers prodding him or hear voices instructing him on what to do.

Schizophrenia affects about one in every one hundred persons in the United States and usually begins in early adulthood. It is a lifelong disorder, although a person may have many years of apparently normal thoughts and behavior between acute flare-ups of the illness.

Someone with schizophrenia may on occasion sleep a great deal. At other times, he may be so fearful that he maintains constant vigilance, working or pursuing some other activity frenetically, sleeping very little. Sometimes night and day get turned around when a person finds himself unable to fall asleep until morning but then sleeps until midday, thus making it harder to sleep the next night. Withdrawal from the everyday world and disregard for the feelings of others in his household further loosen adherence to a regular schedule of sleeping and waking.

Studies of sleep in people with schizophrenia may give doctors clues to the nature of the disorder and suggest better ways to treat it.

Because the waking hallucinations of people with schizophrenia resemble the dreams that the rest of us have during sleep, the notion has been around since ancient times that "the lunatic is a wakeful dreamer." The discovery that most vivid dreaming occurs during REM periods prompted studies of dreaming sleep in people with schizophrenia. The results surprised the researchers: People with schizophrenia did not prove to have higher than normal amounts of dreaming sleep. Most of the time, they seem to have about the same amount of REM sleep as other people, and their REM periods occupy about the same percentage of total sleep time. During acute phases of their illness, they seem to spend a smaller percentage of total sleep time in REM sleep. Further, people with schizophrenia do not show signs of REM sleep while they are awake.

But, although no major abnormalities of REM sleep have been identified, the minor ones tell researchers that the old supposition of a tie between madness and dreams may yet have some validity. Some people with schizophrenia, like those with depression, enter REM sleep "too early" in the night. Such people may have both schizophrenia and depression. When recovering from an acute episode of schizophrenia, they often have sleep problems that are common in depression, including difficulty falling asleep or staying asleep, along with anxiety-laden dreams. Some go through cycles of sleeping more when depressed and less when manic, a history that can aid a physician in assessing the individual's problems.

Furthermore, during REM periods, people with schizophrenia who "hear voices" appear to have higher than normal rates of contraction of muscles of the middle ear. This middle ear muscle activity (MEMA) ordinarily occurs not only during REM periods but also in waking life whenever we speak; it protects the delicate hearing mechanism from the noise that our voices make. Auditory hallucinations in waking life, according to one theory, may occur if the brain prepares for talking but for some still unknown reason is unable to carry through. Because some people with schizophrenia will not discuss their "inner voices," assessing MEMA rates during sleep may provide a clue to their presence while the person is awake, reports Vincent Zarcone, M.D., of Stanford University. The highest rates of MEMA occur in people with paranoid schizophrenia, a form of the disorder in which the patient hears two or three voices talking back and forth to each other in his head, persecuting him and/or supporting him.

Hearing arises in the temporal lobe of the brain, the area of the cerebral cortex near the temples. Because some people with a form of epilepsy involving the temporal lobe also hear voices before having a seizure or as part of the seizure, information about MEMA is prompting further studies to see if a disorder of this part of the brain is involved in at least some cases of schizophrenia.

Long-range studies of the sleep of individuals with schizophrenia are few, because not many of these very disturbed people have been willing to participate. Further, because the drugs prescribed to ease schizophrenia are known to alter sleep, the results of sleep studies are difficult to interpret. But some research findings recently have become available. In a study of six young adults with schizophrenia at different stages of their illness, Dr. Kupfer and his associates found that at the time of the most severe illness, the patients slept the least, just four hours a night. They had less of the deep sleep stage 3–4 and less REM sleep than would have been expected, even considering the number of hours spent asleep. As they got better, their sleep became more normal. The lack of sleep during periods of greatest stress may reflect intense inner turmoil at such times. About 40 percent of people with schizophrenia get less deep sleep than is normal, even when they are free of intense symptoms. Because people with other mental illnesses also frequently get less deep sleep, this finding generally is viewed as a sign of continuing anxiety.

Depriving people with schizophrenia of REM sleep does not worsen their illness, but many fail to recover REM sleep on subsequent nights, as healthy people under similar circumstances ordinarily do. This finding again points to a tie between an abnormality of the REM process and schizophrenia.

The more disturbed the sleep of a person with schizophrenia, the more severely ill he is likely to be. The effectiveness of an antischizophrenic drug can often be assessed by its effect on sleep. If a schizophrenic is receiving an adequate amount of medication, he is probably sleeping reasonably well, although some people with schizophrenia do complain of lifelong poor sleep.

Sleep and Anxiety

Many of us recognize the association between feelings of anxiety and a restless night. Almost any cause of anxiety, pleasant or unpleasant, can make it hard to fall asleep or stay asleep. Most of us attach little importance to a restless night or two, but insomnia that hangs on can make life seem bleak. (See Chapter 7 for more on insomnia.)

Some of us insist, "If only I could sleep well, my problems would be over." While we may be mistaking cause for effect, it's certainly true that persistent loss of sleep will cause almost everyone to feel "blue," to be irritable and to have difficulty concentrating.

Some of us who have difficulty sleeping do not recognize that we are under chronic stress from a troubled marriage or an unpleasant job. Here's where counseling can make a real difference, by enhancing understanding of the daytime problems that are undermining our nights. Some of us benefit from paying more attention to sleep habits, going to bed and getting up at regular hours, for example, or establishing rituals such as turning down the thermostat and setting the alarm clock to help prepare us for sleep. (Good sleep habits are described in Chapter 15, "How to Get a Better Night's Sleep," and Chapter 16, "What to Do If You Can't Sleep—or Can't Stay Awake.")

People with such severe anxiety that they have sleep terrors or wake up with worried thoughts or anxious dreams may benefit from both counseling and medications prescribed by the doctor.

Summing Up

Because anyone whose mind is troubled probably also has troubled sleep, and troubled sleep seems likely to further disturb a troubled mind, the study of how the two affect each other may help researchers find better ways to recognize and treat mental illnesses and perhaps, one day, discover a way to prevent them.

PART III

BETTER SLEEP

15

HOW TO GET
A BETTER
NIGHT'S SLEEP

Everyone wants "a good night's sleep." The last words many of us say or hear at the end of the day are "Good night!" or "Sleep well! Pleasant dreams!" The morning often begins with the question, "How did you sleep last night?"

This concern with sleep is prompted by the belief that sleep restores. We fear that a bad night will keep us from functioning at our best the next day. The worry "Will I sleep well tonight?" makes some of us hesitate to sleep away from home or stay late at parties. The desire for more sleep provokes heavy use of alcohol and sleeping pills, "solutions" doctors say are not only ineffective over the long run but also possibly dangerous.

Dos and don'ts to ensure good sleep are legion. You may have learned many of them from your mother, and she from hers. Until recently, folk wisdom was *all* we had to rely on. But now that scientists have learned to measure and interpret the activity of the sleeping brain, there is a sound rationale for advice on how to foster good sleep at night and full wakefulness during the day.

Tips That Really Work

GET ENOUGH SLEEP.

Only you can determine how much sleep you need in order to feel alert in the daytime. Even though most adults get between seven and eight hours of sleep a day, that amount may be too little or too much for you.

If you're not getting enough sleep now, you probably fall asleep easily whenever you're sitting quietly—watching television, for example, or listening to a lecture. "Such situations don't cause sleepiness, they unmask it," says William Dement, M.D., of Stanford University. If you're spending more time than you need to in bed, you probably lie awake for some time or wake and doze and wake again (a pattern that may lead you to suspect that you have insomnia, rather than that you are a normal short-sleeper).

Most American adults, however, don't seem to get enough sleep to achieve their optimal alertness. When given a twenty-minute opportunity to nap five or six times during the day, a procedure known as the Multiple Sleep Latency Test, most college-age and older adults fall asleep in about ten minutes. Under the same circumstances, pre-teenage children don't fall asleep at all. As any parent can testify, such youngsters are virtually always "on the go"; when they do fall asleep during the day, they're probably ill.

One experiment showed that after as few as three nights, adults who got one extra hour of sleep were less sleepy on the nap test and did better on tests of addition, memory and coordination.

Figure out your own sleep needs by getting a regular, fixed amount for about a month. Then add or subtract thirty minutes for two to four weeks and assess the impact that makes. Some people may also feel better with a regular midday nap. Indeed, a large part of the world's population enjoys napping, a practice that bows to our natural midafternoon dip in performance. (Also see Chapter 3, "How Much Sleep Do We Need?")

KEEP A REGULAR SCHEDULE.

If you go to sleep and get out of bed around the same time each day, you'll sleep more soundly. If you nap, do it at the same time each day, too. The time of day or night when you sleep doesn't matter; people can sleep well at any hour, if they do so consistently.

You wouldn't expect a clock to work on twenty-three-hour or twenty-seven-hour days. But some of us try to make our inner clocks do just that. If you go to bed at midnight and get up at seven on weekdays, but stay up until three Friday or Saturday night and then sleep late the next morning to catch up, you're disrupting a host of inner rhythms.

Sleeping late on Sunday morning, for example, temporarily shifts the time you are asleep and awake. Moreover, you make Sunday an abbreviated day; if you're awake a shorter time, it's harder to fall asleep and stay asleep that night. You're liable to suffer the well-known "Sunday night insomnia." That, in turn, produces "Monday morning blahs." If you want to be alert Monday morning, get enough sleep every day, and keep your weekend schedule close to that of your weekdays.

For most of us, some flexibility in sleeping and waking is tolerable, just as most of us suffer no repercussions from dining at six one night and eight the next. But if you are prone to have trouble sleeping, regularity in bedtimes may be beneficial to you, as regularity of mealtimes and exercise is to someone with diabetes.

You don't have to be rigid about it, though; there are many occasions on which you may want or be obliged to stay up past your usual bedtime. Cinderella might not have captured the affections of her prince if she'd left before the last dance!

The best way to anchor your schedule of sleeping and waking is to get up at the same time, regardless of when you go to sleep. Give yourself a good reason to get up in the morning—a place you must go, someone you must see. Even if you miss some sleep one night, the next night you'll be sleepier than usual and probably will fall asleep easily. You don't have to pay back every hour of stolen wakefulness with equal time; your body will take as much extra sleep as it needs. Sleeping more than an hour or two extra to make up for lost sleep is more likely to make you feel groggy than well rested.

Naps, incidentally, make regular nappers feel more alert but may make occasional nappers feel cranky. Sporadic napping seems to fragment sleep at night, whereas avoiding naps seems to consolidate it.

PAY ATTENTION TO WHAT, AND WHEN, YOU EAT.
Specific foods have been reported to promote drowsiness and others to promote alertness. Some of us may be more sensitive to

such foods than others, and it may take some experimentation to find out which foods, if any, have an effect on you. Following are some facts to keep in mind:

Avoid drinking coffee, tea and cola drinks containing caffeine late in the day. They may make it harder for you to fall asleep. As a stimulant, caffeine has a peak effect two to four hours after it is consumed and it may continue to affect you for as long as seven hours. Hence, it may cause you to awaken during the night.

A big meal makes most of us sleepy for a short time. It's not necessarily the type of food we eat but rather the fact of eating that may be responsible. Sleepiness may be the body's way of slowing us down while the complicated process of digestion begins. If your lunchtime coincides with your midafternoon peak of sleepiness, you may be even more sleepy than usual. Note, however, that if you consume a big meal just before bedtime, you may feel so uncomfortably full that you find it hard to fall asleep.

A low-sodium diet may disturb sleep, at least initially. A recent weight gain brings sounder sleep, while loss of weight sometimes triggers frequent awakenings during the night.

Animal studies by Charles Ehret, Ph.D., of the Argonne National Laboratory, suggest that protein foods foster alertness and carbohydrates, sleep. This finding is one of the cornerstones of his regimen to prevent jet lag, described in Chapter 11, "The Time of Our Lives."

Many people with the sleep disorder of narcolepsy report that eating carbohydrates, particularly simple sugars, such as those in candy and cookies, causes excessive sleepiness. Some people who do not have narcolepsy also believe they are more alert during the day if they avoid sugary foods. Of course, in the late evening, sleepiness is desirable, and carbohydrates often are suggested as a bedtime snack.

Whether or not you are accustomed to eating at bedtime may affect your sleep more than what you eat. Regular bedtime snackers sleep better after eating, and those who do not usually snack sleep better after not eating, according to a 1980 study by Kirstine Adam at Edinburgh University. When people departed from their usual habits, their sleep was disturbed.

A few years earlier, British scientists had reported that a popular malted milk drink consumed at bedtime made people move around less during sleep and wake less often. Dr. Adam disputes this widely cited study, suggesting that the participants may have been those who usually snacked at bedtime and as a result slept better with the drink than without it.

Hunger pangs may make you restless and cause you to awaken sooner than usual. If you do like to eat regularly at bedtime, foods that combine carbohydrates and fat (for staying power) have the strongest scientific rationale. Milk or malted milk, along with either a peanut butter sandwich or cheese and crackers, fits this bill.

Milk contains L-tryptophan, a substance that may by itself promote good sleep. Note, however, that there may not be enough L-tryptophan in a cup of milk to significantly affect most people's sleep, although some people may be exquisitely sensitive to the substance. Pleasant associations with childhood may account in part for milk's soporific effect. Whether milk is warm or cold, the L-tryptophan content is the same.

If you have certain illnesses, eating at bedtime may or may not be wise; follow your doctor's advice. Some people with ulcers, for example, may prevent pain during the night with a bedtime snack, such as milk. However, those with heartburn and choking caused by the reflux of gastric acid into the esophagus are better off avoiding food for several hours before sleeping. (These illnesses are discussed in greater detail in Chapter 13, "In Sickness and Health.")

EXERCISE REGULARLY, PREFERABLY IN THE LATE
AFTERNOON.

Trained athletes don't need more (or less) sleep than sedentary folks, but they do appear to get proportionately more deep sleep than nonathletes. Getting an adequate amount of deep sleep is a key factor in making you feel rested the next day.

Athletes who skip their customary exercise get less deep sleep than usual. Nonathletes who exercise vigorously for a day may end up that night with aches and pains that interfere with sleep, but if they keep at it, sleep improves, as a study among employees at the National Aeronautics and Space Administration headquarters in Washington, D.C., shows. One year after entering a physical fitness program that involved thirty minutes of exercise three times a week, nearly all participants reported feeling healthier and 30 percent specifically singled out having better sleep.

Exercise seems to have a more beneficial effect on sleep if performed in the late afternoon rather than in the morning. Exercising vigorously in the evening may leave you too aroused to fall asleep. Simple stretching or other relaxation exercises just before bedtime are good sleep-inducers.

KNOW THAT SEX MAY HELP (OR HURT) YOUR SLEEP.
Satisfying sexual activity may relax you and hence make it easier for you to fall asleep. If, however, you don't achieve orgasm, you may find it harder to fall asleep. When sexual relations are troubled, getting into bed may trigger in both partners feelings of tension and anger that disrupt sleep. And an argument with your spouse may, understandably, give you insomnia.

When couples who are used to sleeping together sleep apart, both partners are likely to have a harder time falling asleep and to wake more often. Nonetheless, couples who sleep together get slightly less of the deepest stages of sleep than either partner does when sleeping alone. Possibly that's because everyone moves about thirty times during a night's sleep. Over the years, couples do synchronize their movements to accommodate each other, but nonetheless each partner may disturb the other's sleep. Men usually are more disruptive because they are heavier and their movements are more forceful.

If one partner is a "lark" and the other an "owl," one may stay up later than he or she desires, while the other may suffer "insomnia" from going to bed too early. Although many couples choose to go to bed at the same time, sometimes not doing so may foster better sleep.

If your bed partner snores loudly or thrashes about and disturbs your sleep, consider sleeping in separate beds. Be sure that his or her doctor knows about these activities, because they may indicate sleep disorders.

CREATE YOUR OWN BEDTIME RITUALS.

Wind down an hour or so before bedtime. Give yourself a bedtime routine to ease your transition from wakefulness to sleep.

Sheila, a lawyer, closes her briefcase and picks up a novel every night around ten. "Reading fiction separates day and night for me," she says. Some people tell themselves that it's time to sleep by watching the late news on television, walking the dog or soaking in a warm bath. Young children may beg to hear the same story or to be tucked in with a favorite teddy bear and security blanket.

Choose bedtime rituals that you can do even when you're sleeping away from home. These might include brushing your hair a specific number of strokes or washing your face a certain way. The poet Tennyson reportedly said his own name over and over to induce sleep. Be aware that once you establish a sleep ritual, disturbing it may give you grief.

One important caveat: "While bedtime routines often prove beneficial for good sleepers, they may be detrimental to poor sleepers," notes Peter Hauri, Ph.D., director of the Sleep Disorders Center at the Dartmouth Medical School. "If brushing your teeth previously has been followed by many nights of frustration and arousal, this act then may trigger a bad night," he adds. "If poor sleepers change their customary routines or sleep away from home, they may sleep better for a while."

USE YOUR BEDROOM ONLY FOR SLEEPING.

Some of us snack, study, read and listen to music on the bed, even if not actually between the sheets. Many of us treat the bedroom as an office; we pay bills and fill out tax returns there, spreading out paperwork on the bed. We talk on the phone and watch television while in bed. Some of us use bedtime as a quiet time to rehash the day's events and plan—or worry about—tomorrow. "Such activities are not conducive to falling asleep," asserts Richard Bootzin, Ph.D., of Northwestern University. "Reserve your bed for sleep," he says. Sex is the primary exception to this rule. If you associate light reading with falling asleep—and are able to stop after a few minutes—reading may be okay, too.

For some of us, however, the basic problem is not that the bedroom and bed are cues to stay awake. Rather, it is that we try too hard to fall asleep. We toss and turn, anxiously wondering, Will I ever get to sleep? If this is your problem, "distractions can help you get to sleep faster," says Dr. Hauri. "Read, listen to music or watch television. Keep your mind occupied. Give in to the urge to fall asleep only when you cannot fight it any longer. Get up at your regular time; after a few days on this regimen, you probably will be so sleepy that you will fall asleep quickly at bedtime."

CREATE A "SAFE" SLEEPING ENVIRONMENT.

Secure locks, a smoke and fire alarm and perhaps even a burglar alarm may help give you peace of mind. Install a phone in your bedroom and get a bedside lamp that's easy to turn on in the dark, in case you need it. Children often are insecure if they are too far from their parents; a basement or an attic bedroom, a floor or more away, is not recommended for young children.

DON'T COUNT ON SMOKING AT BEDTIME TO RELAX YOU.

Nicotine is a stimulant. Hence, it may make you awaken more frequently during the night. Smoking in bed also poses the danger that you might fall asleep with your cigarette still lighted and start a fire.

DON'T RELY ON ALCOHOL.

The drunken porter in Shakespeare's *Macbeth* claims drink is a great provoker of "nose-painting, sleep, and urine." Although alcohol may help a tense person relax and hence fall asleep more easily, it's generally considered to do more harm than good. Alcohol makes it harder to stay asleep during the night.

To avoid alcohol's effects, don't drink after seven in the evening. If you do choose to drink, recognize that alcohol may disturb your sleep.

USE SLEEPING PILLS ONLY WITH YOUR DOCTOR'S ADVICE.
Benefits of sleeping medications fade quickly. After you stop taking them, your sleep may temporarily be worse than before. (Be reassured that most cases of such insomnia seldom last longer than three weeks.)

Don't drink and take a sleeping pill the same night. The mixture could be fatal. Since many sleeping pills have a carry-over effect into the next day, if you take a sleeping pill and then have a cocktail or two the next day, the alcohol may hit you harder than usual.

Don't use sleeping pills at all if you are pregnant, have difficulty breathing when awake or asleep (and particularly if you snore), or have liver or kidney disorders. (See Chapter 8 for more about sleeping pills.)

KEEP YOUR BEDROOM DARK.
Even though your eyes are closed, light can have an arousing effect. Use blinds, opaque shades or heavy curtains; if you can't get your room dark enough, consider using eyeshades. There are important exceptions: If you get up frequently during the night and have to get out of bed to go to the bathroom or check on someone who's ill, for instance, keep a flashlight nearby or use a night-light to minimize the risk of hurting yourself in the dark. Children often sleep better with a night-light; it eases their fear of the dark.

BLOCK OUT NOISE.
Music that is pleasant in the living room may annoy you when you are in bed. Continuous noises, such as the hum of your air conditioner, fan or refrigerator or the ticking of your clock, may bother you only if you can't fall asleep. Sporadic and unpredictable noises, such as airplane flyovers or street traffic, are more disruptive of sleep than constant noises.

The louder the noise and the longer it lasts, the more likely it is to arouse you. Noise may disturb your sleep even if you don't awaken fully. A quick whisper may make you move to a lighter sleep stage; if you're already in a light sleep stage, you may wake up.

"The more meaningful a noise is to you, the more attention you pay to it," says Michael Bonnet, Ph.D., of the Veterans Administration Hospital, Loma Linda, California. Your baby's whimper may disrupt your sleep more than a thunderstorm or a passing fire engine. An obstetrician on call comes fully awake at the first ring of the phone. "Smoke and fire alarms at present emit a beep about the level of normal speech, sufficient to awaken most adults. However, these alarms might wake people even faster if they contained a computer chip that shouted a significant message such as *Fire!*," Dr. Bonnet suggests.

Your mood is likely to be worse and your irritability higher the next day if your sleep is disturbed by noise, and your general health may suffer, too. People who sleep near airports or major highways eventually awaken less often than they did on first moving to the noisy neighborhood, but they continue to sleep more lightly than people sleeping in quieter surroundings. Not surprisingly, people living in noisy areas also have higher blood pressure. Even when they move away, their sleep patterns remain disturbed for months. People also get less sleep if they are exposed to continuous noise during the day, even though they get away from it at night.

Certain sounds, however, may actually facilitate sleep. Many people have observed that a loudly ticking clock or lullaby soothes a baby at bedtime. Recordings of heart sounds are said to have a similar effect. In a laboratory study, low tones that switched on and off every two seconds made people fall asleep faster than either complete silence or the monotonous hum of a fan motor, Wilse Webb, Ph.D., and H.W. Agnew, Jr., Ph.D., of the University of Florida reported. You can create the same relaxing effect for yourself when you are ready to fall asleep by repeating a soothing sound such as *mmmmm* at regular intervals. (People who practice meditation are already familiar with this technique; they immerse themselves in the meditative state by repeating a word such as "one.") In the Florida study, counting the tone signals brought sleep almost as fast as simply listening to them, a finding that validates that time-honored way of coaxing slumber, counting sheep.

To muffle unwanted noises, soundproof your bedroom with

heavy curtains and rugs and insulate windows and doors. If you are still bothered by your neighbor's stereo or barking dog or the rumble of the subway, consider using earplugs. Of course, if you live alone, you don't want to block out protective noises such as the smoke alarm or the phone. The noise or activity of your own dog or cat moving about your bedroom may disturb your sleep more than you realize.

Consider the benefits of "masking" noises, sometimes referred to as "white" noises. A fan or an air conditioner may diminish the likelihood of your hearing street sounds and thus may help protect your sleep. Relaxing sounds are available on records, tapes and in sound synthesizers. These include music, the sounds of waves lapping on the shore, rain pattering on a roof and gentle breezes.

DON'T MAKE YOUR ROOM TOO HOT OR TOO COLD FOR YOU. Benjamin Franklin advocated coolness; he even proposed readying extra beds so that a person could slip from a warm bed to a cool one during the night, after walking about the bedroom nude to allow the skin to cool. Some people like their bedroom windows open, even in midwinter; others insist, no matter what the temperature, that "night air" is unhealthy. There's no scientific support for any of these notions.

With today's emphasis on energy conservation, many people now set their thermostats during the winter at 65°F or lower at night and pile on the blankets. Although warmth at bedtime probably will make you relax and fall asleep more easily, feeling too warm or too cool during the night will disturb your sleep. People move around less during sleep when they're cold than when they're warm enough; frigid sheets deter the sleeper from abandoning a comfortably warm spot.

At room temperatures above 75°F, people tend to wake more often, stay awake longer, get less deep sleep and dreaming sleep and have less total sleep time than at lower temperatures. In one study, as the room temperature was turned down from 72°F to 63°F and then to 54°F, sleepers reported more emotional and unpleasant dreams. Many people find room temperatures in the upper 60s quite satisfactory, but the "best" temperature for you is the one that makes you comfortable.

As you get older, your body's temperature-regulating mechanisms tend to become less efficient. To help counter sluggish circulation on cold nights, use an electric blanket or wear socks to bed, along with warm nightclothes. You lose one ninth of your body heat through your head; wearing an old-fashioned nightcap can help keep you cozy.

SLEEP IN A WELL-VENTILATED AND HUMIDIFIED AREA.

One drawback to current energy conservation efforts is the indoor air pollution that may develop in tightly sealed buildings. As people breathe in rooms without adequate ventilation, oxygen in the air decreases and carbon dioxide increases. During sleep, when breathing normally slows, it may be harder to get an adequate amount of oxygen. The hazard is greatest for people with breathing problems. For them, an open window and a fan may be advisable to improve ventilation.

If the air's too dry, your skin and the linings of the nose and throat may feel scratchy. If it's too humid, you'll feel sweaty and warm. In both cases, you're likely to sleep more fitfully than you would in a properly humidified room. A humidifier in your bedroom in winter and an air conditioner in summer may be helpful.

CHOOSE A COMFORTABLE BED.

Like many other factors affecting sleep, the "right" bed for you is the one you prefer, often simply the one to which you are most accustomed. There's no mystique about mattresses; people around the world remain healthy and sleep comfortably on straw mats, animal skins and in hammocks. There is no scientific evidence that innersprings, foam, a waterbed or any particular surface will make you sleep better. A couple sleeping together need a bed that provides adequate space for each person to move during the night.

Firm surfaces may be advised for someone with back problems; they keep the spine from sagging into unnatural bends and tiring back muscles. If you suffer from heartburn and choking caused by the reflux of gastric acid into the esophagus, or from breathing difficulties, you may sleep better if your head and upper trunk are elevated about six inches.

Whether to use a pillow—soft or firm, down or foam or none at all—is also a matter of personal preference unless, again, medical needs such as chronic neck strain play a role. Satin sheets may be fun for romance, but they're not conducive to sleep because they're slippery and they don't absorb perspiration as well as more porous materials, such as cotton. With reference to nightclothes, you'll probably sleep better if you don't roll over on buttons or bows or feel the pull of a tight collar. Hair curlers may cause enough discomfort to lighten sleep.

Although, contrary to a recently publicized notion, positions you assume to fall asleep or during sleep don't reveal your type of personality any better than your characteristic daytime postures do, there may be a good reason to discourage certain sleep positions. Sleeping on the stomach is best avoided by people with back problems, for example, because it tends to increase the arch in the lower back and cause unnecessary strain. Sleeping with hand or arm under the pillow may cause tissue congestion, which aggravates rheumatoid arthritis, or pressure on the nerves, which leads to tingling and numbness in the fingers. People with certain breathing problems will breathe more easily if they sleep on their sides. Do-it-yourself measures to help maintain proper posture, such as sewing a pocket for a Ping-Pong ball on the back or front of pajamas, or placing pillows or foam blocks in strategic positions, may be useful; ask your doctor if he or she recommends them.

TRY NOT TO WORRY ABOUT YOUR SLEEP.
The impact of losing part or all of a night's sleep seems to be similar to that of skipping a meal or fasting for a day. Doing without some sleep—or food—now and then apparently won't hurt you. Yet missing sleep stirs anxieties that missing food does not.

Hundreds of devices designed to aid sleep can be purchased: vibrating mattresses, white-noise machines, videotapes to be played in the bedroom featuring a half hour of tranquil nature scenes and sounds, radios with "snooze control" timers to turn them off automatically, blanket supports, chin straps to prevent snoring, anatomically molded pillows, and more. Some of these devices may help us, particularly if we believe that they will.

Fortunately, we may discover, like Dorothy in *The Wizard of Oz*, that what we are seeking—the secret of good sleep—has been in our possession the whole time. We need not stalk after sleep. We can entice it to come to us. Give the recommendations outlined in this chapter a fair trial. Then relax. As the poet Richard Wilbur suggests in "Walking to Sleep":

> *As a queen sits down, knowing the chair will be there,*
> *Or a general raises his hand and is given the field glasses,*
> *Step off assuredly into the blank of your mind,*
> *Something will come to you.*

16

WHAT TO DO IF YOU CAN'T SLEEP— OR CAN'T STAY AWAKE

Complaints about sleep fall into two main categories: "I don't sleep well" and "I'm sleepy all day long." If you can't sleep, you're all too aware of it, but if your sleep is broken by many partial or very brief awakenings, you may be troubled more by discomfort during the day than by worries about lost sleep. If you feel lethargic, you may suspect that you are sleeping poorly, but if you suffer symptoms such as a headache or attacks of muscle weakness, you might not be aware of the "sleep connection."

This entire book aims to help you identify your problem. It *cannot*, however, substitute for your doctor. Many of the more than 120 discrete disorders of sleep have symptoms in common, even though their causes and their remedies vary considerably. A self-diagnosis could be wrong and could lead you to try remedies that won't help you; at the same time it might cause you to put off seeking proper care.

Sleep specialists frequently cite the tale of the overweight man who is constantly sleepy during the day. He decides he needs more sleep at night and, in hopes of getting it, takes sleeping pills. Months pass before he visits his doctor, who directs him to a sleep disorders center. During a night in the sleep laboratory, he stops breathing hundreds of times; his heartbeat wavers from a normal 70 beats per minute to dangerous extremes of as low as 30 beats per minute and as high as 160 beats per minute. The pauses in breathing, of which he was oblivious, not only were robbing him of sleep and causing his daytime sleepiness but also were threatening his life.

Another familiar case is that of the woman who insists she has terrible insomnia because it takes her three or four hours to fall asleep each night. She blames concern about her hard-driving boss, her mother's illness and her son's poor grades. In reality, she is not an insomniac at all. She has disturbing thoughts simply because she is lying in bed awake for a long time. The problem is not in her sleep but rather in the timing of her sleep. Her sleep schedule is out of sync with the rest of her life. The clue is that she needs two alarm clocks to awaken her each morning. If allowed to sleep longer, she would sleep quite well.

You can get a better handle on *your* problem by following these four important steps:

Step 1: Assess Your Sleep

Start today to keep a sleep/wake diary. (See the sample diary in the Appendix.) You'll record the time that you go to bed, how long it takes to fall asleep, whether you awaken during the night, when you get out of bed in the morning, how well you concentrate on tasks during the day, and more. Most people find that a diary makes them more conscious of the impact of their daily lives on their sleep and vice versa. The log will also help you to see if there's a particular pattern in your sleep difficulties.

Don't put off starting your diary, because "this is not a typical week." Ask yourself when you last had a "typical" week. A trip, party, work deadline, staying up for the late show, or other events may—or may not—alter your sleep. Documenting the effect of such activities day by day may help you to anticipate the ones that are likely to disturb your sleep. Therefore, you'll be able to deal with them better. *Keeping a sleep/wake diary is a critical first step to better sleep.*

Step 2: Practice Good Sleep Hygiene

The term "hygiene," favored by sleep specialists, may sound musty, but the concept of health maintenance that it stands for is current and sound. In our busy lives, we sometimes overlook the basic principles of good health. Getting enough sleep, keeping a regular schedule, exercising, creating a safe, quiet, dark environment that fosters sleep, and following other commonsense practices may make a real difference in your life. (For details, see Chapter 15, "How to Get a Better Night's Sleep.")

Step 3: Search Out Stresses in Your Life

If you doubt that your customary habits are ruining your sleep or causing unusual lassitude during the day, perhaps you're under unusual stress. Have you changed jobs, gotten married or divorced, become a parent, been ill or suffered the death of someone close to you? Such experiences cause some people to sleep less and others to sleep more; most people in such circumstances feel "worn down," fatigued and in need of more sleep.

Sleep problems can often be linked to a specific event. When the stressful situation is temporary, such problems usually disappear quickly. Students sleep better after exams than before them, for example. Even when stress continues, sleep problems often lighten after a few days or weeks. If you get passed over for a job promotion, you may continue to seethe, but a month later you'll probably sleep better than you did the day you heard about it. Yet many people with long-standing sleep problems insist, "Stress made things much worse. I never have gotten back to my normal self."

"Most of us know that when we sleep poorly for a few days or weeks, daytime mood and functioning suffer," observes Peter Hauri, Ph.D., director of the Sleep Disorders Center at the Dartmouth Medical School. "Getting a good night's sleep becomes an increasingly important preoccupation. We try harder and harder to fall asleep. This attempt, in itself, causes increased arousal and interferes with the process of falling asleep. After a siege of bad nights, we may anticipate trouble sleeping as soon as we enter the bedroom, prepare for bed and lie down."

If your problem is annoyingly frequent or severe, or if it has continued unabated for more than one month, it's time to seek help.

Step 4: See Your Doctor

Your doctor may be able to determine if you have a sleep disorder from the facts you provide, including your answers to a sleep questionnaire (such as those in use at many sleep disorders centers) and your sleep/wake diary. A complete physical exam and, possibly, hormone function tests or other laboratory tests may help identify—or rule out—certain disorders.

Ask your bed partner or roommate about your sleep, and, if possible, take him or her with you when you see your doctor. A woman who has rhythmic kicks during the night knows about them only secondhand, for example, but her husband can describe her problem quite well. If you know that you snore, tape-record the first hour of a night's sleep. (The recorder will shut off automatically.) Listen for extremely noisy snoring interrupted by silences that last ten seconds or longer and then are followed by gasps. This pattern suggests sleep apnea. Take the tape when you visit the doctor.

If your doctor thinks you have a sleep disorder, he or she may prescribe treatment or recommend that you go to a sleep disorders center for further study. Sometimes a diagnosis cannot be made until after sleep has been monitored in a sleep laboratory and brain waves, muscle activity, breathing and other aspects of sleep have been evaluated. (For what to expect at a sleep disorders center, see Chapter 17.)

What to Do If You Can't Sleep

Some people with insomnia have psychiatric disorders, such as depression and anxiety. Others have illnesses that are induced by sleep and that can be verified only by study during sleep; these include sleep apnea and periodic leg movements. Still others have problems tied to dependency on sleeping pills or alcohol. (The many causes of insomnia are discussed in Chapter 7, "Insomnia.") Sometimes, however, people appear to be "healthy" insomniacs. Their problem persists even though no reason for it can be found.

Until very recently, most people with this problem had a simple choice: either put up with it, or take sleeping pills. During the past few years, since it has been learned that most sleeping pills lose their effectiveness in as little as two weeks, physicians' attitudes toward prescribing sleeping pills have changed dramatically. Today, pills are viewed as beneficial for short-term or occasional use, even in people with chronic insomnia.

Insight into persistent insomnia has encouraged the development of new ways to deal with it. "Treatment for someone with insomnia has many similarities to rehabilitation for someone who has suffered a stroke," suggests Merrill Mitler, Ph.D., senior staff scientist at the Scripps Clinic and Research Foundation. "The stroke victim may need to learn to walk or talk all over again. The insomniac may need to learn new ways to fall asleep or to get back to sleep if he awakens during the night."

There are no easy or instant cures for chronic insomnia. Warm milk at bedtime won't solve this problem. Compare your task with that of losing weight. Getting rid of twenty extra pounds takes time. To keep them off, you probably need to adopt new eating habits. To overcome insomnia, you may have to make substantive changes in your daily life. The methods described below have proved successful with thousands of poor sleepers.

One caution—these are *not* "home remedies" to try before you seek help. If your problem is long-standing, you need to be absolutely certain that you are, indeed, a "healthy" insomniac. The strategies you follow should be tailored to your individual needs.

You can improve your odds of resolving your problem by proceeding under the direction of a knowledgeable health professional. Your doctor may make specific recommendations or may refer you to a sleep disorders center. Additionally, you can locate behavioral therapists at medical centers and universities, usually in departments of psychiatry or psychology, as well as at many community mental health centers. The methods described here frequently are advised by such professionals.

FOCUS YOUR THOUGHTS.

The solitude and quiet of the bed provide many of us with the welcome opportunity for uninterrupted, reflective thought. Some of us luxuriate in this experience. One writer says that the tranquility of the dark helps her to collect ideas that are floating at the periphery of her consciousness. A business executive deliberately concentrates on his most pressing decision, hoping to awaken in the morning with his priorities resolved; frequently, he does.

We may review what we've accomplished during the day and plan for tomorrow, perhaps even jotting down a note or two on a pad kept at the bedside for this purpose. Some of us habitually spend just a few minutes this way; others muse for an hour or even longer. At some point, we decide it's time for sleep and drift off.

Some of us, however, are unable to let go easily. Perhaps we focus more on our failures than on our successes. We chafe about what we should have done today. We fret about the obstacles we must face tomorrow. If worried thoughts make it hard for you to fall asleep or bother you if you wake during the night, master the skill of self-distraction. By consistently returning to a specific topic, you will endow it with the power to ease you into the night.

Counting sheep is an old favorite; moreover, it really works. We associate counting with making progress. The regular tones that sound in your head as you count have been shown in sleep-laboratory studies to speed falling asleep. The pastoral scene engages your mind, squeezing out unwelcome thoughts. For similar reasons, some people find it helpful to imagine that they are slowly painting large figure 3's in white paint on a black wall with a tiny brush. Although few other methods of mental imagery have been scientifically investigated, the concept of self-distraction, sometimes called self-hypnosis, is a time-tested one.

Here's a sampler of twelve ways to occupy your mind:

1. Name animals, birds, countries or other objects in specific categories alphabetically. Traveling from Afghanistan to Bulgaria to China and onward may aid your trip to slumberland as well.

2. Spell your name backward, or visualize writing it over and over in inks of different colors.

3. Compose letters to the editor.

4. Make up clues for crossword puzzles.

5. Practice multiplication tables.

6. Count backward from 1,000 by threes.

7. Create a bedtime fantasy in which all your wishes come true.

8. Sing a favorite song in your mind, or listen to music through a pillow speaker.

9. Try prayer; people have relied on it for centuries to banish worldly thoughts at bedtime.

10. Go for a mental stroll down a familiar, pleasant path.

11. Think of a situation in which you could barely keep your eyes open but had to ward off sleep—standing guard duty, for instance, or driving late at night. Savor your relief when the task is done. Now, surrender to your sleepiness.

12. Recall a time when you fell asleep easily and pleasurably, on a warm, sunny beach listening to the waves softly lapping the shore, or tucked into your childhood bed; mentally transport yourself back in time. Situations you have actually experienced are believed to have a more potent effect than scenes you fabricate.

A twenty-seven-year-old woman who complained of intrusive thoughts that had made it difficult for her to fall asleep "for as long as I can remember," gained relief with a technique known as chunking. Gila Lindsley, Ph.D., of the West-Ros-Park Mental Health Center, Boston, asked the woman to keep a notebook by her bedside. Every night for a week, she recorded on a separate page one key word that captured each thought that ran through her mind. At the end of the week, she was instructed to categorize the hundreds of pages into stacks. She quickly reduced them to ten piles and labeled the stacks with summary words or phrases. Over the next weeks, she was asked to practice classifying every extraneous thought that bothered her, day or night, and to condense the ten categories to seven, a number that psychological theorists say is more easily remembered. As her mastery of this skill grew, she fell asleep much faster. Grouping thoughts into meaningful "chunks" apparently stopped the frenetic whirr of ideas that had been keeping her awake.

If all else fails, concentrate on trying to stay awake. This paradoxical instruction isn't facetious advice. In laboratory studies, people who ordinarily took an hour or more to fall asleep were wired for a night's sleep-recording. The researcher turned out the lights, went around the corner and then returned to say, "Something's wrong with our equipment. Please don't go to sleep until we tell you it's fixed." The insomniacs all fell asleep in a few minutes. Whether you can trick yourself this way is arguable. However, by paying attention to your waking sensations and thoughts, you may divert yourself from worry about how long it will take to fall asleep. In this way, *you can use your insomnia productively, rather than being victimized by it.*

TRY STIMULUS CONTROL.

For most of us, falling asleep is the last of a series of ritual events that includes walking the dog, locking the doors, donning nightclothes and brushing teeth. Most of us sleep better in our own beds than anywhere else.

If that's not true for you, if you doze easily on the living room couch, but find you are wide awake when you get into bed, or if you sleep better away from home, your bedroom and bedtime may be acting as stimuli to keep you awake. Sofia, an accountant, does tax returns in her bedroom; even after the lights are out, she can "see" the piles of unfinished paperwork. Roger, a member of his community's volunteer fire company, is always "on call" for emergencies.

Stimulus control, an approach developed by Richard Bootzin, Ph.D., chairman of the department of psychology at Northwestern University, aims to strengthen the role of bed and bedroom as cues for sleep and to weaken their role as cues for activities that may interfere with sleep. This approach puts you in control of your sleep behavior and calls for permanent changes in your sleeping habits. It works for people who have trouble falling asleep at the beginning of the night, as well as for those who have trouble getting back to sleep if awakened during the night. These are the rules to follow:

• Lie down intending to go to sleep *only* when you are sleepy. "Tune in to your body's demands," says Dr. Bootzin. "It's not necessary to get in bed at the same time every night." For most people, however, a fairly regular schedule promotes readiness to sleep at about the same time each night.

• Use your bed and bedroom only for sleep and sex. Some of us find reading or watching television in bed a relaxing preliminary to sleep. But if you have trouble falling asleep, do not read, watch television, eat, pay bills, do needlepoint, talk on the phone or do anything else in bed. Such activities make not sleeping too attractive. In particular, avoid rehashing matters that worry you; instead, set aside a time earlier in the day for quiet reflection. Keep arguments with your spouse out of the bedroom, too. If your profession demands that you be "on call," try to find a colleague to share the burden, so that you can count on some nights without interruptions.

When husbands and wives go to bed at the same time, one may feel that bedtime is consistently "too early" or "too late." The spouse who wants to read or watch television when the other is ready to sleep belongs in another room. "You can maintain an affectionate relationship with different bedtimes," Dr. Bootzin points out. Lovemaking at other times of the day may even prove more romantic because it is less routine.

• Don't stare at the clock, but if you don't fall asleep in ten to fifteen minutes, get up and go to another room. Do anything you want there, but don't snack. Food, for most of us, is such a nice treat that eating during the night acts as a reward for sleeplessness. Further, it's too easy to overeat. It's not necessary, and probably not even helpful, to punish yourself for being awake. Don't force yourself to clean the oven or iron clothes, for example; being out of bed is bad enough. The idea is to make yourself drowsy.
• Go back to bed only when you are sleepy.
• If you still cannot fall asleep quickly, get up again and leave your bedroom. Repeat as often as necessary through the night.
• Set an alarm clock. It's best to get up at the same time every morning, regardless of how much sleep you got during the night. Doing this will help your body acquire a consistent sleep rhythm. Many of us, insomniacs included, enjoy sleeping an hour or two later on weekends. An occasional *minor* indulgence is unlikely to do serious harm to your sleep; don't feel guilty about it. But don't let yourself sleep until noon.

- In the morning, don't read the newspaper and have coffee in bed. The association of your bed with these activities may carry over into the night.
- Don't nap during the day.

On your first few nights practicing this regimen, you may be busy trotting in and out of your bedroom; however, you probably won't get any less sleep than you did before. Furthermore, if you do lose sleep one night, that should make it easier for you to fall asleep the next. "Admittedly, it's a nuisance to get out of bed, particularly in the winter, when your bed is warm and the house is chilly. Anticipate this problem and keep a robe by your bed," Dr. Bootzin says. "Forcing yourself to get up will help you break the habit of not sleeping in bed," he adds. Additionally, you will gain a sense of control over your own sleep.

Within a few weeks, progress should be apparent; three out of four people with "conditioned insomnia" who stick with this regimen learn to fall asleep faster. This approach has helped people who have had insomnia for years. Many say that the quality of their sleep overall is better, too. Incorporating this regimen into your daily life should help you to cope more easily with temporary bouts of insomnia. If you want to chart your achievement, start a sleep log when you start the program.

LEARN TO RELAX.

Learning to relax is hard work, as anyone who's tried it can testify. Numerous relaxation techniques are used for insomnia; all are based on the premise that if you can relax at bedtime, you will fall asleep more easily.

Compared with good sleepers, many insomniacs who are otherwise healthy have higher rates of muscle tension both awake and asleep and describe themselves as more anxious and depressed. If you feel tense and anxious at bedtime, physical and mental relaxation skills may help you. Further, such skills may help you to deal better with other stresses in your life.

One technique, known as autogenic training, relies on self-suggestion. You tell yourself over and over, "My arm is heavy, I am at peace, my arm is heavy." Practice twice a day for about twenty minutes each time, with one session in bed prior to sleep. It usually takes about three to six weeks to learn to make any part of the body "heavy" this way; then you follow the same routine to produce a sensation of warmth.

Another approach, known as progressive, or deep muscle, relaxation, teaches people to recognize muscle tension in order to reduce it. You might be told, for example, "Bend your right hand back as far as possible. Hold it. Notice the strain in the back of your hand and up your arm. Keep holding it while you count slowly to seven. Now let your hand relax completely. Feel the difference?" Over a period of weeks, "tune in" to each muscle group in your body. Some people like to start with the forehead and work down the body to the toes. Set aside two twenty-minute periods a day, one at bedtime, to practice. Eventually, you may not need to tense muscles before you relax them; you will be able to start relaxing from your normal level of tension and become, as the name of the technique suggests, progressively more relaxed.

Transcendental meditation involves focusing attention to free the mind from distracting thoughts. For this experience, you need a comfortable chair in a quiet place. Relax, close your eyes and as you breathe out, repeat in your mind a word or phrase, such as "one," "peace," or "I am calm." Words repeated in this way are sometimes referred to as mantras. If your mind wanders, try to concentrate again on repeating the word or phrase. Experienced meditators have slower heartbeats and rates of breathing and more "relaxed" brain waves than nonmeditators trying simply to stay awake with their eyes closed. Mastery of the technique calls for twenty-minute practice sessions two or three times a day; one of them may be at bedtime.

Yoga, aerobic dancing, gymnastics, swimming, jogging, weight lifting, even walking—all promote physical and mental relaxation. Don't overlook regular exercise as an aid to sleep.

"Relaxation treatments may be effective, not because of the specific training, but because they require people to schedule time to relax," Dr. Bootzin suggests. They reduce daily stress. They may help you to "turn off" at bedtime and distract you from worries that interfere with falling asleep.

The various methods of relaxation all have been shown to shorten the time it takes to fall asleep; however, no single method has been proved consistently superior to the others. If you're a fidgety person, you might prefer muscle relaxation; if you're the quiet type, meditation might be more your style. You make the choice. *Diligent practice is necessary to learn these skills and to maintain them.*

If you think you might benefit from relaxation skills, you can learn more from a wide variety of how-to-do-it books, available at your local bookstore or library. Adult education programs offer courses in relaxation or meditation. Records and tapes with step-by-step instructions are also available and are often advertised in psychology and health magazines. One New York hospital offers on its telephone hotline an eight-minute tape that leads callers through simple relaxation exercises; the hospital is so certain of success that the popular tape includes reminders to hang up before nodding off.

COULD BIOFEEDBACK HELP?

This approach may help you learn to control bodily processes usually regarded as not under voluntary control. If you stand in front of a mirror for hours to master wiggling your ears, you're practicing biofeedback.

Instruction in the different methods of biofeedback is provided by many sleep centers and by many behavioral therapists. These techniques help some people who have insomnia improve their ability to relax and others to learn to induce drowsiness. Sensors applied to the head are connected via wires to a biofeedback monitor. The device picks up minute amounts of electrical activity generated by muscles as they contract, or by the brain. The electrical signals are amplified and converted to an auditory or visual display, such as a beep or a flashing light.

The subject observes changes in these signals and uses trial and error to try to relax muscles or produce brain waves associated with sleep. Eventually, it's hoped, he will learn to achieve these results without the machine and therefore will be able to fall asleep faster. When people are asked, "How do you do it?," they invariably reply, "I don't know; I just sense that what I'm doing is right." Biofeedback is usually taught in hour-long sessions given two or three times a week for about eight weeks. Periodic refresher sessions may be advised. If you would like "proof" that you can alter bodily responses, you may find biofeedback appealing.

Tense people may benefit from learning to relax. But people who are already relaxed will not benefit from trying to relax more; they might even feel frustrated, which could make their insomnia worse. "If you try biofeedback, it's critical to first find out which approach is most likely to help you," stresses Dr. Hauri.

Because some people who prove adept at biofeedback in a laboratory setting continue to have trouble sleeping in their own bedrooms, there's growing interest today in biofeedback equipment for home use. One device, already on the market, helps develop relaxation skills by monitoring small changes in skin temperature that reflect tension. It turns itself off as the user falls asleep, loosening his grip. Check with your doctor first, to see if he or she thinks home devices will be useful to you.

LOOK INTO BEHAVIORAL SELF-MANAGEMENT.

This comprehensive approach teaches you strategies that may not only help you to sleep better but also improve your ability to take charge of other aspects of your life.

One self-management program for poor sleepers is a six-month undertaking. Developed by Thomas Coates, Ph.D., of the University of California School of Medicine, San Francisco, and Carl Thoresen, Ph.D., of Stanford University, it begins with a two-to-four-week period of assessment in which you address the issues outlined at the beginning of this chapter, that is, your health and life-style. You also start a sleep/wake diary.

In the next month, you learn relaxation skills and other techniques. "Cognitive restructuring," for example, teaches you to use thoughts conducive to good sleep. Lying in bed, you might tell yourself, "If I continue to relax, I should fall asleep soon." You become a "personal scientist" to try to discover the causes of your good nights and your bad ones.

You decide how your sleep might be improved and begin making changes. You might write a contract with yourself, stating, for example, "I agree not to talk on the phone after ten at night."

Over the next few months, you continue to search for, and change, factors that make your sleep worse and to keep up those that make your sleep better. "You will never be 'cured' of your insomnia," the researchers emphasize. But you should be able to fall asleep faster, return to sleep sooner if you wake during the night and enjoy your sleep more, if you continue to practice the strategies that you have learned will help you.

Among their dramatic "success stories" is that of a fifty-eight-year-old woman who had had insomnia for more than thirty years. Her improvement was documented with all-night sleep recordings; five years later, it continues. She no longer thinks of herself as an insomniac. She asserts, "My body has learned to tumble into bed and go to sleep. I know I have the resources to manage poor sleep when it occurs."

JOIN A "POOR SLEEPERS" GROUP.

There's no Poor Sleepers Anonymous yet, but many medical centers, universities and community health programs and some physicians run groups for insomniacs who are otherwise in good health. Such programs allow you to share your problems and progress and to learn from others.

A Stanford University program, based on the behavioral self-management approach, has helped many poor sleepers to sleep better and to abandon their use of sleeping pills.

Some insomniacs get together just for fun. A New York City ecology group, Friends of the Parks, sponsors bicycle tours in the early morning hours. The City of Baltimore's "insomniac tours" have captured national attention; the popular "ghost tour" includes a visit to the grave of Edgar Allan Poe and a reading by candlelight of one of his spookier tales.

What to Do If You Are Always "Too Sleepy"

As with insomnia, the first step is to find out the cause. In a nationwide study of thousands of patients coming to sleep disorders centers, two disorders—sleep apnea and narcolepsy—proved responsible for seven out of every ten cases of excessive sleepiness. (See Chapters 9 and 10.)

Other causes of excessive sleepiness include periodic leg movements and the restless legs syndrome; a person with these problems usually knows he has had a fretful night and hence complains of insomnia, but sometimes he has no awareness of any trouble while he sleeps and instead focuses on sleepiness during the day. Metabolic and endocrine disorders, such as diabetes and thyroid disease, occasionally cause sleepiness. Many women feel unusually sleepy just before their menstrual periods, and excessive sleepiness is often an early indication of pregnancy.

As we grow older, we become less able to sustain sleep for long periods. We sleep less at night and nap more during the day. Boredom, living alone with few social contacts, and limited mobility may make a person sleepy.

The use of sleeping pills at night may undermine alertness the next day. Alcohol can have a similar effect. In manic-depressive disease, people may alternate periods of normal or very short sleep with periods of excessive sleep.

In sum, it's possible for doctors to put a "tag" on most cases of daytime sleepiness; then they can proceed with specific treatment. Perhaps only one person in one hundred has sleepiness that persists, without any discoverable underlying reason. Of course, there's small comfort in this number if it applies to you. The following guidelines may help.

DEFINE YOUR FEELINGS MORE PRECISELY.

Most of us tend to use the words "sleepy" and "tired" indiscriminately. Yet the feelings of sleepiness that we experience in the late evening are quite distinct from the physical tiredness we feel after jogging or chopping wood or the mental tiredness we have after a long day at the office. Sleepiness is sometimes described by sleep authorities as a "drive" state, because it leads us to seek sleep. Tiredness, on the other hand, may be relieved by resting or turning to another activity.

What you are feeling may be neither sleepiness nor tiredness but rather a reaction to a stressful situation. Another, more serious cause of feeling fatigued is a psychiatric depression. Some of us use tiredness as a psychological defense to protect ourselves from problems we can't see a way to resolve. We've all known people who simply "took to bed."

People who spend long periods in bed, dozing on and off, are prone to develop disorders of their sleep/wake schedule. Their bodies are never sure whether it's time to sleep or time to be awake; as a result, they do neither well. Someone with this problem may complain of both insomnia and sleepiness.

As a practical first step, put rules of good sleep hygiene to work in your life (see Chapter 15). Consider psychological or psychiatric help. Getting further insight into your problem may help you overcome it.

TAKE REGULAR NAPS.

Naps have a bad reputation, at least in Western society; most people associate them with laziness. But many productive persons nap; one of them, Winston Churchill, wrote in *The Gathering Storm*, "I always went to bed for at least one hour as early as possible in the afternoon and exploited to the full my happy gift of falling almost immediately to sleep. By this means I was able to press a day and a half's work into one."

You'll fall asleep fastest at the natural low point of your daily cycle of sleepiness and alertness. Those of us who sleep at night usually feel most drowsy in the early to mid afternoon. Some entire cultures bow to this daily rhythm; sleep disorders centers in countries such as Italy seem to have fewer patients complaining of excessive daytime sleepiness than those in the United States or England, where regular napping is less prevalent.

People who regularly take a thirty-minute to sixty-minute nap report feeling more energetic afterward and do better on tests of mental performance. However, people who nap only occasionally often find they are "undone" by the experience.

The loss of the ability to get a long, unbroken period of nighttime sleep, which often occurs as we get older, may be offset considerably by a judiciously scheduled daytime nap. Regular naps help people with narcolepsy control their tenacious sleepiness.

GET MORE SLEEP. (YES, YOU!)

It's easy to shortchange yourself on sleep. If you're trying to be a "supermom" who shines at the office, dishes up tasty meals for your family, keeps your home company-perfect and doesn't want to neglect community activities or friends, you're probably the last person in your home to go to bed and the first one up in the morning. Are you getting enough sleep?

Or if you're going to school while working, or holding two jobs, you're also a prime candidate for this problem. If you're a shift worker, you're at high risk, too, because your body clock often is out of sync with your scheduled time for sleep and work.

The impact of insufficient sleep is sometimes subtle: Irritability, difficulty concentrating, even loss of appetite and painful muscles are symptoms that may reflect chronically inadequate sleep. *Insufficient sleep is the major cause of persistent sleepiness in otherwise healthy people.*

Many people who need nine, ten or more hours of sleep every day don't want to "waste" that much time in bed. But some of us need that much sleep in order to feel alert during the day. There is no fixed amount of sleep that's right for everybody. Some of us need more sleep than others, just as some of us need more calories than others to maintain the same weight. If you fall asleep in sedentary situations—when you watch television or listen to lectures, for example—you're probably not getting enough sleep.

If you feel terrific when you have the opportunity to sleep as long as you like—on vacations of more than a few days, for instance—the solution to your problem is clear: Get more sleep. It may be hard to pass up the late show or to leave a party before midnight. The trade-off is increased well-being and productivity while you are awake. Only you can decide if it's worth it.

17

COULD A SLEEP CENTER HELP YOU?

By now, you know about the most common sleep disorders and the impact they have on daily life. You've become, we hope, aware that poor sleep habits can undermine your sleep, while good ones can enhance it. You also now know that sleeping pills may not be the best solution for troubled sleep. If you suspect that you may have a sleep disorder, or that someone in your family does, you may want professional help.

"Most people are good judges of when they need care," notes Charles Pollak, M.D., director of the Sleep-Wake Disorders Center at the New York Hospital-Cornell Medical Center. But he also believes that many of us tend to put off seeking attention for too long. "Most people with insomnia, for example, have had it for many years. They keep hoping it will go away," he asserts.

It's time to seek help if any of the following conditions applies to you:

- You feel you are not sleeping properly at night, you feel that there is something abnormal about your sleep (perhaps someone has told you that you snore or sleepwalk) or you feel that you are too sleepy during the day no matter how much sleep you get at night.
- Your problem occurs frequently or is severe (perhaps you have seizures or you often wake during the night drenched with sweat).

- Your problem has continued for a month or more.
- It has caused an accident or near-accident on the road, at work or at home.
- It has jeopardized a job or social relationships.

If your spouse or child suffers from any of these problems, then it is important for you to see that he or she receives help promptly.

To help you examine your sleeping habits, we've included a daily sleep/wake diary at the back of this book. Your next step is to schedule a visit to your doctor. Because he or she knows you well, your doctor can relate sleep problems to your overall health.

The characteristic symptoms of some disorders make it possible for doctors to diagnose them in their office, perhaps with the help of studies of hormone function, breathing patterns and heart rhythms. But sometimes your doctor will need the kind of information that only a sleep disorders center provides.

What to Expect at a Sleep Disorders Center

After you schedule an appointment, most sleep centers will send a sleep/wake diary for you to complete before your visit. You'll review this information with a staff member and discuss your problem further. The initial examination at most sleep centers includes comprehensive medical, psychological and neurological tests. You probably will be asked to complete several questionnaires, to provide details about your problem and the impact that it is having on your life.

Some people whose symptoms appear to indicate sleep disorders turn out not to have such problems at all. Fatigue may be caused by depression or thyroid disease, for example. Because sleep specialists are familiar with a wide range of sleep disorders, they may be able to diagnose your problem after the initial exam.

However, it's more likely that the evaluation of your problem will require a look at your sleep. Recording your sleep may reveal when the problems occur and what goes wrong. The records can also show how your sleep patterns compare with "averages" obtained from the study of hundreds of normal sleepers of the same age.

Some sleep studies can be carried out during the hours you ordinarily are awake. People with narcolepsy, for example, frequently begin sleep with the REM state of sleep, unlike normal sleepers who ordinarily start with a long period of deep NREM sleep; this unusual feature shows up even during naps. But most sleep studies are done during your customary time for sleep. Following are the answers to the questions most frequently asked of sleep specialists.

HOW IS SLEEP MONITORED?

You will probably be asked to come to the sleep laboratory an hour or two before your usual bedtime. After you get ready for bed, a technician will place electrodes and other sensors at strategic spots on your body.

Consider for a moment a checkup in your doctor's office. He or she listens to your heart, takes your blood pressure, asks you to flex and relax certain muscles. You report whether or not you feel pain from a pinprick. Electrodes may be placed on your chest for a recording of heart muscle activity, a test known as an electrocardiogram (ECG), or on the scalp, for a recording of brain activity, known as an electroencephalogram (EEG). The tests performed when you sleep are quite similar.

The sensors attached to your body are connected to color-coded wires that plug into a panel by your bed. These, in turn, are connected to a device known as a polygraph, located in another room. The polygraph amplifies the signals generated by bodily activity. As its name suggests, it produces "many tracings," one for each sensor that you wear. The lines run across a continuous roll of moving paper, making up the record of your night's sleep, which is referred to as a polysomnogram. By turning various dials, the technician overseeing your sleep can adjust the signals, much as you might fine-tune your television set.

The minute electrical signals go in only one direction, to the polygraph; it is not possible for you to receive an electric shock.

WHAT IS MEASURED?

Two measurements are necessary to distinguish REM sleep from NREM sleep, and to detect the various stages of NREM sleep.

They are *brain activity*, monitored by electrodes on your scalp, and *eye movements*, monitored by electrodes near the outer corners of your eyes. For greater precision, many laboratories also monitor *chin movements*, by placing electrodes on the chin.

The other measurements to be made depend on the reason why your sleep is being evaluated. The most customary ones include *heart activity*, checked by electrodes on your chest; *leg movements*, noted by electrodes on your legs; *breathing* (that is, the rate at which air enters and leaves your body), measured by means of a light face mask worn during sleep, or "beads" that are sensitive to changes in temperature of incoming and outgoing air, taped near your nose and mouth; *breathing effort* (or the movement of your chest and diaphragm), assessed with small gauges on elastic bands placed around your body across your chest and abdomen); *blood oxygen saturation* (that is, the changing amount of oxygen in your blood, an indication of how efficiently you breathe), assayed with a device that clips on one earlobe, much like an earring (the assessment of trouble breathing during sleep is described further in Chapter 9, "The Snoring Sickness"); *body temperature*, taken by a probe taped under your arm or worn in your rectum; and *erections of the penis* (an aid to determining the cause of impotence), assessed by small gauges on stretch bands worn on the penis (for more information on this test, see Chapter 13, "In Sickness and Health").

Additional measurements may also be made, for such problems as pressure in the brain, chest pain or seizures.

After the electrodes are attached and you get into bed, the technician will check to see that the recording devices are properly placed. You may receive requests such as these: "With your eyes open, please look straight ahead. Please close your eyes. Open your eyes . . . without moving your head, look to the right . . . look to the left . . . look to the right . . . look to the left . . . look straight ahead . . . look up . . . look down . . . look up . . . look down . . . relax." You may also be asked to blink rapidly five times, grit your teeth or clench your jaw, inhale and hold your breath, exhale and breathe normally, and flex your left or right leg.

AREN'T ALL THE GADGETS UNCOMFORTABLE?

After a few minutes, you probably will be no more aware of the various sensors than you would be of a bandage applied to a small cut.

The electrodes will be fastened to your skin with collodion, a kind of temporary "glue." Sometimes surgical tape is used to hold the electrodes securely in place, and gauze may be wrapped around your head to keep them from being dislodged during the night. After the study, the dried glue can be brushed off or removed with alcohol. If any skin irritation develops, it is usually mild and disappears within a few hours.

You don't have to stay in one position in bed; you can move around freely. If you want to get out of bed during the night, simply unplug the wires from the panel near your bed or ask for assistance from the technician, who will be in an adjacent room monitoring you at all times.

You may be asked to spend more than one night in the laboratory; two nights are customary in many centers. Don't worry if you don't sleep as well there as you do at home; you may be reassured to know that most people do get enough sleep in the laboratory to permit their sleep problems to be assessed.

Although most of us need to sleep for at least one night in an unfamiliar place before we sleep as well as usual, poor sleepers often report that they sleep better in the laboratory than at home, despite the sensors. Some may associate their bed at home with poor sleep; others may like the security of having the technician as a "protector" standing by.

If you ordinarily share a bed with someone else, you may sleep differently in the lab. Although it is not customary for sleep centers to invite a patient's partner to sleep with him or her in the lab, special arrangements are sometimes made, depending on the problem that is being investigated. A parent of a child whose sleep is being monitored may be able to spend the night in the laboratory, too.

WHAT ARE THE ACCOMMODATIONS LIKE?

Most sleep labs try to make the sleeping rooms as homelike as possible, with comfortable furniture, cheery colors, pictures and carpeting. Some have private bathrooms; many have showers.

In most sleep centers an intercom is on at all times so that you can talk directly with the technician. Many centers also use cameras, much like those you've seen in banks, so that your sleep can be observed throughout the night. The cameras aid in documenting difficulty breathing or unusual leg or body movements during sleep. Sometimes sleep is filmed for further study, as an aid to diagnosis. Some people are uncomfortable about being filmed while they sleep; if you feel this way, discuss your concerns in advance.

The technicians are trained not only to monitor sleep but also to provide cardiopulmonary resuscitation and to handle other emergencies. All sleep laboratories are stocked with lifesaving equipment. Many are located in medical centers where further emergency help is available within seconds.

If you're accustomed to bedtime snacks or breakfast immediately upon awakening, check to see if food will be provided. If you have diabetes or special food needs, be sure to make these facts known in advance. At many sleep laboratories, people spending the night don't receive meal service in their rooms but may use the hospital's cafeteria.

WILL I BE GIVEN A DRUG TO HELP ME SLEEP?

Not usually. In fact you may be asked not to use drugs that affect your sleep for at least a week before the sleep study is performed. Please be sure to let the doctor know about all medications that you take; many taken for other purposes, even aspirin, may have an effect on sleep. At some sleep centers, you'll be expected to bring to the laboratory a list of all medications used within the past two weeks. You'll probably be asked to refrain from alcohol, and possibly from caffeine-containing beverages, for the twenty-four hours preceding the test. If you will be having certain evaluations, such as that for heartburn during sleep, you may be asked to follow a special diet before the study.

You'll probably be asked to try to maintain your usual sleep schedule the day before you come to the sleep center and to refrain from taking any extra naps.

WHAT SHOULD I BRING WITH ME?

For both men and women, two-piece pajamas are preferred, to make it easier for the technician to apply the sensors while respecting your privacy. Some sleep specialists advise you to bring the nightclothes you're used to, rather than new ones, to help counter the unfamiliarity of the laboratory setting.

Bring personal toilet articles, clothing for the next day, something to read or work on if you expect to be awake part of the test time and medications that you must take regularly. The laboratory provides bed linens and towels. You can bring your own pillow; many people find doing so makes sleep easier.

As with any hospital stay, it's best to leave valuables at home. Even if you normally wear a watch at all times, you probably will be asked to remove it so as not to color your reactions should you awaken during the night.

HOW WILL THE SLEEP RECORD BE ANALYZED?

Your record—all 1,000 to 2,000 pages of it from the typical eight-hour recording session—will be reviewed by a clinical polysomnographer. This specialist will observe the amount of time you spend in the various sleep stages and awake, and take note of other significant events, such as interruptions in breathing, unusual brain-wave patterns, tooth-grinding, frequent awakenings, and so forth. It usually takes a minimum of four hours to read a record. Today, a number of medical centers are using computers to assist in the examination of the sleep record, but the final analysis is very much a human chore.

WHAT DOES A SLEEP CENTER EVALUATION COST?

Fees vary around the country, but as of this writing, the charge for an evaluation without sleep studies ranges from about $75 to $250. A comprehensive evaluation that includes two recording sessions, with the services of the technical staff who monitor your sleep and the professional staff who review it, costs about $800 to $1,000.

ARE FEES COVERED BY INSURANCE?

Generally, yes, but insurance policies vary considerably. As a rule of thumb, if your policy covers outpatient X-ray exams and ECGs, it is likely to cover studies at a sleep center. Medicare and Medicaid also provide reimbursement.

WHAT ARRANGEMENTS ARE MADE FOR TREATMENT?

The sleep center staff members will review their findings with you and your doctor and will recommend the appropriate treatment. Most problems of sleeping and waking can be treated or managed successfully.

As noted in other chapters of this book, some problems may require treatment with medications. Others may respond to changes in the hours or timing of sleep. Sometimes techniques of behavior modification and stress management are useful; in other cases, psychotherapy is advised. Occasionally, surgery is recommended, most frequently to relieve trouble breathing during sleep.

Usually, you will continue under the direct care and supervision of your personal physician. The sleep center staff will be available for consultation and you may be asked to return to the center periodically, so that your progress can be evaluated.

HOW DO I FIND A SLEEP CENTER?

More than seventy sleep centers are now operating all over the United States. Your doctor can refer you to one in your area. Most sleep centers are affiliated with medical schools; hence, these schools are another good source of information. You'll find a list of sleep centers at the back of this book.

18

GOOD NIGHTS/ GOOD DAYS

Awake! for Morning in the Bowl of Night
Has flung the Stone that puts the Stars to flight.

—*Edward Fitzgerald*
The Rubáiyát of Omar Khayyám

In the sleep laboratory, it's nearly eleven at night. A young woman sits patiently as a technician pastes on her forehead and scalp dime-sized metal cups trailing red, green and yellow wires. Soon she resembles a folkloric bride, the cascade of colored wires sweeping her face. Fifteen minutes later, she slips off the lights and settles down in bed. Despite the strangeness of her surroundings, she takes but seven minutes to travel from wakefulness to sleep, a voyage to a world of inner space that has only recently been discovered and is just beginning to yield its secrets to hardy explorers.

Specialists in the young science of sleep are mapping this new terrain and, after looking at the sleep of thousands of satisfied and troubled sleepers, are able in many cases not only to identify things that go wrong but also to prescribe treatment to set things right.

A principal finding has been that we ourselves, by modifying our daily habits, can do much to guarantee ourselves good, restful sleep at night and full alertness during the day. Besides enhancing the pleasure of living, sound sleep appears to be a good predictor of long life. An American Cancer Society study of over one million Americans showed that people who were free of chronic sleep troubles and who never used sleeping pills lived longer than people with the opposite characteristics.

The burgeoning of interest in sleep by scientists in a wide variety of disciplines promises that advances will continue to come at a rapid pace. Research in progress includes:

- Studies of the sleeping brain. A new radiologic device, the positron-emission transaxial tomography (PETT) scanner, gives scientists a "moving picture" of brain activity during sleep. National Institute of Mental Health scientists have found that metabolic activity slows throughout the brain during NREM sleep, supporting the theory that the brain "rests" at this time. Future studies will assess brain activity during REM sleep.
- Identification of substances that the body manufactures to induce sleep, with the aim of creating more effective, safer sleeping pills that mimic their action. Researchers at Harvard University believe they have isolated a sleep-promoting substance from human urine. They have dubbed it Factor S and report that when it is infused into the brain of rabbits, it induces a 50 percent increase in deep NREM sleep.
- Development of easy-to-perform, inexpensive ways to screen for sleep disorders. These include portable, battery-operated devices that provide around-the-clock measurements of various bodily processes. One such device, worn like a watch, records wrist activity; researchers at the Veterans Administration Medical Center, San Diego, California, say that the rate of wrist movements tells how long a person sleeps and whether his sleep is disturbed. Studies of long-term circadian rhythms in pilots are being conducted with such devices and may help to further improve performance and safety. Studies of body movements confirm that children who are hyperactive while awake are more active than other children even when they sleep, and that people who are depressed move less than mentally healthy people.

Another device, a pocket-sized computer, is being worn for a week or more to monitor heart activity, breathing, the level of oxygen in the blood and other bodily processes in Stanford

University studies of people who are suspected of having sleep apnea.

• Development of ways to record sleep at home. Such systems would eliminate concern about the impact that the sleep laboratory's unfamiliar surroundings has on sleep. At the same time, many more sleep studies could be performed than are now feasible in the typical three- or four-bedroom sleep center. Researchers are studying ways to transmit recordings to the laboratory over the phone. This would enable a technician to monitor the recording and to communicate directly with the sleeper via a microphone that would be part of the transmission unit.

• Use of computers to analyze sleep records to speed diagnosis and search out subtleties of sleep behavior. The sleep of many people who complain of poor sleep, for example, appears no different from that of many people who say they sleep well. Computers may be able to identify possible reasons for the subjective sense of unsatisfying sleep.

• Examination of the tie between our biological rhythms and physical and mental illness, with the hope that resetting inner clocks may correct some of these problems. Moreover, better understanding of biological clocks may offer ways to combat jet lag and to overcome health consequences of shift work, such as disorders of sleep and digestion.

• Investigations of the phenomenon of "lucid dreaming"—that is, dreams in which the dreamer knows that he is dreaming—as a way of learning how dreams are shaped and what purposes they serve.

• Studies of changes in sleep from infancy through old age, to better distinguish variations that are normal from those that indicate sleep disorders.

• And, finally, the development of better ways to help all of us enjoy the restorative benefits of good sleep, night after night and day after day.

APPENDIX

Typical Human Sleep Patterns

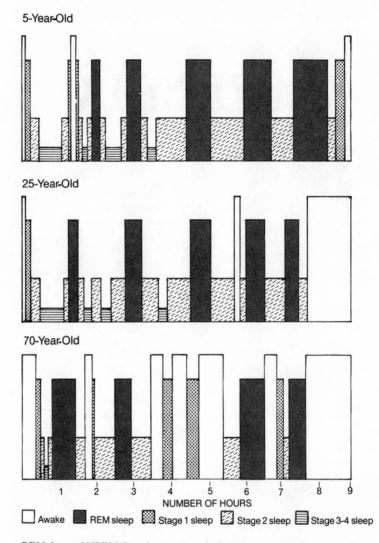

REM sleep and NREM sleep alternate in cycles lasting approximately ninety minutes throughout the night. As sleep progresses, deep sleep periods become increasingly shorter and REM periods, during which we experience our most vivid dreams, grow progressively longer.

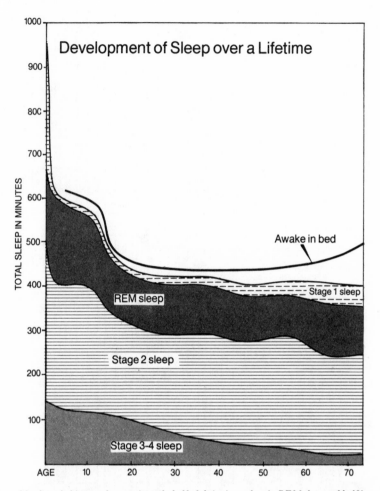

Development of Sleep over a Lifetime

TOTAL SLEEP IN MINUTES

Awake in bed

REM sleep

Stage 1 sleep

Stage 2 sleep

Stage 3-4 sleep

AGE   10   20   30   40   50   60   70

Newborn babies spend approximately half of their time asleep in REM sleep and half in NREM sleep, as shown in the chart above. The average adult spends about 20 percent of his or her time asleep in the REM stage. REM sleep remains stable in healthy people until extreme old age. As we grow older, we get less of the deeper stages of sleep and more of the lighter ones, and we are awake for a greater proportion of our time in bed.

SLEEP/WAKE DIARY

Use the three-day sample below as a guide to prepare your sleep/wake diary. You will need to keep a diary for at least a week to get a good sense of your sleep patterns. Record all times in hours and minutes, e.g., 6:15. Mark all sleep periods, including naps, with a dark line. Note events or activities that seem to harm or help you sleep, e.g., coffee, alcohol, stressful day, day off from work, argument with spouse, trip, and, for women, time of menstrual cycle.

Use the following abbreviations:

M: meals
S: snacks
P: sleeping pills
D: other drugs (number and list separately)
X: exercise
A: alarm clock

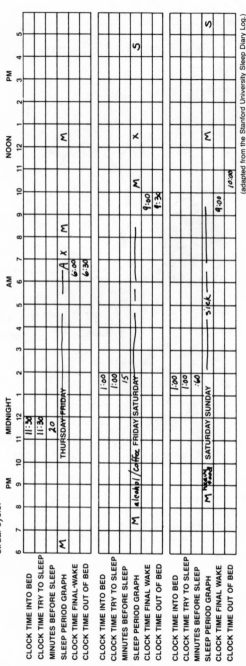

(adapted from the Stanford University Sleep Diary Log.)

SLEEPINESS/ALERTNESS CHART

INSTRUCTIONS:

1. Complete this chart during the time that you are keeping the diary.
2. Select two typical CONSECUTIVE working days.
3. Write in the days and dates you selected at the top of each chart.
4. Throughout your waking hours on these days RATE yourself every two hours according to the scale at the left of the chart.
5. CIRCLE the number indicating your level of alertness or sleepiness for each two-hour time period.
6. CIRCLE "X" for those times when you were asleep.

DAY ONE   Day _____ Date _____

SCALE	MID-NIGHT	AM PERIOD 2	4	6	8	10	NOON	PM PERIOD 2	4	6	8	10	MID-NIGHT
1. Alert. Wide Awake. Energetic.	1	1	1	1	1	1	1	1	1	1	1	1	1
2. Functioning at a high level, but not at a peak. Able to concentrate.	2	2	2	2	2	2	2	2	2	2	2	2	2
3. Awake, but not fully alert.	3	3	3	3	3	3	3	3	3	3	3	3	3
4. A little foggy, let down.	4	4	4	4	4	4	4	4	4	4	4	4	4
5. Foggy. Beginning to lose interest in remaining awake. Slowed down.	5	5	5	5	5	5	5	5	5	5	5	5	5
6. Sleepy. Prefer to be lying down. Woozy.	6	6	6	6	6	6	6	6	6	6	6	6	6
7. Cannot stay awake. Sleep onset soon.	7	7	7	7	7	7	7	7	7	7	7	7	7
X. Asleep.	X	X	X	X	X	X	X	X	X	X	X	X	X

DAY TWO   Day _____ Date _____

SCALE	MID-NIGHT	AM PERIOD 2	4	6	8	10	NOON	PM PERIOD 2	4	6	8	10	MID-NIGHT
1. Alert. Wide Awake. Energetic.	1	1	1	1	1	1	1	1	1	1	1	1	1
2. Functioning at a high level, but not at a peak. Able to concentrate.	2	2	2	2	2	2	2	2	2	2	2	2	2
3. Awake, but not fully alert.	3	3	3	3	3	3	3	3	3	3	3	3	3
4. A little foggy, let down.	4	4	4	4	4	4	4	4	4	4	4	4	4
5. Foggy. Beginning to lose interest in remaining awake. Slowed down.	5	5	5	5	5	5	5	5	5	5	5	5	5
6. Sleepy. Prefer to be lying down. Woozy.	6	6	6	6	6	6	6	6	6	6	6	6	6
7. Cannot stay awake. Sleep onset soon.	7	7	7	7	7	7	7	7	7	7	7	7	7
X. Asleep.	X	X	X	X	X	X	X	X	X	X	X	X	X

(adapted from the Stanford University Sleepiness Scale)

GLOSSARY
OF SLEEP TERMS

apnea

A pause in breathing that lasts ten seconds or longer. A person with the sleep apnea syndrome, a potentially lethal disorder, has many apneas during sleep.

arousal

"Partial" arousal is an abrupt change from a "deep" stage of NREM sleep (stage 3–4) to a "lighter" one (stage 2 or 1). "Full" arousal means awakening. During an arousal, your muscle tone increases, your heart beats faster and you move around.

awakening

"Spontaneous" awakenings most often start while you are in REM sleep, although you may awaken from NREM sleep, as well. When you are awake, your brain waves are of the alpha or beta patterns (see brain-wave rhythms), your muscle tone is high and you can

move your eyes and blink
voluntarily.

B

brain-wave rhythms

Patterns of electrical activity of the
brain. They include:

Alpha waves:

Most consistent and predominant
during relaxed wakefulness,
particularly when your eyes are
closed or you are in the dark.
Alpha waves cycle eight to
thirteen times per second.

Beta waves:

Usually associated with alert
wakefulness. They are faster than
alpha waves, cycling about
thirteen to thirty-five times per
second.

Delta waves:

Occur chiefly in deep sleep stage
3–4, also known as slow wave
sleep. Delta waves cycle less than
four times per second.

Theta waves:

Associated with the light sleep
stages 1 and 2. These cycle four to
eight times per second.

C

cataplexy

A sudden, dramatic drop in muscle
tone and loss of deep reflexes,
which leads to muscle weakness
or paralysis; an attack may cause a
person to collapse. It is usually
triggered by an emotional
stimulus such as laughing or
being startled, or by some sudden
physical exertion. Cataplexy is a
symptom of narcolepsy, a

neurologic disorder that causes excessive sleepiness.

chronobiology   The study of the impact of time on living things.

circadian   About a day. One example of a circadian rhythm is the daily alternation of sleeping and waking.

D

dreams   Periods of intense vivid imagery during sleep, often associated with rapid eye movements.

H

hypnagogic images (or hallucinations)   Vivid images that occur at the beginning of sleep. These are particularly intense when sleep begins with a REM period, as frequently occurs in narcolepsy. Such images may also occur just before awakening; then, they are called hypnapompic images.

hypnagogic jerk   A "startle" reaction or sudden body jerk that many of us normally experience just as sleep begins. It may awaken us briefly.

hypnotic   Literally, "causing sleep." Used as a noun, the term is a synonym for "sleeping pill."

I

insomnia   Literally, "no sleep." But most people who say they have insomnia describe it as "poor sleep." Their problem is trouble falling asleep or staying asleep.

L

latency period

An interval. Sleep latency is the interval from "lights out" until sleep begins. REM latency is the period from the beginning of sleep to the first appearance of rapid eye movement (REM) sleep.

M

microsleep

A lapse from wakefulness into sleep that lasts just a few seconds.

multiple sleep latency test (MSLT)

This test measures how sleepy you are by observing how long it takes you to fall asleep during your normal waking hours. It is used to diagnose various sleep disorders and to evaluate sleeping pills.

myoclonus

A muscle contraction that produces a jerk or twitch. Some people experience periodic leg movements that repeatedly interrupt their sleep.

N

narcolepsy

A neurological disorder that causes irresistible sleepiness.

nightmare

An anxiety-filled dream that often wakes the sleeper from REM sleep. It is distinguished from "sleep terror," which is a sudden, partial arousal from NREM sleep that may cause the sleeper to cry out in fright but that seldom includes vivid images.

nocturnal penile tumescence (NPT) test

Assessment during sleep of the hardening and expansion of the penis. Penile erections occur during REM sleep in healthy males of all ages. Documenting these erections aids in the diagnosis of impotence.

NREM sleep   See sleep stages.

P

polysomnogram   A continuous recording of physiological activity during sleep. The two basic activities that are measured are brain waves and eye movements, but chin muscle activity, breathing, heart rate and numerous other functions are often recorded, too.

R

rebound insomnia   Disrupted sleep that may occur for a few nights after a person stops taking sleeping pills.

REM rebound or recovery   An increased amount of REM sleep for a few nights after a period of REM deprivation. REM rebound may occur after several days without sleep, or upon withdrawal from certain drugs, including some sleeping pills, that suppress REM sleep. Increased amounts of REM sleep may be reflected by disturbing dreams.

REM sleep   See sleep stages.

restlessness   Persistent or recurrent body movements, arousals and brief awakenings during sleep.

S

sleep paralysis   An inability to move voluntarily, occurring just at the beginning of sleep or on awakening. May last from a few seconds to a few minutes. Occurs in one in twenty healthy people but is more common in those with narcolepsy.

sleep stages

REM sleep:

Named for the rapid eye movements that typically occur during this time. It is a period of intense brain activity, often associated with dreams. Muscle activity is suppressed. REM sleep usually represents about 20–25 percent of total sleep time in a young adult.

NREM sleep:

Non-rapid-eye-movement sleep. NREM and REM periods alternate during sleep in cycles that last approximately ninety minutes. REM sleep periods become progressively longer and NREM sleep lighter, as sleep continues. NREM sleep has four stages, which occur in predictable percentages in young adults. They include: *stage 1*—the transition between wakefulness and sleep (about 5 percent of total sleep time); *stage 2*—light sleep (about 45–55 percent of total sleep time); *stage 3*—deeper sleep (about 5 percent of total sleep time); *stage 4*—deepest sleep (about 15 percent of total sleep time). Stages 3 and 4 are often combined and referred to as stage 3–4. Both stages usually appear only in the first

third of the sleep period.
Sleepwalking and sleep terror
attacks usually start in these
stages.

somnologist
A specialist in the study of sleep
and in the diagnosis and
treatment of sleep disorders.

(This glossary is adapted from "Diagnostic Classification of Sleep
and Arousal Disorders," in the journal *Sleep*, Volume 2, Number
1, 1979.)

DIRECTORY OF SLEEP DISORDERS CENTERS

The centers listed here are members of the Association of Sleep Disorders Centers. For information about sleep disorders centers that may have opened in your area since this list was compiled, write the ASDC at P.O. Box 2604, Del Mar, California 92014, or call the department of psychiatry or neurology at a medical school in your area.

ACCREDITED CENTERS

Alabama
Alabama Regional Sleep
Disorders Center   (205) 934-7464
P.O. Box 500, University Station
Birmingham, AL 35294

Arizona
Sleep Disorders Center   (602) 239-5815
Good Samaritan Medical Center
1111 East McDowell Road
Phoenix, AZ 85062

California
Sleep Disorders Center   (213) 206-8005
Department of Neurology
UCLA School of Medicine
Los Angeles, CA 90024

Sleep Disorders Center   (213) 365-8051, x1497
Holy Cross Hospital
15031 Rinaldi Street
Mission Hills, CA 91345

Sleep Disorders Center   (714) 634-5777
U.C. Irvine Medical Center
101 City Drive South
Orange, CA 92688

Sleep Disorders Program   (415) 497-7458
Stanford University Medical Center
Stanford, CA 94305

Connecticut
Sleep Disorders Center   (203) 735-7421
The Griffin Hospital
130 Division Street
Derby, CT 06418

Florida
Sleep Disorders Center   (305) 674-2613
Mt. Sinai Medical Center
4300 Alton Road
Miami Beach, FL 33140

Illinois
Sleep Disorders Center   (312) 942-5440
Rush-Presbyterian-St. Luke's
1753 W. Congress Parkway
Chicago, IL 60612

Sleep Disorders Center   (312) 962-1780
University of Chicago
950 East 59th Street
Chicago, IL 60637

Maryland
Sleep Disorders Center   (301) 396-8603
Baltimore City Hospital
Baltimore, MD 21224

Michigan
Sleep Disorders Center   (313) 876-2233
Henry Ford Hospital
2799 W. Grand Blvd.
Detroit, MI 48202

Minnesota
Sleep Disorders Center   (612) 347-6288
Neurology Department
Hennepin County Medical Center
Minneapolis, MN 55415

Missouri
Sleep Disorders Center   (314) 645-8510
Deaconess Hospital
6150 Oakland Avenue
St. Louis, MO 63139

New Hampshire
Sleep Disorders Center   (603) 646-7521
Department of Psychiatry
Dartmouth Medical School
Hanover, NH 03755

New York
Sleep-Wake Disorders Center   (212) 920-4841
Montefiore Hospital
111 E. 210th Street
Bronx, NY 10467

Sleep Disorders Center   (516) 444-2916
Department of Psychiatry
SUNY at Stony Brook
Stony Brook, NY 11794

Ohio
Sleep Disorders Evaluation Center   (614) 421-8296
Department of Psychiatry
Ohio State University
Columbus, OH 43210

Oklahoma
Sleep Disorders Center   (405) 271-6312
Presbyterian Hospital
N.E. 13th at Lincoln Blvd.
Oklahoma City, OK 73104

Pennsylvania
Sleep Disorders Center   (412) 624-2246
Western Psychiatric Institute
3811 O'Hara Street
Pittsburgh, PA 15261

Sleep Disorders Center   (215) 874-1184
Department of Neurology
Crozer-Chester Medical Center
Upland-Chester, PA 19013

Tennessee
Sleep Disorders Center   (901) 522-5704
Baptist Memorial Hospital
Memphis, TN 38146

Texas
Sleep Disorders Center   (713) 799-4886
Baylor College of Medicine
Houston, TX 77030

Sleep Disorders Center   (512) 223-4057
Metropolitan Medical Center
1303 McCullough
San Antonio, TX 78212

PROVISIONAL MEMBERS

Arizona
Sleep Disorders Center   (602) 626-6112
University of Arizona
1501 North Campbell Avenue
Tucson, AZ 85724

California
Sleep Disorders Center   (619) 455-8087
Scripps Clinic and Research Foundation
10666 North Torrey Pines Road
La Jolla, CA 92037

Sleep Disorders Center   (213) 325-9110, x2049
Torrance Memorial Hospital
3330 Lomita Boulevard
Torrance, CA 90509

Colorado
Sleep Disorders Center   (303) 839-6447
Presbyterian Medical Center
1719 E. 19th Avenue
Denver, CO 80218

Florida
Sleep Disorders Center   (904) 476-7851, x4128
Sacred Heart Hospital
5151 N. 9th Avenue
Pensacola, FL 32504

Hawaii
Sleep Disorders Center   (808) 523-2311
Straub Clinic and Hospital
888 South King Street
Honolulu, HI 96813

Indiana
Sleep Disorders Center   (812) 479-4257
St. Mary's Medical Center
3700 Washington Avenue
Evansville, IN 47750

Iowa
Sleep Disorders Center   (515) 283-6207
Iowa Methodist Medical Center
1200 Pleasant Street
Des Moines, IA 50308

Kansas
Sleep Disorders Center   (316) 688-2660
Wesley Medical Center
550 North Hillside
Wichita, KS 67214

Louisiana
Tulane Sleep Center   (504) 588-5231
Psychiatry and Neurology
Tulane Medical School
New Orleans, LA 70118

Massachusetts
Sleep Disorders Clinic   (617) 735-6242
Boston Children's Hospital
300 Longwood Avenue
Boston, MA 02115

Sleep Disorders Unit   (617) 735-4020
Harvard University School of Medicine
Beth Israel Hospital—330 Brookline Av.
Boston, MA 02215

Sleep-Wake Disorders Unit   (617) 856-3802
University of Massachusetts
55 Lake Avenue North
Worcester, MA 01605

Minnesota
Sleep Disorders Center   (612) 932-6083
Methodist Hospital
6500 Excelsior Boulevard
Minneapolis, MN 55426

Sleep Disorders Center   (507) 284-8403
Division of Pulmonary Medicine
Mayo Clinic
Rochester, MN 55901

Sleep Disorders Center   (612) 291-3174
St. Joseph's Hospital
69 West Exchange Street
St. Paul, MN 55102

Mississippi
Sleep Disorders Center   (601) 987-3902
Division of Somnology
University of Mississippi
Jackson, MS 39216

Missouri
Sleep Disorders Center   (314) 771-6400
St. Louis University Medical Center
1221 South Grand Boulevard
St. Louis, MO 63104

North Carolina
Sleep Disorders Center   (919) 684-6003
Division of Neurology
Duke University Medical Center
Durham, NC 27710

New York
Sleep Disorders Center   (716) 464-3000
St. Mary's Hospital
89 Genesee Street
Rochester, NY 14611

Sleep Disorders Center   (716) 275-2776
University of Rochester Medical School
601 Elmwood Avenue
Rochester, NY 14642

Sleep-Wake Disorders Center   (914) 997-5751
New York Hospital-Cornell
21 Bloomingdale Road
White Plains, NY 10605

Ohio
Sleep Disorders Center   (513) 861-7770
Jewish Hospital
515 Melish Avenue
Cincinnati, OH 45229

Sleep Disorders Center   (216) 444-5567
Department of Neurology
Cleveland Clinic
Cleveland, OH 44106

Oregon
Sleep Disorders Program   (503) 229-8311
Good Samaritan Hospital
2222 NW Lovejoy Street
Portland, OR 97210

Pennsylvania
Sleep Disorders Center   (814) 533-1000
Mercy Hospital of Johnstown
1127 Franklin Street
Johnstown, PA 15905

Sleep Disorders Center   (215) 842-4250
Department of Neurology
The Medical College of Pennsylvania
Philadelphia, PA 19129

Tennessee
Sleep Disorders Center   (615) 971-6011
St. Mary's Medical Center
Oak Hill Avenue
Knoxville, TN 37917

Texas
Sleep-Wake Disorders Center   (214) 696-8563
Presbyterian Hospital
8200 Walnut Hill Lane
Dallas, TX 75231

Sleep Disorders Center   (713) 468-4311
Sam Houston Memorial Hospital
P. O. Box 55130
Houston, TX 77055

Utah
Sleep Disorders Center   (801) 226-2300
Utah Neurological Clinic
1999 N. Columbia Lane
Provo, UT 84604

DEVELOPING CENTERS

Arkansas
Sleep Laboratory   (501) 661-5525
Department of Pulmonary Medicine
Univ. of Arkansas Med. Center
Little Rock, AR 72201

Colorado
Sleep Disorders Center   (303) 388-4461
National Jewish Hospital
3800 East Colfax Avenue
Denver, CO 80206

Illinois
Sleep Disorders Center   (312) 649-2650
Northwestern Memorial Hospital
250 East Superior Street
Chicago, IL 60611

Kentucky
Sleep Disorders Center   (502) 636-7459
Humana Hospital Audubon
One Audubon Plaza Drive
Louisville, KY 40217

New Jersey
Sleep/Wake Studies   (201) 456-4687
University of Medicine and Dentistry
100 Bergen Street
Newark, NJ 07103

Sleep Disorders Center   (201) 463-4416
Rutgers Medical School
Box 101
Piscataway, NJ 08502

New York
Sleep Disorders Center   (212) 694-5341
Columbia Presbyterian Medical Center
617 West 168th Street
New York, NY 10032

Sleep Disorders Center   (315) 476-7461
VA Medical Center
Irving Avenue
Syracuse, NY 13210

Ohio
Sleep Disorders Center   (216) 368-7000
Psychiatry Department
St. Luke's Hospital
Cleveland, OH 44118

Sleep Disorders Center   (216) 421-3732
Mt. Sinai Medical Center
1800 East 105th Street
Cleveland, OH 44106

Texas
Sleep Disorders Center   (512) 452-0361
Shoal Creek Hospital
3501 Mills Avenue
Austin, TX 78731

West Virginia
Sleep Disorders Laboratory   (304) 234-0123
Department of Neurology
Ohio Valley Medical Center
Wheeling, WV 26003

CANADIAN CENTERS

Sleep Disorders Clinic   (514) 333-2070
Hôpital du Sacre-Coeur
5400 ouest, Boul. Gouin
Montreal, Qu., CANADA H4J 1C5

Sleep Disorders Clinic-Neurology   (613) 231-4738
Ottawa General Hospital
501 Smyth Road
Ottawa, CANADA K1H 8L6

Sleep Disorders Center   (416) 486-3309
Sunnybrook Medical Center
2075 Bayview Avenue
Toronto, CANADA

Sleep Disorders Clinic   (416) 369-5109
Department of Psychiatry
Toronto Western Hospital
Toronto, CANADA M5T 2S8

OTHER CENTERS

Laboratorio de Estudio del Sueno y la Vigilia
Departamento de Neurofisiologia Clinica N.C.—F.L.E.N.I.
Ayacucho 2166
1112 Buenos Aires, ARGENTINA

Sleep Center
Department of Medicine
The University of Sydney
Sydney, New South Wales 2006, AUSTRALIA

Department of Neurology
Charles University
Katerinska 30
12000 Prague 2, CZECHOSLOVAKIA

Service: Sommeil-Rêve
Hôpital Neurologique
39, Boulevard Pinel
69500 Bron, FRANCE

Centre Medical Gui de Chauliac   67 63-90-50, x3944
Centre du Sommeil
34059 Montpellier Cedex, FRANCE

Sleep Disorders Clinic
Loewenstein Rehabilitation Center
Post Office Box 3
43100 Ra'Anana, ISRAEL

Clinica delle Malattie Nervose et Mentali   51 58-51-58
Universita di Bologna, Via Ugo Foscolo 7
Bologna, ITALY

Centro del Sonno   51 213-40-41
Universita di Milano
Ospedale S. Raffaele
20090 Milano, Segrate, ITALY

Department of Neuropsychiatry
Osaka University Medical School
1-1-50 Fukushima
Osaka, JAPAN 533

Department of Neuropsychiatry
Kurume University School of Medicine
67 Asahi-machi
Kurume, JAPAN 830

Department of Psychiatry
Tokyo University School of Medicine
7-3-1 Hongo, Bunkyo-ku
Tokyo, JAPAN 113

Sleep Disorders Clinic
Department of Internal Medicine
University of the Orange Free State
339, Bloemfontein 9300, SOUTH AFRICA

Sleep Disorders Center
First Moscow Medical Institute
Moscow, U.S.S.R.

INDEX

About the Author

LYNNE LAMBERG is a free-lance medical journalist. She writes a regular health news column for *Better Homes and Gardens* magazine and contributes articles to *American Health* and other leading periodicals. Her work appears in the *Encyclopaedia Britannica Medical and Health Annual* and the *World Book Encyclopedia*'s *Science Year* and *Medical Update* annuals. Additionally, she has completed special assignments for the Johns Hopkins Medical Institutions and the National Cancer Institute.

A native of St. Louis, Missouri, Ms. Lamberg now lives in Baltimore, Maryland. She holds a B.A. from Washington University in St. Louis and an M.A. from the Annenberg School of Communications of the University of Pennsylvania in Philadelphia.